The Nature of Concepts

The Nature of Concepts examines a central issue for all the main disciplines in cognitive science: how the human mind creates and passes on to other human minds a concept. This excellent cross-disciplinary collection presents some of the most recent approaches to concepts, and discusses their structure, evolution, representation and relationship with the external world.

Concepts can be abstract (e.g. justice), mathematical (e.g. a square), linguistic (e.g. a verb), scientific (e.g. a mammal) or even *ad hoc* (e.g. things to eat on a diet). As this book shows, the concept of 'concepts' – and the range of theoretical approaches – is very broad indeed. Among these approaches, two familiar ones are shown to be complementary rather than contradictory: both classical and prototype models can have psychological reality. In other chapters, contributors discuss the structure of concepts in relation to different parts of the human environment, such as the linguistic and pre-linguistic environments, the natural environment, different parts of the cultural environment, and the scientific environment.

The Nature of Concepts will be of interest to cognitive scientists, psychologists and linguists who wish to become or remain acquainted with recent developments in the field of the study of concepts.

Philip Van Loocke is a Senior Research Associate of the Fund for Scientific Research (Flanders/Belgium) and Visiting Professor in Epistemology at the University of Ghent, Belgium.

Routledge Frontiers of Cognitive Science
Series advisor Tim Valentine

The Nature of Concepts

Evolution, structure and representation

Edited by Philip Van Loocke

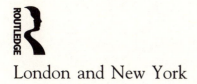

London and New York

First published 1999
by Routledge
11 New Fetter Lane, London EC4P 4EE

Simultaneously published in the USA and Canada
by Routledge
29 West 35th Street, New York, NY 10001

Typeset in Goudy by
The Florence Group, Stoodleigh, Devon
Printed and bound in Great Britain by
T J International Ltd, Padstow, Cornwall

British Library Cataloguing in Publication Data
A catalogue record for this book is available from the British Library

Library of Congress Cataloging in Publication Data
A catalogue record for this book has been requested

ISBN 0–415–17963–7

Contents

Figures

Contributors

Michael A. Arbib, USC Brain Project, University of Southern California, Los Angeles, USA

Andy Clark, Department of Philosophy, Washington University, St Louis, USA

Yosef Grodzinsky, Department of Psychology, Tel Aviv University, Israel

Markus F. Peschl, Department of Philosophy of Science, University of Vienna, Austria

Steven Pinker, Department of Brain and Cognitive Systems, Massachusetts Institute of Technology, Cambridge, MA, USA

Henry Plotkin, Department of Psychology, University College London, UK

Alan Prince, Department of Linguistics, Rutgers University, New Brunswick, NJ, USA

Giacomo Rizzolatti, Instituto di Fisologia Umana, Universita di Parma, Italy

William S. Robinson, Department of Philosophy, Iowa State University of Science and Technology, Iowa, USA

Christian Scheier, AI Lab, Computer Science Department, University of Zürich, Switzerland

Paul Thagard, Department of Philosophy, University of Waterloo, Ontario, Canada

Wolfgang Tschacher, University Psychiatric Services, University of Bern, Switzerland

Philip Van Loocke, Lab for Applied Epistemology, University of Ghent, Belgium

Acknowledgements

This book is a result of the project "Concepts: representation and evolution" of the Lab for Applied Epistemology at the University of Ghent. During this project, the editor was supported as a senior research associate by a grant of the Flemish Fund for Scientific Research. Participants in this project, in alphabetical order, were Michael Arbib, Andy Clark, Terry Dartnall, Liane Gabora, Ben Goertzel, Yozef Grodzinsky, Mark Hubey, Markus Peschl, Steven Pinker, Henry Plotkin, William Robinson, Lee Spector, Paul Thagard, Wolfgang Tschacher, Fernand Vandamme and Philip Van Loocke. The editor wishes to thank all participants for many fruitful discussions.

Earlier versions of the present chapters appeared in *Philosophica, Communication and Cognition* and in *CC-ai*. We wish to thank the Institute of European and American Studies, Academia Sinica, Taipei, Taiwan for their kind permission to reprint the main part of Andy Clark's paper, which appeared in *Mind and Cognition: Collected papers from 1993 symposium on mind and cognition*.

Introduction

The structure and representation of concepts

Philip Van Loocke

This is a book about concepts – about their structure and its relationship with the structure of the external world. A central issue is how concepts are represented in the brain of living systems. In order to cope with its environment every living system must categorize "things" or "events" into classes that provoke similar reactions. A simple living system may categorize its environment into things to approach versus things to avoid, or into things to eat and things to mate with. These are concepts. But the word "concept" is not confined to such categories; concepts can be abstract (e.g. justice), mathematical (e.g. a square), linguistic (e.g. a verb), scientific (e.g. a mammal) or even *ad hoc* (e.g. things to eat on a diet). As this book shows the concept of "concepts" is very broad indeed.

Concepts are represented in physical systems which exist in a larger physical world. A minimum condition for a system to possess concepts is for there to be a coherence between the operation part of the system and the external world. As soon as it is recognized that such coherences occur it is meaningful to try to formulate a theory about concepts.

The law-like nature of the human physical, biological or social environment sometimes gives rise to fairly well-demarcated structures. In such cases, developing "classical" categories can be useful. Examples frequently mentioned are "mother", "bachelor", "odd number", etc. All exemplars of such a category must share a set of necessary and sufficient conditions. During the last two decades, another type of concepts has been put forward. Prototype models assert that concepts are organized around one or more prototypes. Categories have graded degrees of membership, and the relations between instances of a category can be described as a family resemblance structure. The most famous instance of such a category, due to Wittgenstein (1953), is "game". Though "good" members of the category have characteristic features, these features are not defining. In many domains of the human environment, underlying laws are obscured by the complexities inherent in these domains. As chaos theory has demonstrated, even simple laws may lead to remarkable complexities when several degrees of freedom interact. Further, objects are cluttered in ways that testify to the myriad of contingent historical processes that led to their creation and preservation. In such cases, a cognitive system at best can construct prototype categories with relatively vague demarcation. Nevertheless, the external world sometimes has enough structure to enable idealized models with idealized laws to be constructed. Thus, the concept "mother" occurs in evolutionary models as the producer of the larger of the two kinds of gametes in sexual reproduction, it occurs in the ethology of mammals as the adult that provides the greater minimal parental investment, etc. Such models are constructed most straightforwardly on the basis of classical categories. They are addressed, for instance, when inferences must be produced. Idealized models are not only a product of formal schooling or scientific activities, but are a general characteristic of human conceptual organization, since also pre-school children and non-literate cultures appear to construct types of idealized models (Keil, 1989; Gelman *et al.*, 1994).

In some cases, an object may belong to a prototype category as well as to a classical category: the fact that it participates in a family membership structure does not exclude that a corresponding concept occurs in an idealized theory of the world. Steven Pinker and Alan Prince show in Chapter 1 that both models complement each other, and that both have psychological reality. An unexpected example of this fact is found in the English past tense system: regular verbs appear to define a classical category, whereas irregular verbs form prototype categories.

To the extent that concepts are used in idealized models of the world, the human conceptual system contains more structure than its environment. The amount of internal structure in the human conceptual system has been minimized during the last decade by connectionism in two respects. First, several connectionist authors take for granted the prototype nature of concepts, and leave no place for classical categories. Second, patterns that contain the information about concepts are supposed to be massively distributed. Though there are several sub-directions in connectionism, many assume that different pieces of information integrated in a concept are not nicely grouped in the brain, but smeared out in mixed form. There is an important part of the human environment, however, that is strongly structured: the linguistic environment. For this environment, Yosef Grodzinsky shows in Chapter 2 that different characteristics of verbal concepts are represented in a modular way. Hence, even if connectionist approaches to representation are able to describe patterns associated with concepts in some subsystems, other subsystems remain for which a more classical, modular approach is adequate.

The synergetics approach is complementary to Grodzinsky's chapter. This perspective emphasizes the continuity of the human conceptual system with the natural environment. The natural human environment can be described in terms of sets of non-linear, coupled differential equations. Synergetics uses the same type of equations to describe processes in the human cognitive system. In this respect, there is a stylistic difference between synergetics and most connectionist approaches. The latter give a strongly dominant importance to terms like connections, units with their specific update rules, etc., that have little place in descriptions of a natural environment. In synergetic approaches, the description of a cognitive system and of its environment are more on an equal footing. Nevertheless, after analysis of synergetic equations, attractor dynamics appear that are familiar from connectionism. In Chapter 3, Wolfgang Tschacher and Christian Scheier argue that a synergetic emphasis on the coherence between cognitive systems and their environment can avoid different "classical" problems in artificial intelligence.

Evolution has selected particular coherent brain patterns and accompanying dynamical relations between such patterns. Though they are on a scale that is larger than the participating cells, their occurrence enhances the survival of the individual cells. For this reason, nature has developed systems that include downward causation, and in which indeterminacies at the cell level are filled in by processes taking place at higher levels (Popper and Eccles, 1977). Synergetics describes coherences at the larger level. The non-linearities in the equations that are used suggest, along with an amount of coherence and organization, a degree of indeterminism that is epistemological to some, and ontological according to others (Prigogine, 1984). This incomplete determination leaves room for influences from processes taking place at smaller scales. The extent to which such upward causation is relevant differs from domain to domain. It may be larger in domains where indeterministic search processes play an important constructive role, and smaller when the structural organization of patterns must be quite constrained, like in the case of linguistic processes.

As we have noticed, one of the functions of the coherent patterns in a brain is the construction of models for various parts of the environment. The nature of the code that is used in these constructions has been the subject of much debate in cognitive science. Recently, the active nature of this construction process has been emphasized. Even in ordinary perception, higher brain areas appear continuously to propose series of candidate constructions; interactions between these areas and areas that are closer to the input select among the candidates that are proposed (Kosslyn and Sussman, 1995). Much of the original human environment is of a biological nature. As is well known, nature itself uses DNA codes to construct this part of our environment. The codes a brain uses to reconstruct the environment, however, are not the codes that objectively generate this environment. Rather, the codes studied in cognitive science are simpler. For instance, in order to reconstruct biological environments, fractals, boolean networks and chaos methods have been studied extensively (Barnsley, 1993). In Chapter 4, Philip Van Loocke proposes a new type of growing fractal, and suggests that it is suited to help recoding processes in functional modules that specialize in representing biological information. If it is possible to demarcate functional modules that have such tasks (Pinker, 1994), then specialized recoding processes may be useful (Clark and Thornton, 1997). In the case of man, however, other types of representation must also have acquired importance, since linguistic communication requires representations that are more specifically constrained than present complex systems methods allow.

Communication, and hence culture, has influenced the dynamics of cohering patterns in a profound way (Donald, 1991). The relation between culture and concepts is one of the tenets in the work of H. Plotkin. In an important direction of evolutionary epistemology, concepts, or aggregations of concepts, are named "memes", and a subject of debate is whether the evolution of memes has parallels with the evolution of genes. Such an approach has an important advantage that is paralleled in biological evolution theory. Darwin did not know about DNA, or chromosomes. Nevertheless, his theory enabled explanation of important properties of phenotypes. With this precedent in mind, one may try to found a science of conceptual evolution, even if the nature of representations in the brain is not yet understood in a detailed way (Gabora, 1996).

In Chapter 5, Henry Plotkin points out that abstract schemas or higher order structures rather than individual concepts function as important types of memes. For instance, a concept that relates to a specific school is not a meme; a better meme candidate is the higher knowledge structure that specifies that schools are places where children go, where they learn to read and write, where they are taught by teachers, and so on. Around such stable memes, clouds of large numbers of less stable and more superficial memes may cluster. Below the relatively stable cultural memes are a number of culturally universal meme structures. An instance of such a meme is the "social force" that stimulates the participation of humans in groups and that supports consensus formation.

The relation between concepts and social–cultural environment is also prominent in the chapter by Michael Arbib and Giacomo Rizzolatti (Chapter 6). It shows that verbal concepts, and properties of their representations, may have an evolutionary predecessor in meaningful social action. The authors show how this evolution can be reconstructed by studying neural representations in monkey and man. The basis of their proposal is that it is possible to trace an evolutionary path from manual skills to language. More specifically, it is demonstrated that monkeys possess a system that matches observation with execution in the following sense. When a monkey perceives a meaningful hand movement, a subset of F5 neurons discharges. The neurons that discharge (the "mirror neurons") form a subset of the F5 neurons that discharge when the observed act is executed by the monkey itself. Hence, the recognition of a hand movement involves activating part of the pattern that is activated when the monkey itself carries out the movement. This suggests that the process of "internalization" of socially meaningful information is far reaching. In order to understand a social act, it is analyzed in terms of the monkey's own past experience with similar acts.

Concepts are heavily determined by cultural tradition. Some of the relatively stable cultural tradition may influence the formation of concepts. This generates a question about the relation between the concepts actually used by the human cognitive system and the opinions about concepts that are implicit and explicit in a cultural environment. The extent to which such opinions, commonly called "folk psychology", are simplifications of more scientific views has been widely debated in the past decades. In Chapter 7,

Andy Clark differentiates between two extreme stances concerning the relation between folk concepts and scientifically identified representations. According to the first stance, concepts that are commonly used in folk psychology must fit scientific developments. If these developments justify the use of folk concepts, we can continue using them. If scientific insights show folk concepts to be illusory constructions, we should change our way of thinking, and replace folk concepts by new, scientifically justified terms. Then, it would be a humanistic duty to re-educate the folk and to furnish them with scientifically justified mental tools. Hence, according to the first view, folk concepts ("mind") are a scientific kind: science must be allowed to prescribe the terms used in our daily thinking. According to the second view, it does not matter if science fits the concepts that we constantly use. Persons can ascribe concepts to each other even if, on a deeper level, they turn out not to use such concepts. This is the ascriptivist position. As long as ascribing concepts to a person helps to predict his or her behavior, it is permissible to make the ascription. In this view, "mind" is not a scientific concept.

Clark works out an intermediate position. There is a subset of folk concepts that must be confronted with science. If it turns out that these folk concepts do not correspond with deeper level neuropsychological facts, they should be adapted. The concepts at issue relate to how cognitive systems deal with concepts. Folk psychology assumes, for instance, that people have a memory from which items can be recalled. It assumes that a cognitive system sometimes can generalize from past experience. It asserts that a belief-producer is conscious, and so on. Among such assumptions there are assertions that are compatible with science, or assertions that can be made compatible on condition of minor modifications. Hence, even if most folk concepts would not fit deep level representations in any perspicuous way, a subset of folk concepts about concepts remains defensible when confronted with science. Consequently, there is a core within folk psychology that should not be treated in a mere ascriptivist way. Further, given this fact, it can be defended that only systems that satisfy the properties and conditions contained in this core must be regarded as concept-manipulating or belief-holding systems.

Nevertheless, many folk concepts may be remote from the deep level structures that have causal significance in neuropsychological functioning. This point remains when such concepts are combined in beliefs. As William Robinson points out in Chapter 8, beliefs are properties ascribed to a total cognitive system that is much more complex than this ascription suggests. At every moment, a problem-solving brain maintains several representations active. The next moment, many of these representations may appear to be fruitless sidetracks, and may be abandoned without further elaboration. If a representation remains active longer, or if it has large causal effect, it may be called a "dominating" representation, but it is never the only one that is active. Usually, if we ascribe a belief in terms of folk concepts to a person, we make a simplification of the complex and composite inner dynamics of his or her cognitive system. This point remains when particular "self-evident" beliefs are considered.

One can try to relate actual human concepts to "folk concepts" about the use of concepts, but when comparing actual concepts with human environments, one can also compare properties of actual concepts of individuals with properties of concepts in a specific sphere of present culture: the sphere of science. In Chapter 9 of this book, Markus Peschl argues that scientific concepts can be considered from the same evolutionary perspective as pre-scientific ones. An organism develops a representation of its environment in order to increase its fitness, not in order to create a mirror for the environment. There are significant respects in which this property remains when highly abstract scientific concepts are developed. A theory, as a construct of a nervous system, can be considered as a point in a special instance of a weight space, called a theory space. Scientific activities during episodes of "normal" science can be described as searching the weight space for points that correspond to better fitting theories. In episodes of new paradigm construction, the weight space itself is varied according to a process that can be compared with variations in the genetically defined characteristics of the nervous system itself.

The exposition of Peschl uses the basic terms of connectionism in order to draw attention to parallels between evolution in individual and in collective, scientific systems of concepts. In Chapter 10, Paul Thagard develops a framework to analyze and characterize such evolution. In fact, the history of science contains many examples of theories in which structures of concepts are made as explicit as possible, and in which as many inferences as possible are drawn from properties of concepts and from their relations. This clarity enables changes between successive conceptual structures to be studied in great detail. There are different ways in which such changes can be described. For instance, one can posit a functional "lexical module" in which a fairly new lexical structure is realized with every fundamental conceptual change. On a more specific level, it can be postulated that concepts are subject to processes of differentiation and of coalescence, and that during developments of theories, properties of concepts are re-analyzed in terms of relations between concepts. P. Thagard's analysis is deeper. He differentiates between nine degrees of conceptual change, illustrated with the evolution of the concept "tuberculosis". The nine degrees include a criterion that refers to exemplars, and two principles that refer to causal explanations in which the concepts participate. Furthermore, one rule refers to the part–whole relations in which the concept occurs and other criteria can be formulated in terms of the conceptual hierarchy in which the concept is embedded. Like the first chapter, the final chapter of this book illustrates that different structural properties of concepts that are described by different principles are complementary rather than exclusive.

References

Barnsley, M. (1993), *Fractals everywhere*, Cambridge: Academic Press

Clark, A., Thornton, C. (1997), Trading spaces: computation, representation, and the limits of uninformed learning, *Behavioral and Brain Sciences*, 20, 57–65

Donald, M. (1991), *The origins of the modern mind*, Cambridge, MA: Harvard University Press

Gabora, L. (1996), A day in the life of a meme, *Philosophica*, 57(1), 53–90

Gelman, S., Coley, J., Gottfried, G. (1994), Essentialist beliefs in children: The acquisition of concepts and theories, in L. Hirschfeld and S. Gelman (eds), *Mapping the mind: domain specificity in cognition and culture*, New York: Cambridge University Press

Keil, F. (1989), *Concepts, kinds, and cognitive development*, Cambridge, MA: MIT Press

Kosslyn, S., Sussman, A. (1995), Roles of imagery in perception: Or, there is no such thing as immaculate perception, in M. Gazzaniga, *The cognitive neurosciences*, Cambridge, MA: Bradford

Pinker, S. (1994), *The language instinct*, London: Penguin Books

Popper, K., Eccles J. (1977), *The self and its brain*, New York: Springer-Verlag

Prigogine, I. (1984), *Order out of chaos*, New York: Bantam Books

Wittgenstein, L. (1953), *Philosophical investigations*, New York: Macmillan

1   The nature of human concepts

Evidence from an unusual source

Steven Pinker and Alan Prince*

Abstract

What kind of categories do human concepts represent? *Classical* categories are defined by necessary and sufficient criteria that determine whether an object is in a category or not in it. A popular contemporary view is that concepts correspond instead to *prototype* categories. *Prototype* categories lack necessary and sufficient conditions; their members need not be absolutely "in" or "out of" the category but can be members to greater or lesser degrees; their members display family resemblances in a number of characteristic properties rather than uniformly sharing a few defining properties; and they are organized around "prototypical" exemplars. This distinction raises several questions. Is one type of category psychologically real, the other an artifact (of formal schooling, or of the experimental methodologies used to study them)? If both are psychologically real, do they serve different functions in cognition? Are they processed by the same kind of computational architecture? And do they correspond to fundamentally different kinds of things in the world? We suggest that some answers to these questions can be found in an unusual place: the English past tense system.

This paper is about an extensive parallel we have discovered between a part of language and a part of cognition, and about the possibility that the parallel is not a coincidence. The parallel involves the difference between a *classical category* and a *prototype* or *family resemblance category*, a topic of controversy for many years in cognitive psychology, philosophy, linguistics, and artificial intelligence.

Classical categories are defined by necessary and sufficient criteria, and membership in them is all-or-none. Examples include squares, grandmothers, odd numbers, and the vertebrate class *Aves*. Family resemblance categories differ from classical categories in a number of ways:

- They *lack necessary and sufficient conditions* for membership. For example, the category "chair" includes objects that have legs and that lack them (e.g. beanbag chairs), and objects that can be sat upon and that cannot (e.g. delicate museum pieces).

- They have *graded degrees of membership*. A robin is a better example of the family resemblance category "bird" than an eagle is; and a penguin a worse example.
- The category can be summarized by an ideal member or *prototype*, sometimes but not always an actual exemplar of the category. The more similar other members are to the prototype, the "better" examples they are. The sparrow, which is used to illustrate the entry for "bird" in many dictionaries, might be a prototype of the bird category.
- There can be *unclear cases* – objects that may or may not be members of the category at all. One example is the fossil species Archaeopteryx, characterized by one paleontologist as "a piss-poor reptile, and not very much of a bird" (Konner, 1982). Garlic is an unclear example of the category "vegetable," as is ketchup, as we see in the famous controversy that followed the proposal of the Reagan administration that ketchup be classified as a vegetable in meeting nutritional guidelines for school lunch menus.
- They often display a *family resemblance* structure (Wittgenstein, 1953).[1] The members of a family of people generally do not have a single feature in common. Instead, a pool of features such as hair color, mouth shape, or nose size is shared by various sets of family members. Similarly, the members of family resemblance categories have different features that run through different subsets: green color is shared by spinach, celery, and broccoli, but not carrots or cauliflower; stems and bunches of florets are shared by broccoli and cauliflower but not carrots.
- Good members tend to have *characteristic nondefining features*. For example, gray hair and a domestic lifestyle characterize many grandmothers, but someone can be a grandmother without possessing either property, such as Elizabeth Taylor.

Evidence for family resemblance categories

Human concepts pick out categories of objects; what kind of category do they pick out? There is a large body of evidence, summarized in Brown (1977), Smith and Medin (1981), and Rosch (1973, 1978, 1988), that has been taken to show that human concepts correspond to family resemblance categories. First, semanticists and philosophers have generally failed in their attempts to find necessary and sufficient conditions for most natural concepts that are labeled by words (see Fodor, Garrett, Walker, and Parkes, 1980). Second, psychologists have found that subjects can give ratings of the goodness of membership of a list of exemplars with respect to a category that are reliable and in close agreement with one another. Similarly, there is good agreement about prototypes and unclear cases. Third, these judgments are not unanalyzable gut feelings but can be predicted in a systematic way using a feature calculus, in which the features possessed by a given exemplar (assessed independently, for example, by asking subjects to list the attributes of the object) are compared with those possessed by the other members of the category. Fourth, judgments of goodness of membership have strong effects on performance in various psychological tasks. For example, people can verify that prototypical members are members of a category faster and more accurately than peripheral members, and when asked to recall instances of a category, they name prototypical members first. Fifth, developmental psychologists have found that children often learn the names for prototypical exemplars of a category before learning other exemplars, and apply superordinate terms such as *bird* to its prototypical members first. Sixth, linguists have found that certain adverbials called *hedges* are sensitive to prototypicality: one can say that a sparrow, but not a penguin, is a bird *par excellence*, and that a penguin, but not a sparrow, is *technically* or *strictly speaking* a bird.

Evidence against family resemblance categories

On the other hand, there is also evidence that certain aspects of human concepts do not correspond to family resemblance categories. Some of the empirical effects that have been interpreted as demonstrating family resemblance classes also occur for categories that people clearly treat as being classical. Armstrong, Gleitman, and Gleitman (1983) have found that subjects show a great deal of agreement with one another in rating the degree of membership of exemplars of categories like "female" and "odd number." For example, they agree that a mother is a better example of a female than a comedienne is, and that 13 is a better example of an odd number than 23. Similarly, Armstrong, *et al.* found that people take less time and are more accurate at deciding that 13 is an odd number than that 23 is, and that a mother is a female than that a comedienne is. Since these subjects surely knew that "female" and "odd number" in reality have sharp boundaries and all-or-none membership (and Armstrong, *et al.* discovered, in an independent questionnaire, that their subjects believed as such), it calls into question whether the analogous results that Rosch and others obtained for "bird" or "tool" really tell us anything about people's representations of those concepts.

Moreover, most judgments of membership in family resemblance categories based on characteristic features are highly corrigible when people are asked to engage in careful reasoning about it. For some purposes people are willing to consider a penguin as a full-fledged bird and Elizabeth Taylor a full-fledged grandmother. In fact characteristic nondefining features can be quickly abandoned, even by young children. Children say that three-legged dogs are dogs, that raccoons with stripes painted down their backs are raccoons, not skunks (Rey, 1983; Armstrong, *et al.*, 1983; Keil, 1989).

People not only shelve their perception of similarity when pressed as to what an object "really is," but also when making everyday inferences about the object based on its category membership. For example, Gelman and Markman (1987) showed three-year-old children a picture of a flamingo, a picture of a bat, and a picture of a blackbird, which looked a lot more like the bat than the flamingo. They told the children that a flamingo feeds its babies mashed-up food but a bat feeds its babies milk, and asked them what the blackbird feeds its babies. With no further information, children go by appearances and predict "milk." But all it took was a mention that flamingos and blackbirds were "birds," and the children lumped them together and predicted "mashed-up food."

Similar demonstrations with adults have shown that inference is often not driven by the similarity criteria that define family resemblance categories (see Murphy, 1993; Medin, 1989; Kelly, 1992; Smith, Langston, and Nisbett, 1992; Rips, 1989; Rey, 1983). For example, when people are asked which two out of three belong together – white hair, gray hair, black hair – they say that black is the odd hair out, because aging hair turns gray then white. But when asked about a white cloud, a gray cloud, and a black cloud, they say that white is the odd cloud out, because gray and black clouds give rain. In another experiment, subjects were asked whether a three-inch disk is more similar to a quarter or a pizza, and whether it is more likely to *be* a quarter or a pizza? Most said it is more similar to a quarter but more likely to be a pizza, presumably because quarters have to be standardized but pizzas can vary. Most people, upon being presented with a centipede, a caterpillar that looks like it, and a butterfly that the caterpillar turns into, feel that the caterpillar and butterfly are "the same animal," but the caterpillar and centipede are not, despite appearances to the contrary.

Possible resolutions

There are several possible resolutions of this conflicting evidence.

First, human concepts could basically pick out family resemblance categories. Classical categories would be special cases or artifacts resulting from explicit instruction, such as in formal schooling. Alternatively, human concepts could basically pick out classical categories. Family resemblance categories would be artifacts of experimental tasks asking subjects for graded judgments or asking them to make categorization decisions under time pressure. A third, compromise position, would say that human concepts correspond to both classical and family resemblance categories. Classical categories are the "core" of the concept, used for reasoning. Family resemblance categories are "identification procedures" or "stereotypes," used for identification of category exemplars on the basis of available perceptual information, or for rapid approximate reasoning. Although most theorists have tended toward compromise positions, something close to the mainly family resemblance view can be found in Lakoff (1987), Rosch (1978), and Smith, Medin, and Rips (1984); something close to the mainly classical view can be found in Rey (1983), Fodor (1981), and Armstrong, *et al.* (1983), and tentative proposals favoring the core-plus-identification-procedure compromise can be found in Smith and Medin (1981), Armstrong, *et al.* (1983), and Osherson and Smith (1981).

This leads to several open questions.

(1) Is one type of category psychologically real, the other an artifact or special case?
(2) If both are psychologically real, can they be distinguished by function (e.g., reasoning versus categorization)?
(3) If both are psychologically real, are they handled by the same kind of computational architecture?
(4) If either or both are psychologically real, do they correspond to ontological categories?

Rey (1983) stresses the importance of distinguishing the "metaphysical" problem of what kinds of categories the world contains (as characterized by the best current scientific characterization of that aspect of the world), and the "epistemological" or psychological question of what kinds of categories people use to understand the world. That is, are classical (or family resemblance) categories incorrectly imposed by people on the world because of limitations of the way the mind works, or is there some sense in which the world contains classical (or family resemblance) categories, which people can accurately represent as such, presumably because the mind evolved to grasp aspects of the world accurately?

We will attempt to shed light on these questions by examining an unusual source of evidence: English past tense forms.

An unexpected test case: English past tense forms

English verbs come in two types: those that have regular past tense forms, and those that have irregular past tense forms. Consider them as two categories: "regular verbs," such as *walk/walked, talk/talked, jog/jogged, pat/patted, kiss/kissed*, and *play/played*, and "irregular verbs," such as *hit/hit, go/went, sleep/slept, make/made, ring/rang, bring/brought, stink/stunk*, and *fly/flew*.

In fact the irregular verbs are not a single class but a set of subclasses, which can be subdivided according to the kind of change that the stem undergoes to form the past tense (Jespersen, 1942; Curme, 1935; Bybee and Slobin, 1982a; Pinker and Prince, 1988):

- No change: *hit, fit, slit, split, quit, knit, spit, shit, bid, rid, forbid, shed, spread, wed, let, set, upset, wet, cut, shut, put, burst, cast, cost, thrust, hurt*
- Lax the vowel: *bleed, breed, feed, lead, mislead, read, speed, plead, meet, hide, slide, bite, light, shoot*
- Devoice the final d: *bend, send, spend, lend, rend, build*
- Lax the vowel, add a -t: *lose, deal, feel, kneel, mean, dream, creep, keep, leap, sleep, sweep, weep, leave*
- Change the vowel, add a -d: *flee, say, hear, sell, tell, foretell, do*
- Change the rhyme to -ought: *buy, bring, catch, fight, seek, teach, think*

- Change e or similar vowel to o: *freeze, speak, steal, weave, get, forget, swear, tear, wear, bear, forbear, forswear, awake, wake, break, choose*
- Change -ing to -ang or -ung: *ring, sing, spring, drink, shrink, sink, stink, swim, begin, cling, fling, sling, sting, string, swing, wring, stick, dig, win, spin, stink, slink, run, hang, strike, sneak*
- Change the vowel to u: *blow, grow, know, throw, draw, withdraw, fly, slay*
- Miscellaneous vowel changes: *take, mistake, forsake, shake, partake, bind, find, grind, wind, rise, arise, write, smite, ride, drive, strive, fall, befall, hold, behold, come, become, eat, beat, see, give, forgive, forbid, sit, spit, lie*
- Complete replacement (suppletion): *be, go, undergo*

Let us consider some properties of the irregular subclasses.

Properties of the irregular subclasses

1 Characteristic nondefining features

The irregular subclasses tend to be characterized by phonological properties other than those that define the change from stem to past form. Consider the subclass that changes an *o* vowel to *u*, I [*blow, grow, know, throw, draw, withdraw, fly, slay*]. In principle, any verb with an *o* or similar vowel could be included in the subclass. In fact, all the verbs in the subclass end in a vowel, usually a diphthong, and most begin with a consonant cluster.

Similarly, the subclass that changes *ay* to *aw* – *bind, find, grind, wind* – could include any verb with the vowel *ay*, but in fact, all the verbs happen to end in -*nd*. The subclass that changes a final *d* to *t* – *bend, send, spend, lend, rend, build* – could include any word ending in *d*, but in fact, most of the verbs rhyme with -*end*. Finally, the subclass that changes the vowel *e* to *u* – *take, mistake, forsake, shake* – could include any word with an *e*, but in fact all the verbs rhyme with -*ake* and begin with a coronal consonant.

Note that the characteristic nondefining features are arbitrary, not lawful, with respect to the sound pattern of English. No rule of phonology excludes *loon* as the past tense of *loan* or *choud* as the past of *chide*.

2 Family resemblance

Irregular subclasses display a family resemblance structure (Bybee and Slobin, 1982a; Bybee and Moder, 1983). Consider the subclass that changes an *I* to an *^*. Most of the verbs end with velar nasal consonant: *shrink, sink, stink, cling, fling, sling, sting, string, swing, wring, slink*. Some end in a consonant that is velar but not nasal: *stick, dig, sneak, strike*. Others end in a vowel that is nasal but not velar: *win, spin, swim, begin*.

Similarly, within the subclass that changes a final diphthong to *u*, some begin with <consonant–sonorant> cluster, and contain the diphthong *ow*: *blow, grow, throw*. But one member, *know*, contains the *ow* diphthong, but does not begin with a consonant cluster. Others begin with a consonant cluster, but have a different diphthong or no diphthong at all: *draw, withdraw, fly, slay.*

3 Prototypicality

Bybee and Moder (1983) point out that for many of the subclasses, one can characterize a prototype, based on the kinds of characteristic phonological properties that go into defining the family resemblance structure. According to Bybee and Moder, the prototype of the *ing* → *ung* subclass is:

$$\text{S} \quad \text{C} \quad \text{C} \quad \text{i} \qquad \begin{matrix} \text{[velar]} \\ \text{[nasal]} \end{matrix}$$

where "C" stands for a consonant. This prototype is maximally similar to the most members of the existing subclass, but more interestingly, it predicts subjects' generalization of the $I → \wedge$ change to novel verbs. Bybee and Moder asked subjects to rate how natural a variety of putative past tense forms sounded for each of a set of nonce stems. The independent variable was the similarity of the stem to the prototype listed above. They found that subjects were extremely likely to accept the vowel change for stems like *spling, strink,* and *skring,* which match the schema for the prototype exactly. They were only slightly less willing to accept *struck* and *skrum* as the past of *strick* and *skrim,* which differ from the prototype in one feature. Somewhat lower in acceptability were *spruv* for *spriv,* and similar past forms for *sking, smig, pling,* and *krink. Glick, krin, plim, shink* were even less likely to admit of the vowel change, and *trib, vin,* and *sid,* the forms furthest from the prototype, were the least acceptable of all. The results have been replicated by Prasada and Pinker (1993), and with analogous German forms by Marcus, Brinkmann, Clahsen, Wiese, and Pinker (1995).

4 Graded goodness-of-membership

Within most of the subclasses, there are some verbs that clearly accept the irregular past tense form, but others, usually of low but nonzero frequency, for which the specified past tense form is less than fully acceptable, being accompanied by a sense of unusualness or stiltedness. Below we contrast, for a variety of subclasses, some "good examples" of the past tense form with "poor examples" of the same kinds of forms. Intuitions vary from person to person for the "poor" examples, as is true for nonprototypical exemplars of conceptual categories; the perceptions of "poorness" we report here are true for most of the speakers of American English we have consulted, and are documented quantitatively by Ullman (1993):

(1) **Good examples**   **Poor examples**
   hit, split   spit, forbid
   bled, fed   pled, sped

burnt, bent	learnt, lent, rent
dealt, felt, meant	knelt, dreamt
froze, spoke	wove, hove
got, forgot	begot, trod
wrote, drove, rode	dove, strove, smote, strode

5 Unclear cases

For some verbs associated with a subclass, the mandated past tense form is so poor in people's judgment that it is unclear whether the verb can be said to belong to the subclass at all. Sometimes these are verbs restricted to idioms, clichés, or other specialized usages. For example, the expression *forgo the pleasure of*, as in *You will excuse me if I forgo the pleasure of reading your paper until it's published*, sounds fairly natural. Because the verb has a transparent morphological decomposition as [for + go], the form *forgoed* is clearly unacceptable, but the irregular past tense form, as in *Last night I forwent the pleasure of grading student papers*, is decidedly peculiar if not outright ungrammatical (this intuition has been corroborated by ratings from subject in a study by Ullman and Pinker, in preparation). Likewise, the sentence *The Vietnam War is rending the fabric of American society* is a natural-sounding cliché, but? *The Vietnam War rent the fabric of American society* is distinctly less natural. One occasionally hears the idiom *That conclusion does not sit well with me*, but many people balk at *That conclusion has not sat well with many people*. *That dress really becomes you* is a natural English sentence; *When you were ten pounds lighter, that dress really became you* is almost unintelligible.

In other cases grammatical phenomena conspire to make the past tense form of a verb extremely rare. The transitive verb *stand* meaning "to tolerate" is fairly common but because it is usually used as the complement of a negated auxiliary, as in *She can't stand him*, the verb is almost always heard in its stem form. In constructions where the past is allowed to reveal itself, the verb sounds quite odd: compare *I don't know how she stands him* with *?I don't know how she stood him*; similarly, *I don't know how she bears it* versus *?I don't know how she bore it*.

Conclusions about the irregular subclasses

Subclasses of irregular verbs in English have characteristic nondefining features, family resemblance structures, prototypes, gradations of goodness of membership, and unclear or fuzzy cases. Since these are exactly the properties that define family resemblance categories, we conclude, in agreement with Bybee and Moder (1983), that the irregular subclasses are family resemblance categories.

This is a surprising conclusion. Linguistic rules are traditionally thought of as a paradigm case of categorical, all-or-none operations, and might be thought to correspond to classical categories if anything did. The fact that entities subject to grammatical operations can have a clear family resemblance structure thus has far-ranging implications for some theorists. For example, for Rumelhart and McClelland (1986) this phenomenon is part of their argument for a radically new approach to studying language, based on a computational architecture in which rules play no causal role. For Lakoff (1987), it is part of a call for a radically new way of understanding human cognition in general.

It seems clear that at least one kind of linguistic object, English irregular past tenses, falls into family resemblance categories. An important question at this point is: Do all linguistic objects fall into family resemblance categories?

Properties of the regular class

More specifically, we might ask, do English regular verbs fall into family resemblance categories? One answer, favored by Bybee (Bybee and Moder, 1983; Bybee, 1991) and by Rumelhart and McClelland (1986), is "yes": the regular class just has more members, and more general characteristic features. Let us examine this possibility.

A confounding factor: the Blocking Principle

The regular and irregular classes interact in a specific way, and it is necessary to take account of this interaction so that the properties of the irregular subclasses do not confound our examination of the properties of the regular class. The interaction is governed by what has been called the "Blocking Principle" (Aronoff, 1976) or the "Unique Entry" Principle (Pinker, 1984): if a verb has an irregular past tense form, its regular form is pre-empted or "blocked". Thus the fact that *go* has an irregular past *went* not only allows us to talk of past instances of going using *went*, but it prevents us from using **goed*. The verb *glow*, in contrast, does not have an irregular past **glew*, so its regular past *glowed* is not blocked.

We saw in a previous section how some irregular past forms are "fuzzy" or marginal in their grammaticality. As a result of blocking, these gradations of goodness can cause the appearance of complementary gradations of goodness of the corresponding regular. Thus because *pled* is a marginal past tense form for *plead* but one that we nonetheless recognize, the regular form *pleaded guilty* sounds fairly good but may be tinged with a bit of uncertainty for some speakers. Conversely, *?wept* is a fairly good past tense form of *weep*, though not maximally natural (compare, for example, *kept* for *keep*). As a result *??weeped* does not sound terribly good, though it is not perceived as being completely ungrammatical either (compare **keeped*). This effect has been documented by Michael Ullman (1993; see also Pinker, 1991 and Pinker and Prince, 1994) who asked subjects to rate the naturalness of irregular and regularized past tense forms for 40 verbs whose irregular pasts were somewhat fuzzy in goodness. The two sets of ratings were consistently negatively correlated.

What we now try to do is put aside this reciprocity effect due to blocking, and see if it is possible to determine whether the regular class has family resemblance category properties independent of those of the irregular subclasses with which it competes.

1 Independence of the phonology of the stem

The first salient property of the regular class is that it has no sensitivity to the phonological properties of its stems. As a result, it has no phonologically char-acterized prototype, gradations of membership, or characteristic features.

First, the phonological conditions that govern the irregular subclasses can be entirely flouted by regular verbs. In the extreme case, homophones can have different past tense forms: *ring/rang* versus *wring/wrung*, *hang/hung* (suspend) versus *hang/hanged* (execute), *lie/lay* (recline) versus *lie/lied* (fib), *fit/fit* (what a shirt does) versus *fit/fitted* (what a tailor does). More generally, there are regular counterexamples to the membership criteria for each of the irregular subclasses:

(2) shut/shut   jut/jutted
     bleed/bled   need/needed
     bend/bent   mend/mended
     sleep/slept   seep/seeped
     sell/sold   yell/yelled
     freeze/froze   seize/seized
     grow/grew   glow/glowed
     take/took   fake/faked
     stink/stunk   blink/blinked
     ring/rang   ring/ringed

This shows that the phonologically defined fuzzy boundaries of the irregular subclasses do not create complementary phonological fuzzy boundaries of the regular classes. The effect of the Blocking Principle is that specific irregular *words* block their corresponding regulars. Though most of those words come from regions of phonological space whose neighbors are also often irregular, those regions do not define complementary fuzzy "holes" in the space from which the regulars are excluded; a regular form can occupy any point in that space whatsoever. Moreover, it is not just that there *already* exist regular verbs in the language that live in irregular phonological neighborhoods; regular class can *add* members that violate *any* irregular membership criteria. The reason has been spelled out by Kiparsky (1982a, b), Pinker and Prince (1988), Kim, Pinker, Prince, and Prasada (1991), Kim, Marcus, Pinker, Hollander, and Coppola (1994). Irregular forms are verb roots, not verbs. Not all verbs have verb roots: a verb that is intuitively derived from a noun (e.g. *to nail*) has a noun root. A noun or an adjective cannot be marked in the lexicon as having an "irregular past," because nouns and adjectives do not have past tense forms at all; the notion makes no sense. Therefore, a verb created out of a noun or adjective cannot have an irregular past either. All such verbs are regular, regard-less of their phonological properties:

(3) He braked the car suddenly. ≠ broke
    He flied out to center field. ≠ flew
    He ringed the city with artillery. *rang
    Martina 2-setted Chris. *2-set
    He sleighed down the hill. *slew
    He de-flea'd his dog. *de-fled
    He spitted the pig. *spat
    He righted the boat. *rote
    He high-sticked the goalie. *high-stuck
    He grandstanded to the crowd. *grandstood

This makes it possible, in principle, for *any* sound sequence whatsoever to become a regular verb. There is a lexical rule in English that converts a name into a verb prefixed with *out*, as in *Reagan has finally out-Nixoned Nixon.* Like all verbs derived from non-verbs, it is regular. Since any linguistically possible sound can be someone's name, any linguistically possible sound can be a regular verb, allowing there to be regular homophones for any irregular. For example:

(4) Mary out-Sally-Rided Sally Ride.
    *Mary out-Sally-Rode Sally Ride.

   In grim notoriety, Alcatraz out-Sing-Singed Sing-Sing.
   *In grim notoriety, Alcatraz out-Sing-Sang Sing-Sing.
   *In grim notoriety, Alcatraz out-Sang-Sang Sing-Sing.
   *In grim notoriety, Alcatraz out-Sing-Sung Sing Sing.
   *In grim notoriety, Alcatraz out-Sung-Sung Sing Sing.

This effect has been demonstrated experimentally in several kinds of subject. Kim, *et al.* (1991) asked subjects to rate the regular and irregular past tense forms of a set of verbs that were either derived from nouns that were homophonous with an irregular verb or were derived directly from the irregular verbs. For verbs with noun roots, the regular form was given higher ratings; for verbs with verb roots, the irregular form was given higher ratings. Similar effects have been demonstrated in non-college-educated subjects (Kim, *et al.*, 1991), children (Kim, *et al.*, 1994), and German-speaking adults (Marcus, *et al.*, 1995).

Perfectly natural-sounding regular past tense forms exist not only when the verb root is similar to an irregular, but when it is *dissimilar* to existing regular roots, and hence lacks a prototype that would serve as the source of an analogical generalization. Prasada and Pinker (1993) replicated Bybee and Moder's (1983) study but also presented novel *regular* words of differing similarity to existing English regular words. For example, *plip* is close to one of the prototypes for regular verbs in English, because it rhymes with *slip, flip, trip, nip, sip, clip, dip, grip, strip, tip, whip,* and *zip,* whereas *smaig* rhymes with no existing verb root, and *ploamph* is not even phonologically well-formed in English. Nonetheless people rated the prototypical and peripheral forms as sounding equally natural (relative to their stems), and produced the prototypical and peripheral forms with the same probability when they had to produce them.

2 No prototypes, gradation of membership, or unclear cases caused by low frequency or restricted contexts

Unlike irregular past tense forms, regular past tense forms do not suffer in well-formedness on account of frequency, familiarity, idiomaticity, frozenness, or restricted syntactic contexts. Pinker and Prince (1988) noted that though the verb *perambulate* may be of low frequency, it is no worse-sounding in its past tense form than it is in its stem form; there is no feeling that *perambulated* is a worse past tense form of *perambulate* than *walked* is of *walk*. In fact, a verb can be of essentially zero frequency and still have a regular past tense form that is judged as no worse than the verb itself. Though *fleech, fleer,* and *anastomose* are unknown to most speakers, speakers judge *fleeched, fleered,* and *anastomosed* to be perfectly good as the past tense forms of those verbs. These observations have been confirmed experimentally by Ullman (1993), in a study in which people judged the naturalness of hundreds of verbs and their past tense forms. Subjects' ratings of regular pasts correlate highly with their ratings of the corresponding stems, but not with the frequency of the past form (partialing out stem rating). In contrast, ratings of irregular pasts correlate less strongly with their stem ratings but significantly with past frequency, partialing out stem rating.

Unlike irregular verbs, when a regular verb gets trapped in a frozen or restricted expression, putting it into the past tense makes it no worse. For example, the verb *eke* is seldom used outside contexts such as *She ekes out a living*, but *She eked out a living*, unlike *forwent the pleasure of*, does not suffer because of it. Similarly: *He crooked his finger; She stinted no effort; I broached the subject with him; The news augured well for his chances.* The regular verb *to afford*, like the irregular verb *to stand*, usually occurs as a complement to *can't*, but when liberated from this context its past tense form is perfectly natural: *I don't know how she afforded it.* Similarly, both *She doesn't suffer fools gladly* and *She never suffered fools gladly* are acceptable.

The phenomena discussed in this section and the preceding one show why the apparent gradedness of acceptability for regular forms like *pleaded* or *weeped* can be localized to the gradedness of the corresponding irregulars because of the effects of the Blocking Principle and are not inherent to the regular verbs *per se*. The gradedness of certain irregulars generally comes from low frequency combined with similarity to the prototypes of their subclasses (Ullman, 1993). But for regular verbs that do not compete with specific irregular roots, there is no complementary landscape of acceptability defined by phonology and frequency; all are equally good.

3 *Default structure*

As we have seen, the regular past tense alternation can apply regardless of the stem's:

- phonological properties
- verb-root versus non-verb-root status
- frequency
- listedness (familiarity)
- range of contexts

Apparently, the regular class is the *default* class. More generally, there is a sense in which the category of regular verbs has no properties; it is an epiphenomenon of the scope of application of the regular rule.

Conclusions about the regular class

These phenomena invite the following conclusion. The class of regular verbs in English is a classical category. Its necessary and sufficient conditions are simply the conditions of application of the regular rule within English grammar. Those conditions for membership can be stated simply: a verb, unless it has an irregular root. The category has no other properties.

Psychological implications

We have shown that by the standard criteria the irregular subclasses are prototype or family resemblance categories, and the regular class is a classical category. If we take this conclusion seriously, it has several immediate implications.

Psychological reality

First, both family resemblance categories and classical categories can be psychologically real and natural. Classical categories need not be the product of explicit instruction or formal schooling: the regular past tense alternation does not have to be taught, and indeed every child learns it and begins to use it productively in the third year of life (Marcus, Pinker, Ullman, Hollander, Rosen, and Xu, 1992). The fact that children apply the regular alternation even to high-frequency irregular stems such as *come* and *go*, which they also use with their correct irregular pasts much of the time, suggests that children in some way appreciate the inherently universal range of the regular rule. And like adults, they apply the regular suffix to regular verbs regardless of the degree of the verbs' similarity to other regular verbs (Marcus, *et al.*, 1992), and to irregular-sounding verbs that are derived from nouns and adjectives (Kim, *et al.*, 1994). Gordon (1985) and Stromswold (1990) have shown that children as young as three make qualitative distinctions between regular and irregular plural nouns related to their different formal roles within the grammar, without the benefit of implicit or explicit teaching inputs (see Marcus, *et al.*, 1992, and Kim, *et al.*, 1994 for discussion).

The regularization-through-derivation effect (*flied out, high-sticked*) provides particularly compelling evidence that classical categories do not have to be the product of rules that are explicitly formulated and deliberately transmitted. The use of the regular rule as a default operation, applying to any derived verb regardless of its phonology, is a grass-roots phenomenon whose subtleties are better appreciated at an unconscious level by the person in the street than by those charged with formulating prescriptive rules. Kim, *et al.* (1991) found that non-college-educated subjects showed the effect strongly, and in the recent history of English and other languages there are documented cases in which the language has accommodated such regularizations in the face of explicit opposition from editors and prescriptive grammarians. For example, Mencken (1936) notes that the verb *to joy-ride*, first attaining popularity in the 1920s, was usually given the past tense form *joy-rided*, as we would predict given its obvious derivation from the noun *a joy-ride*. Prescriptive grammarians unsuccessfully tried to encourage *joy-rode* in its place. Similarly, Kim, *et al.* (1994) showed that children display the effect despite the fact that most have rarely or never heard regularized past tense forms for irregular-sounding verbs in the speech of adults.

On the other side, family resemblance categories are not necessarily artifacts of reaction time studies or rating studies, as Fodor (1981) and Armstrong, *et al.* (1983) have suggested. Children generalize family resemblance patterns of irregular subclasses to inappropriate regular and irregular verbs in their spontaneous speech, as in *brang* for *brought* and *bote* for *bit*, and their generalizations appear to be sensitive to the frequency and family resemblance structure of the subclasses (Xu and Pinker, 1995; Bybee and Slobin, 1982a; Rumelhart and McClelland, 1986; Pinker and Prince, 1988). The irregular subclass structure also affects dialectal variation and historical change in adult speech (Bybee and Slobin, 1982b; Mencken, 1936; Prasada and Pinker, 1993) with new irregular forms occasionally entering the language if their stems are sufficiently similar to existing irregular stems.

Psychological function

A further corollary is that classical categories and family resemblance categories do not have to have different psychological functions such as careful versus casual reasoning, or reasoning versus categorization of exemplars. What is perhaps most striking about the contrast between the regular and irregular verbs is that two kinds of entities live side-by-side in people's heads, serving the same function within the grammar as a whole: regular and irregular verbs play indistinguishable roles in the syntax and semantics of tense in English. There is no construction, for example, in which a regular but not an irregular verb can be inserted or vice versa, and no systematic difference in the temporal relationships semantically encoded in the past tense forms of regular and irregular verbs.

More specifically, it is difficult to make sense of the notion that family resemblance categories are the product of a set of identification procedures used to classify exemplars as belonging to core categories with a more classical structure. The suggestion that "irregulars are used in perceptually categorizing members of the regular class" is uninterpretable. The irregulars are a class of words that display one kind of category structure; the regulars do not display it.

Perhaps a closer analogy would be between membership conditions for the irregular subclasses and the operation on the stem that generates the past tense form. One might say that a family resemblance structure characterizes the membership of each subclass, but once an item is a member (for whatever reason), it is transformed into a past tense form by a classical all-or-none operation such as laxing the vowel. But even here, the core identification distinction does not easily apply, because the changes that the member stems of a class undergo, and not just the properties of the stems, have a heterogeneous structure. Within the subclass of irregulars ending in *ing/ink*, *sing* goes to *sang* while *sting* goes to *stung* and *bring* goes to *brought*. Similarly, within the subclass that adds a [d] to the past tense form some verbs have their vowel laxed (e.g., *hear/heard*), some have their final consonant deleted (e.g., *make/made, have/had*), some undergo the *e–o* ablaut that is frequent across the various subclasses (e.g., *sell/sold*), and one undergoes a unique vowel change (*do/did*). Furthermore, within a class there can be graded differences of acceptability among different possible change operations: *?spit/spat* for *spit*, *?begot/??begat* for *beget*, *bid/?bade* for *bid*. In sum, both the membership conditions and the operations of the irregular subclasses display family resemblance category effects. Later we will show that the core/identification distinction does not work well for conceptual categories either.

Underlying psychological mechanism

Though classical and family resemblance categories, in the case of the past tense, do not differ in psychological function – what they are used for – they do differ in psychological structure – what mental processes give rise to them. Our main claim is that the psychological difference between regulars and irregulars is a fundamental one, and is of a piece with the psychological difference between classical and family resemblance categories in general, including conceptual categories.

As we have seen, the classical category consisting of regular verbs is defined completely and implicitly by the nature of a rule in the context of a formal system, in this case, a rule within English grammar that applies to any word bearing the part-of-speech symbol "verb" unless it has an irregular root. The category is not a generalization or summary over a set of exemplars; indeed, it is blind to the properties of the exemplars that fall into the category. It falls out of the combinatorial rule system that allows humans to communicate propositions (including novel, unusual, or abstract propositions) by building complex words, phrases, and sentences in which the meaning of the whole is determinable by the meanings of the parts and the way in which they are combined.

Family resemblance categories, in contrast, are generalizations of patterns of property correlations within a set of memorized exemplars. Consequently, factors that affect human memory affect the composition of the irregular class. A well-known example is word frequency. Irregular verbs tend to be higher in frequency than regular verbs (Ullman, 1993; Marcus, *et al.*, 1995), and if an irregular verb's frequency declines diachronically, it is liable to become regular (Hooper, 1976; Bybee and Slobin, 1982b; Bybee, 1985). Presumably this is because irregulars are memorized; to memorize an item one has to hear it; if opportunities for hearing an item are few, its irregular form cannot be acquired and the regular rule can apply as the default. This is also presumably the cause of the fuzziness of the past tenses of irregular verbs that are used mainly in nonpast forms, such as *forgo* or the idiomatic meanings of *stand* or *become*.

A related account could help explain the genesis of the family resemblance structure of the irregular verbs. Rosch and Mervis (1975) found that people find lists of strings that display family resemblance structures easier to remember than lists of strings with arbitrary patterns of similarity. Just as frequency affects the memorizability, hence composition, of the irregular subclasses, so might family resemblance structure. The current subclasses may have emerged from a Darwinian process in which the irregular verbs that survived the generation-to-generation memorization cycle were those that could be grouped into easy-to-remember family resemblance clusters.

In sum, the properties of the regular and irregular classes of verbs in English show that both classical categories and family resemblance categories can be psychologically real, easily and naturally acquired, and not subject to a division of labor by function along the lines of reasoning versus identification of exemplars. Rather, they differ because they are the products of two different kinds of mental processes: a formal rule system, and a memorized partially structured list of exemplars. We now point out two less obvious conclusions based on properties of the regular and irregular classes: classical and prototype categories are suited to different kinds of computational architectures, and the mental mechanisms giving rise to classical and family resemblance categories are suited to representing inherently different kinds of entities in the world. Finally, we return to human conceptual categories like "bird" and "mother," seeing whether we can gain insight by generalizing our findings about classical and prototype categories.

Computational architecture

The acquisition of English past tense morphology has recently been implemented in a computer simulation model by Rumelhart and McClelland (1986). The architecture of the simulation, its behavior, and its fidelity to human data have been discussed in detail (Pinker and Prince, 1988, 1992; Lachter and Bever, 1988; Sproat, 1992; Prasada and Pinker, 1993; Marcus, *et al.*, 1992, 1995).

The RM model makes use of a device called a "pattern associator." This device is paradigmatic of Parallel Distributed Processing (PDP) or Connectionist architectures that are currently a central topic of debate in cognitive science (Rumelhart and McClelland, 1986; McClelland and Rumelhart, 1986; Pinker and Mehler, 1988). Our discussion will refer to pattern associators in particular, not to all PDP architectures.

A pattern associator is a feedforward two- or three-layer network that is designed to take an input representation and map it onto an output representation; in this case, a stem and a past tense form, respectively. There is a set of input nodes, each corresponding to a possible property of an input form. An input is encoded by a separate device, an encoder, that dissolves it into its properties: a node is turned on corresponding to each property that the input possesses, and the unique identity of the input item itself is not registered on any node (this is sometimes called "distributed representation"). Likewise, the pattern associator has a set of output nodes, each representing a property of the output form when activated. Every input node is connected to every output node by a weighted link. When a set of input nodes is activated, each node sends its activation level, multiplied by the link weight, to the output nodes it is connected to. Each output node sums its weighted inputs, compares the result to a threshold, and turns on if the threshold is exceeded, with a likelihood related to the difference.

The model "learns" by adjusting the weights on its links. During "training" trials, an input is provided to the model, it is allowed to generate an output, and the output pattern is compared to the target "correct" output pattern provided by a "teacher." The discrepancies between actual and target outputs are registered, and the weights on the links leading to the discrepant output nodes are adjusted to lessen the likelihood of such an error when similar input patterns are presented in the future. For an output node that is off but should be on, the weights on the links from currently active input links are incremented and the node's threshold is lowered. For an output that is on but should be off, the weights on links from active input nodes are lowered, and the threshold on the node is raised. The procedure is repeated for other inputs; node adjustments from different inputs are superimposed in a single set of link weights, which represent the aggregate correlational structure between properties of the inputs and properties of the outputs in the training set.

Two properties of pattern associators are crucial in understanding their behavior: items are represented by their properties, and statistical contingencies between every input property and every output property across a set of items are recorded and superimposed.

Before being applied to the case of learning past tense forms, pattern associators had been studied in detail, including their ability to learn and identify members of conceptual categories (McClelland and Rumelhart, 1985), and they are known to do certain things well. They can often reproduce a set of associations in a training set, and generalize to new cases based on their similarity to existing ones. They are sensitive to input pattern frequencies in ways similar to humans. Furthermore they reproduce many of the effects displayed by people when dealing with family resemblance categories. McClelland and Rumelhart (1985) and Whittlesea (1989) have devised pattern associators that are fed patterns of data concerning properties of a set of nonlinguistic objects. They found that the models do fairly well at duplicating the effects of frequency, prototypicality, family resemblance, gradations of membership, and influence of particular exemplars on human classification times and error rates. Since such effects are known to be related to co-occurrence frequencies among objects' features (Smith and Medin, 1981), this is not surprising.

Thanks to these abilities, the pattern associator that Rumelhart and McClelland applied to learning past tense forms handled the irregular verbs with some success. The model was fed a set of 420 verbs (each one presented as a pair consisting of its stem and its past form), including 84 irregular verbs, about 200 times each. Following this training it was able to approximate the past tense forms for all of them given only the stem as input. Furthermore, it was able to generalize to new irregular verbs by analogy to similar ones in the training set, such as *bid* for *bid*, *clung* for *cling*, and *wept* for *weep*. In addition, it showed a tendency to extend some of the subregular alternations to regular verbs based on their similarity to irregulars, such as *kid* for *kid* and *slept* for *slip*, showing a sensitivity to the family resemblance structure of the irregular subclasses. Finally, its tendencies to overgeneralize the regular *d* ending to the various irregular subclasses is in rough accord with children's tendencies to do so, which in turn is based on the frequency and consistency of the vowel changes that the verbs within each subclass undergo (Pinker and Prince, 1988; Sproat, 1992).[2]

However, pattern associators do not seem to perform as well for other kinds of mappings. In particular, they are deficient in handling regular verbs. For one thing, their uniform structure, in which regulars and irregulars are handled by a single associative mechanism, provides no explanation for why the regular class has such different properties from the irregular classes; it falsely predicts that the regular class should just be a larger and more general prototype subclass.

Moreover, the pattern associator fails to acquire the regulars properly. Pinker and Prince (1988) pointed out that the model is prone to *blending*. Competing statistical regularities in which a stem participates do not block each other, they get superimposed. For example, the model produced erroneous forms in which an irregular vowel change was combined with the regular ending, as in *sepped* as the past of *sip* or *brawned* for *brown*. It would often blend the *t* and *id* variants of the regular past tense form, producing *stepted* for *step* or *typted* for *type*. Sometimes the blends are quite odd, such as *membled* for *mailed* or *toureder* for *tour*.

Furthermore, Pinker and Prince noted that in contrast to the default nature of the regular rule, the RM model failed to produce any past form at all for certain verbs, such as *jump, pump, glare,* and *trail.* Presumably this was because the model could not treat the regular ending as an operation that was capable of applying to any stem whatsoever, regardless of its properties; the ending was simply associated with the features of the regular stems encountered in the input. If a new verb happened to lie in a region of phonological space in which no verbs had previously been supplied in the training set (e.g. *jump* and *pump,* with their unusual word-final consonant cluster), no coherent set of output features was strongly enough associated with the active input features, and no response above the background noise could be made. Pinker and Prince's diagnosis was tested by Prasada and Pinker (1993) who presented typical-sounding and unusual-sounding verbs to the trained network. For the unusual-sounding items, it produced odd blends and chimeras such as *smairf-sprurice, trilb-treelilt, smeej-leefloag,* and *frilg-freezled.*

The model is inconsistent with developmental evidence. Children first use many irregulars properly when they use them in a past tense form at all (e.g., *broke*), then begin to overregularize them occasionally (e.g., *broke* and *breaked*) before the overregularizations drop out years later. Since pattern associators are driven by pattern frequency, the only way the RM model could be made to duplicate this sequence was first to expose it to a small number of high-frequency verbs, most of them irregular, presented a few times each, followed by a large number of medium-frequency verbs, most of them regular, presented many times each. Only when the model was swamped with exemplars of the regular pattern did it begin to overregularize verbs it had previously handled properly. However, the onset of overregularization in children is not caused by a sudden shift in the proportion of regular verbs in the speech they hear from their parents: the proportion remains largely unchanged before, during, and after the point at which they begin to overregularize (Pinker and Prince, 1988; Slobin, 1971; Marcus, *et al.*, 1992). Nor is it caused by a rapid increase in the proportion of verbs in their vocabulary that is regular; the percentage of children's vocabulary that is regular increases quickly when they are *not* overregularizing, and increases more slowly when they *are* overregularizing (Marcus, *et al.*, 1992).

The results support the traditional explanation of overregularization, which appeals not to frequency but to different internal mechanisms: children at first memorize irregular and regular pasts, then they discover that a regularity holds between many regular stems and their past forms and create a rule which they apply across the board, including instances in which a memorized irregular form does not come to mind quickly enough; the rule is available to fill the gap, resulting in an overregularization. Consistent with this interpretation, Marcus, *et al.* (1992) found that children begin to overregularize at the age at which they first start using *regular* forms consistently in the past tense; that, presumably, is the point at which the regular rule has been acquired. As mentioned, the fact that the regular rule is applied even to high-frequency irregular stems, which remain high in frequency in children's input throughout development, shows that children treat the regular rule as having an unlimited range.

Proponents of connectionist models of language have offered two kinds of counterarguments, but both are inadequate. One is that the RM model was a two-layer perceptron, and that three-layer models, whose hidden layer's weights are trained by error-back-propagation, perform much better (see, e.g., Plunkett and Marchman, 1991, 1993; MacWhinney and Leinbach, 1991). However, Sproat (1992), Prasada and Pinker (1993), and Marcus (1995) have shown that hidden-layer models have the same problems as the original RM model. The other is that the effects of regularity in English come from the fact that regular verbs are in the majority in English, fostering the broadest generalization. German presents the crucial comparison. Marcus, *et al.* (1995) reviewed the grammar and vocabulary statistics of German in detail, and documented that the participle *-t* and plural *-s* are found in a *minority* of words in the language, compared to irregular alternatives, but nonetheless apply in exactly the "default" circumstances where access to memorized verbs or their sounds fails, including novel, unusual-sounding, and derived words (i.e., the *flied-out* examples have exact analogues in German). The findings were verified in two experiments eliciting ratings of novel German words from German adults. The cross-linguistic comparison suggests that default suffixation is not due to numerous regular words reinforcing a pattern in associative memory, but to a memory-independent, symbol-concatenating mental operation.

In sum, pattern associators handle irregular subclasses reasonably well, but handle the regular class poorly, both in terms of computational ability and psychological fidelity. We suggest that this is a symptom of the relative suitability of this architecture to handle family resemblance and classical categories in general. The reasons, we suggest, are straightforward:

- Classical categories are the product of formal rules.
- Formal rules apply to objects regardless of their content – that is what "formal rule" means.
- Pattern associators soak up patterns of correlation among objects' contents – that is what they are designed to do.
- Therefore, pattern associators are not suited to handling classical categories.

We conclude that the brain contains some kind of non-associative architecture, used in language, and presumably elsewhere.

Epistemological categories versus ontological categories

Rey (1983) has pointed out that even if people can be shown to use prototype (or classical) categories, it doesn't mean that the world contains prototype (or classical) categories – that is, that the lawful generalizations of how the world works, as captured by the best scientific description, make reference to one kind of category or the other. That raises a question: if there is a psychological distinction between the representation of prototype and classical categories, is it because these representations accurately reflect different kinds of categories in the world? Or does the human system of categorization arise from some limitation or quirk of our neurological apparatus that does not necessarily correspond to the lawful groupings in the world?

The question of what kinds of categories are in the mind and what kinds of categories are in the world are clearly related. If the mind evolved to allow us to grasp and make predictions about the world, the mental system that forms conceptual categories should be built around implicit assumptions about the kinds of categories that the world contains, in the same way that a visual algorithm for recovering structure from motion might presuppose a world with rigid objects and might work best in situations where the assumption is satisfied.

Because the English past tense system shows classical and family resemblance categories, but must have a very different ontology from that underlying concepts of tools, vegetables, animals, and other entities that ordinarily compose conceptual categories, an analysis of the source of classical and family resemblance categories in the past tense system may help us to identify the distinctive conditions in which these two kinds of categories arise.

Where do the properties of the regular and irregular classes come from?

The properties of the regular class are simply products of the regular rule. From any speaker's perspective, the class exists "in the world" in the sense that other speakers of the language possess the rule and use it in speaking and understanding. This in turn comes from the basic requirement for parity in any communicative system. Language can only function if the rule system that generates forms is shared by a community of speakers. Thus one person's use of a past tense rule (or any rule) in production presupposes that that same rule is in the head of the listener and will be used to interpret the produced form. Similarly, use of a rule in comprehension presupposes that the speaker used it in programming his speech. So the answer to the question "What class of entities in the world is picked out by a rule-generated class, such as the regular verbs?" is "The class of entities that can be generated by a replica of that rule in other speakers' minds."

For the irregulars, the issue is more complex. Of course, irregulars, like regulars, are usable only because they are shared by other speakers. But unlike the case of regulars, where the rule is so simple and efficient that it naturally fits into a grammar shared by all members of a community, the composition of the irregular class is so seemingly illogical that one must ask how other speakers came to possess it to begin with.

In a previous section we suggested that the family resemblance structure of the irregular past tense subclasses is related to the fact that irregulars must be memorized and human memory has an easier time with family resemblance categories (Rosch and Mervis, 1975). Interestingly, the obvious Darwinian metaphor in which the most easily memorized verbs survive does not apply to the psychology of the child doing the learning. Note that family resemblance structure is not a property that some individual verbs have and others lack, but a property of *an entire class* of verbs. But unlike the subjects of Rosch and Mervis's experiment, children are not given two classes to learn, one with a random organization, the other with a family resemblance structure, with the latter being better retained in memory. One might suppose that the similarity of a verb to other verbs affects how easy it is for the child to memorize that verb, and that in the aggregate, a family resemblance structure arises. But this, too, does not properly characterize the acquisition of irregular forms. There is relatively little change in the composition of the subclasses between one generation and the next; children end up pretty much learning the same irregulars that their parents learned. Moreover, if the childrens' memory really shaped their irregular classes, we would expect them to arrive at classical categories, not family resemblance categories. For example, a rule that said "all verbs ending in *ing* go to *ang*" would have much higher inter-item similarity than the current English *ing* class, so verbs like *bring* would be even easier to memorize. In fact, given children's ability to regularize the irregular verbs by assimilating them to the regular rule (*bringed*) or generalizing a subregularity (*brang*), children would be in a position to obliterate irregularity altogether if their memory were all that fragile.

A more accurate version of the Darwinian metaphor would point to effects of memory not in the child doing the learning in a given generation but in the children (and adults) of previous generations whose learning shaped the input to the current generation. Even though each generation reproduces the previous generation's irregulars with high accuracy, changes occasionally creep in. These can be characterized as a kind of convergent evolution toward certain attractor states. For example, some lower-frequency irregular verbs may be consistently regularized in a given generation, and this might be more likely for verbs that are most dissimilar from other irregulars and hence most weakly protected from forgetting. (Marcus, *et al.*, 1992, documented that irregulars that are more dissimilar from other irregulars are more prone to being overregularized by children.) In the other direction, some regulars might be attracted into an irregular class because of their high similarity to existing irregulars, as is happening with *sneak-snuck* (cf. *stick-stuck, string-strung*, etc.). If some of these occasional forgettings and analogies get fixed in a language community in a contagion-like process (see Cavalli-Sforza and Feldman, 1981) and accumulate across generations, classes of verbs with a family resemblance structure can arise. The past tense forms *quit* and *knelt*, for example, are fairly recent additions to the language, and are presumably irregular because of their similarity to verbs like *hit* and *feel*. This process can be seen even more clearly in the more rapid process of dialect formation in smaller communities, where forms such as *bring-brang, slide-slud*, and *drag-drug* are common (see Mencken, 1936).

Though this convergent evolution process surely occurs, it cannot explain the entire structure of the irregulars in English. First, it does not capture the historical facts completely. The language never contained arbitrary irregular classes whose members were attracted into or drifted out of prototype classes because of fussy learners, leaving the next generation with a slightly more orderly class than they had found. Rather, as we shall see, the strong subclasses are in evidence from the earliest sources. Second, the account posits a kind of harmony between properties of the memory of one generation and properties of the memory of succeeding generations: the errors of forgetting and assimilation of generation n result in a stimulus set that is easier for generation $n + 1$ to acquire without error, because the memory of both generations is biased towards remembering items that are similar along multiple dimensions to other items. But in doing so it just begs the question of why memorization of categories in any generation should be biased toward partial similarities to begin with. Why does memory work that way? Why not do away with remembering patterns of irregularity altogether and give the next generation a nice regular class?

In the history of English, *divergence* has been the more prominent trend. That confronted learners in each generation with the task of learning classes whose family resemblance structure was not simply caused by the psychology of previous generations of learners. In Old English, there were seven "strong" past tense classes, in which the vowel of the stem was altered, and three "weak" classes, in which a suffix containing d was added, which sometimes caused a modification of the stem vowel for phonological reasons. Most of the modern irregulars derived from verbs in the strong classes. The modern regular rule, and most of the irregulars that end in t or d such as *meant* and *made*, evolved from the weak classes. The Old English strong classes had themselves evolved out of classes that can be traced back to Proto-Germanic, and before that, to Proto-Indo-European. Many scholars believe that the Proto-Indo-European classes were defined by regular rules: the number and type of segments following the vowel within the stem determined the kind of change the vowel underwent (Johnson, 1986; Bever and Langendoen, 1963; Prokosch, 1939; Campbell, 1959). By the time of Old English the patterns are more complicated, but they were still more pervasive and productive and tolerated fewer arbitrary exceptions than the alternations in the modern English irregular subclasses. That is, many stems that are now regular but fit the characteristic pattern of an irregular subclass in fact used to undergo the irregular change: *deem/dempt, lean/leant, chide/chid, seem/sempt, believe/beleft, greet/gret, heat/het, bite/bote, slide/slode, abide/abode, fare/fore, help/holp*, and many others. Furthermore, there was a moderate degree of productivity within the classes (Johnson, 1986).

Beginning in the Middle English period, there was an even greater decline in the productivity and systematicity of the past tense subclasses, with the exception of one of the weak suffixing processes. The main causes were the huge influx of new words from Latin and French that needed a general, condition-free past tense operation, and the widespread shifts in vowel pronunciation that obscured regularities in the vowel-change operations. The weak suffixing operation was already being used for verbs derived from nouns in Old English, which did not fit the sound patterns defining the strong classes of verbs, so their extension to borrowed words was natural (see Marcus, *et al.*, 1995 for further discussion).

In sum, there has been a consistent trend in the history of English since the Proto-Indo-European period for the strong classes, originally defined by phonological properties of their stems, to become lists of items to be learned individually. This had an interesting consequence. Originally, lists would have been relatively homogeneous, owing to their once having been generated by rule-like operations. But then, a variety of unrelated processes, operating on individual items, destroyed the homogeneity of the classes. Here are some examples:

Phonological change   *Blow, grow, throw, know, draw, fly, slay* all begin with <consonant–sonorant> cluster except for *know*. The reason that *know* is exceptional leaps from the page in the way it is spelled. As it was originally pronounced, with an initial *k*, it did fit the pattern; when syllable-initial *kn* mutated to *n* within the sound pattern of the language as a whole, *know* was left stranded as an exception within its subclass.

Morphological category collapse   In Old English, past tenses were distinguished by person and number. For example, *sing* had a paradigm which can we simplify as follows:

(5)

	Singular	**Plural**
1st	*sang*	*sung*
2nd	*sung*	*sung*
3rd	*sang*	*sung*

When the number distinctions collapsed, each verb had to pick a form for its past tense as if playing musical chairs. Different verbs made different choices; hence we have *sing/sang/sung* alongside *sling/slung/slung*. The contrast between *freeze/froze* and *cleave/cleft* has a similar cause.

Attrition   Earlier, the class in which *t* changed to *d* had the following members: *bend, lend, send, spend, blend, wend, rend, shend, build, geld, gild, gird* (Bybee and Slobin, 1982b). The class is succinctly characterized as containing a vowel followed by a sonorant followed by *d*. In modern American English, the verbs *geld, gird, gild, wend, rend* and *shend* are now obsolete or obscure. The residue of the class has 5 members, 4 rhyming with *end* and 1 with *ild*. Although logically it still can be characterized as ending in a vowel–sonorant–*d* cluster, the presence of regular verbs ending in *eld* and *ird*, and the highly specific nature of the rhyme with *end*, makes it more natural to represent the class as containing verbs that rhyme with *end* but with one exception.

Idiosyncratic pronunciation shifts   In Old and Middle English, many verbs had variant pronunciations. If past tense forms are simply associated with their stems, rather than being generated from them by a rule, it should be possible for one pronunciation to drift out of the language while its corresponding past tense form survives. For example, *run* could once be pronounced as *rin*. The forms *ran* and *has run* would thus fit perfectly into the pattern *sing/sang/has sung*, *ring/rang/has rung*, and so on. *Rin* is no longer possible in standard English, but *ran/has run* has survived. Similarly, *spit* used to have the pronunciations *spete* and *spitte*. The former yields the past tense form that became *spat*, the latter the form that became *spit*. Both past tense forms survive as fuzzy or marginal exemplars in American English, but of course only *spit* survives as its stem.

We conclude that a class of items that originally is homogeneous on account of its being generated by a rule can acquire a family resemblance structure by divergent evolution once the rule ceases to operate and the effects of unrelated processes acting on individual members accumulate through history. Superimposed on these patterns is a convergent process in which the accumulated effects of the analogizing and forgetting tendencies of previous generations of learners cause partly similar forms to accrete onto an existing class. Thus a learner in a single generation is confronted with family resemblance structures as products of these divergent and convergent historical processes, and these structures can be said to exist in the world independent of his or her psychology.

Implications for conceptual categories

We have suggested that classical and family resemblance categories can be found in a surprising realm, English past tense forms, and that within it the two kinds of categories have distinct linguistic properties, psychological representations, underlying computational architectures, and real-world counterparts. Do these discoveries offer insight into the role of classical and family resemblance categories in the domain of conceptual categories like birds and mothers? Perhaps the best way to start would be to consider what conceptual categories are for.

The function of conceptual categories: inference of unobserved properties

No two objects are exactly alike. So why do we use conceptual categories? Why don't we treat every object as the unique individual that it is? And why do we form the categories we do? Why lump together salmon, minnow, and sharks, as opposed to sharks, leaves, and spaghetti? These are elementary questions, but possible answers to them have not informed research on conceptual categories as much as would be desirable. Often it is suggested that people need categories to reduce memory or processing load, but given that the cortex has in the order of a trillion synapses and that long-term memory is often characterized as "infinite," the suggestion carries little force. Furthermore for many categories (e.g., months, baseball teams, one's friends) both the category and every individual member of it are stored in memory. Rey (1983) provides a list of the main functions that concepts are supposed to perform, including stability of concepts at different times in a given individual or at the same time for different individuals, the ability of a concept to serve as the basis for a word's meaning, the basis for things to belong to categories in the world, and the basis for people to know which things belong to which categories in the world. But none of the functions had anything to do with why we form conceptual categories at all, or why some categories in the world are natural bases for concepts and others unnatural.

Bobick (1987), Shepard (1987), and Anderson (1990) have attempted to reverse-engineer human conceptual categories, seeking principles motivating the choice of particular representations for concepts in terms of their function in people's dealings with the world. They have independently proposed that categories are useful because they allow us to infer objects' unobserved properties from their observed properties (see also Rosch, 1978, and Quine, 1969.) Though we cannot know everything about an object, we can observe some things; the observed properties allow us to assign the object to a category, and the structure of the category then allows us to infer the values of the object's unobserved properties. Categories at different levels of a hierarchy (e.g., cocker spaniels, dogs, mammals, vertebrates, animals, living things) are useful because they allow a variety of tradeoffs between the ease of categorization and the power of the licensed inference. For low-level, specific categories, one has to know a lot about the object to know that it belongs in the category, but one can then infer many unobserved aspects of the nature of the object. For high-level, general categories, one need know only a few properties of an object to know it belongs to the category, but one can infer only a few of its unobserved properties once it is thus categorized.

To be concrete: knowing that Peter is a cottontail, we can predict that he grows, breathes, moves, was suckled, inhabits open country or woodland clearings, spreads tularemia, and can contract myxomatosis. If we knew only that that he was a mammal, the list would include only growing, breathing, moving, and being suckled. If we knew only that he was an animal, it would shrink to growing, breathing, and moving. On the other hand, it's much harder to tag Peter as a cottontail than as a mammal or an animal. To tag him as a mammal we need only notice that he is furry and moving, but to tag him as a cottontail we have to notice that he is long-eared, shorttailed, long hind-legged, and has white on the underside of his tail. To identify *very* specific categories we have to examine so many properties that there would be few left to predict. Most of our everyday categories are somewhere in the middle: "rabbit," not mammal or cottontail; "car," not vehicle or Ford Tempo; "chair," not furniture or Barcalounger. They represent a compromise between how hard it is to identify the category and how much good the category does. These compromises correspond to Rosch's (1978) notion of the "basic level" of a category.

We can get away with inductive leaps based on categories only because the world works in certain ways. Objects are not randomly distributed through the multidimensional space of properties that humans are interested in; they cluster in regions of co-occurring properties that Bobick calls "natural modes" and Shepard calls "consequential regions." These modes are the result of the laws of form and function that govern the processes that create and preserve objects. For example, the laws of geometry dictate that objects formed out of mult-iple parts have concavities at the part boundaries. The laws of physics dictate that objects denser than water will be found on lake bottoms rather than lake surfaces. Laws of physics and biology dictate that objects that move quickly through fluid media have streamlined shapes, and bigger objects tend to have thicker legs. Knowing some of the coordinates of an object in prop-erty space, the existence of natural modes allows us to infer (at least probabili-stically) some of its unknown coordinates.

Classical categories: inferences within idealized lawful systems

All this raises the question of what kinds of regularities in the world generate natural modes that humans can exploit by forming concepts. In the most general sense, regularities in the world are the result of scientific and mathematical laws (e.g., of physics, geometry, physiology). Laws can be captured in formal systems, given a suitable idealization of the world. By "formal system" we mean a symbol manipulation scheme, consisting of a set of propositions and a set of inference rules that apply to the propositions by virtue of their form alone, so that any knowledge not explicitly stated in the propositions cannot affect the inferences made within it. Formal systems, we suggest, are the contexts in which classical categories are defined. Therefore, under whatever idealization of the world a set of scientific or mathematical laws applies, the world contains classical categories. For example, when the texture, material, thickness, and microscopically ragged edges of real-world objects are provisionally ignored, some can be idealized as plane geometry figures. Under this idealization, objects with two equal sides can be assigned to the category "isosceles triangle". Once the object is assigned to that category, one can make the inference that it also has two equal angles, among other things. Frictionless planes, ideal gases, randomly interbreeding local populations, and uniform communities of undis-tractable speaker-hearers are other idealizations under which regularities in the behavior of objects can be captured in formal systems. A smart organism could use formal systems as idealizations of the world to infer unknown prop-erties from known ones. In the psychology of categorization, no less than in the history of science, idealization or selective *ignoring* of salient correlational structure is crucial to apprehending causal laws.

We suggest, then, that wherever classical categories are to be found in human cognition, they will be part of a mentally represented formal system allow-ing nontrivial deductions to be made. Given the function of concepts, why else would one bother to assign an object to a classical category? What is unnatural, then, about traditional experiments in concept formation, such as those of Hull (1920), Bruner, Goodnow, and Austin (1956), and Hunt (1962), in which subjects learn categories like "red square with two borders," is not that the categories have sharp boundaries or necessary and sufficient conditions, but that the categories are not part of a system allowing interesting inferences to be drawn – they are unnatural because they are literally useless.

Though one tends to think of formal systems as the province of systematic education in modern societies, there are a variety of kinds of formal systems capturing inference-supporting regularities that could be accessible to people, including those in preindustrial and preagricultural societies. For example, bodies of folk science need not resemble their counterparts in modern scientific systems, but they can reproduce some of their visible predictions with alternative means. Mathematical intuitions too are incorporated into many other systems of common knowledge. Here are some examples:

- Arithmetic, with classical categories like "a set of 3 objects," supporting inferences like "cannot be divided into two equal parts," independent of the properties of objects that can be grouped into threes.
- Geometry, with classical categories like "circle," supporting inferences like "all points equidistant from the center" or "circumference is a constant multiple of diameter," regardless of whether previously encountered circles are sections of tree trunks or drawings in sand.
- Logic, with classical categories like "disjunctive proposition," supporting inferences like "is true if its second part is true" or "is false if the negations of both its parts are true."
- Folk biology, with classical categories like "toad of kind x," which support inferences like "extract of mouth gland when boiled and dried is poisonous," regardless of its similarities to nonpoisonous toads or its dissimilarities to other poisonous toads.
- Folk physiology, with the famous all-or-none category "pregnant," supporting the inferences "female," "nonvirgin," and "future mother," regardless of weight or body shape.

In addition, the world of humans contains other humans, and there is reason to expect mentally represented formal systems to arise that govern the conduct of humans with one another. Given the fuzziness and experience-dependent individual variation inherent to family resemblance categories, it is not surprising that conflicts of interest between individuals will often be resolved by reasoning within systems that have a classical structure, allowing all-or-none decisions whose basis can be agreed to by all parties. There is a rationale to assigning drinking privileges to people after their twenty-first birthday, arbitrary though that is, rather than attempting to ascertain the emotional maturity of each individual when he or she asks for a drink. Furthermore, Freyd (1983) and Smolensky (1988) have suggested that certain kinds of socially transmitted knowledge are likely to assume the form of discrete symbol systems because of constraints on the channels of communication with which they must be communicated between individuals and transmitted between generations. It is not hard to identify formal systems involved in social interactions that define classical categories:

- Kinship, with classical categories like "grandmother of X," supporting inferences like "may be the mother of X's uncle or aunt" or "is the daughter of one of X's great-grandparents," regardless of hair color or propensity to bake muffins.
- Sociopolitical structure, with classical categories like "president" or "chief," supporting inferences like "decisions on entering wars are carried out," regardless of physical strength, height, sex, and so on.
- Law, with classical categories like "felon," supporting inferences like "cannot hold public office," regardless of presence or absence of a sinister appearance, social class, and so on.
- Language, with the category "verb," supporting the inference "has a past tense form suffixed with *d* unless it has an irregular root," regardless of its phonological properties.

It is unlikely to be a coincidence that humans uniquely and nearly universally have language, counting systems, folk science, kinship systems, music, and law. As we have seen, classical categories deriving from formal systems require a neural architecture that is capable of ignoring the statistical microstructure of the properties of the exemplars of a category that an individual has encountered. One can speculate that the development of a non-associative neural architecture suitable to formal systems was a critical event in the evolution of human intelligence.

Family resemblance categories: inferences within historically related similarity clusters

In a previous section we showed that learners of English are presented with a family resemblance structure and must cope with it if they are to speak the same language as their parents. Are there cases where learners of conceptual categories are similarly forced to cope with a family resemblance structure in nature if they are to be able to make inferences about it? Many people have noted similarities between linguistic and biological evolution (see, e.g., Cavalli-Sforza and Feldman, 1981), and there is a particularly compelling analogy in the formation of family resemblance categories in the evolution of biological taxa.

It is generally believed that a novel species evolves from a small interbreeding population occupying a local, hence relatively homogeneous stable environment. Through natural selection, the organisms become adapted to the local environment, with the adaptive traits spreading through the population via sexual reproduction. As a result the population assumes a morphology that is relatively uniform – since selection acts to reduce variation (Sober, 1984; Ridley, 1986) – and predictable in part from engineering considerations to the extent that the organism's niche and selection pressures can be identified (Hutchinson, 1959; Williams, 1966; Dawkins, 1986).

Subsequent geographic dispersal can cause the members of the ancestral population to form reproductively isolated subgroups. They are no longer homogenized by interbreeding, and no longer subject to the same set of selection pressures imposed by a local environment. In the first generation following dispersal, the species is still homogeneous. Then, a set of distinct processes destroys the homogeneity of class: genetic drift, local geographic and climatic changes imposing new selection pressures, adaptive radiations following entry into empty environments, and local extinctions. As a result, the descendants of the ancestral species form a family resemblance category – the category of "birds," for example. Robins, penguins, and ostriches share many features (e.g., feathers) because of their common ancestry from a single population adapted to flying, while differing because of independent processes applying to different members of that population through history.

This suggests that as in the case of irregular past tense subclasses, the family resemblance structure of many biological taxa comes from the world, not just the minds of those learning about them. Note that such family resemblance structures are not always identical with classically defined categories, and may be indispensable even in the best scientific theories. Many traditional biological taxa are somewhat arbitrary, serving as useful summaries of similar kinds of organisms. There are, to be sure, some biological categories that are well defined, including species (a population of interbreeding organisms sharing a common genepool), and monophyletic groups or clades (all the descendants of a common ancestor also belonging to the category). But many important biological taxa are neither. For example, fish comprise thousands of species, including coelocanths and trout. But the most recent common ancestor of coelocanths and trout is also an ancestor of mammals. Therefore no branch of the genealogical tree of organisms corresponds to all and only fish; trout and coelocanths are grouped together and distinguished from mammals by virtue of their many shared properties. To some biologists this is reason to deny the scientific significance of the category altogether, but most probably agree with the sentiment captured by Gould when he writes: "A coelocanth looks like a fish, tastes like a fish, acts like a fish, and therefore – in some legitimate sense beyond hidebound tradition – is a fish" (Gould, 1983; p. 363). In other words, biologists often recognize a category that is characterized as a cluster of co-occurring properties. Indeed some taxonomists have tried to characterize taxa using clustering algorithms that use criteria similar to those thought to lead to the formation of prototype conceptual categories in humans (see Ridley, 1986; Bobick, 1987).

Thus we have seen two examples of family resemblance categories that exist in the world, and that have the same genesis: a law-governed process creating a relatively homogeneous class, followed by a cessation of the influence of the process and the operation of independent historical causes that hetero-genize the class, though not to such an extent that the inter-member similar-ities are obliterated entirely. Since objects can escape the direct influence of laws while retaining some of their effects, a smart organism cannot count on always being able to capture the world's regularities in formal systems. For example, no observer knowing only the United States Constitution would be able to explain why presidents are always wealthy white Christian males. Similarly, presumably no observer, not even a scientist equipped with a knowl-edge of physiology and ecology, would be able to explain why penguins have feathers, like robins, rather than fur, like seals. Instead, it will often be best simply to record the interpredictive contingencies among objects' properties to infer unknown properties from known ones. Thus a smart observer can record the contingencies among feathers, wings, egg-laying, beaks, and so on, to note that the world contains a set of objects in which these properties cluster, and to use the presence of one subset of properties to infer the likely presence of others.

Just as irregular subclasses were shaped both by divergent and convergent historical processes, in the domain of conceptual categories there is a conver-gent process that can cause objects to cluster around natural modes even if the objects are not linked as descendants of a more homogeneous ancestral population. For example, there is no genealogical account of chairs that paral-lels the ones we give for languages or species. The similarities among chairs are caused solely by a convergent process, in which a set of properties repeat-edly arises because it is particularly stable and adaptive in a given kind of environment. In contrast, several historically unrelated groups of organisms evolve to attain such a set. Examples include nonhomologous organs such as the eyes of mammals and of cephalopods, the wings of bats and of birds, and polyphyletic groups such as cactuslike plants (which have evolved succulent leaves, spines, and corrugated stems as adaptations to desert climates in several parts of the world). As in the case of divergent evolution discussed above, there is a mixture of shared and distinct properties that are respectively caused by law-governed adaptation and historical accident, though here the influences are temporally reversed. For example, although vertebrate and cephalopod eyes are strikingly similar, in vertebrates the photoreceptors point away from the light source and incoming light has to pass through the optic nerve fibers, whereas in cephalopods the photoreceptors point toward the light in a more "sensible" arrangement. The difference is thought to have arisen from the different evolutionary starting points defined by the ancestors to the two groups, presumably relating to differences in the embryological pro-cesses that lay down optic and neural tissue. Artifacts such as chairs develop via a similar process; for a chair to be useful, it must have a shape and material that is suited to the function of being stable and access-ible (Winston, Binford, Katz, and Lowry, 1983), but it is also influenced by myriad historical factors such as style, available materials, and ease of manu-facture with contemporary technology. Social stereotypes, arising from the many historical accidents that cause certain kinds of people to assume certain roles, are another example.

We might expect family resemblance categories to be formed whenever there is a correlational structure in the properties that people attend to among sets of objects they care about, and that the world will contain opportunities for such clusters to form wherever there are laws that cause properties to be visibly correlated and historical contingencies that cause the correlations to be less than perfect – which is to say, almost everywhere.

Schematic summary

These ideas may be summed up by sketching four schematic worlds. Each contains objects that have three attributes of interest to an organism, and each can assume a small set of values, so an object can be represented as, say, ABC. The organism needs to know as many of the values as possible but can observe only subsets of them.

A random world   In the world schematized in (6), there is nothing to gain by forming categories; every attribute occurs equally often with every other attribute, and the maximum predictive power is achieved by consulting base rate probabilities across all objects.

(6) ABC
    ABF
    AEC
    AEF
    DBC
    DBF
    DEC
    DEF

An ideal law-governed world   In the second world, classical categories are useful. In world (7), an observer can categorize any object as being in one of two classes, "X" and "Y," on the basis of, say, the first attribute, and can predict the values of the other two attributes with certainty.

(7) ABC
    ABC
    ABC
    ABC
    DEF
    DEF
    DEF
    DEF

Such a world can come about if there are laws operating, in particular, X → A B C and Y → D E F, and an observer who internalized the laws can forget the actual groups of objects and consult the laws themselves.

A world evolved by divergent processes   In the third world, prototype categories are useful (8). Knowing that an object has the attribute A one can assign it to the first category and then predict with .67 confidence that it will have a B (as opposed to the .375 base rate for B's in general).

(8) ABC
     ABR
     PBC
     AQC
     DEF
     DER
     PEF
     DQR

Such a world can come about if the classical world in (7) was subject to divergent evolutionary forces in which some of the attributes of each object within a category were subject to unsystematic replacement with other values through history:

(9) ABC
     AB(C → I)
     (A → P)BC
     A(B → Q)C
     DEF
     DE(F → R)
     (D → P)EF
     D(E → Q)F

A world evolved by convergent processes   Finally, another world in which prototype categories would be useful is (10).

(10) ABC
      ABC
      ABC
      ABF
      ABC
      DBC
      AEC
      DBF
      AEF
      DEF

DEC
DEF
DEF
DEF

It could have evolved out of the random world of (6) by a convergent evolutionary process if certain pairs of values were more stable than others and served as attractor states. For example if the selective pressures in (11) were at work, world (10) could have developed through the historical sequence shown in (12).

(11)   AB > AE
       BC > BF
       AC > DC
       DE > DB
       EF > EC
       DF > AF

(12)   ABC → ABC
       ABF → ABC, DBF
       AEC → ABC, AEF
       AEF → ABF, DEF
       DBC → ABC, DEC
       DBF → DBC, DEF
       DEC → AEC, DEF
       DEF → DEF

Interactions between classical and family resemblance categories

The referents of many words, such as *bird* and *grandmother*, appear to have properties of both classical and family resemblance categories. How are these two systems to be reconciled? The distinction between cores used for reasoning and stereotypes used for identification was of no help in the case of English past tense forms, and the distinction does not do much better when applied to conceptual categories. Many classical categories have no family resemblance identification procedure associated with them, for example, the number "–3". Many family resemblance categories have no classical category serving as a core that they identify, such as "seafood" or Wittgenstein's famous example, "game." Furthermore some classical categories can be identified by simple, easily computable, all-or-none tests. For example, odd numbers can be quickly identified by tests such as "divide by 2 and check for remainder" or "see if last digit is 1, 3, 5, 7, or 9"; in fact, the features of the associated family resemblance class, such as "has many odd digits" (which Armstrong, *et al.*, 1983, found to be a feature that led subjects to judge that a given number was a better example of the "odd" class), are not even probabilistically diagnostic. On the other side, family resemblance classes can support nonperceptual reasoning, sometimes quite reliably, such as "presidents are well-off," "vegetables are not served for desert," or "tools have metal in them." We are not denying that categories may have "cores" in the sense that some kinds of knowledge are given priority over others when they conflict, but it does not seem that this distinction can be equated either with quick identification versus reasoning or with classical versus family resemblance categories (Armstrong, *et al.*, 1983, and Rey, 1983, mention some of these problems).

A more likely reconciliation is that people have parallel mental systems, one that records the correlational structure among sets of similar objects, and another that sets up systems of idealized laws. Often a category within one system will be linked to a counterpart within the other. In general we might expect family resemblance categories to be more accessible to observers than classical categories. Most objects in the world are cluttered by the effects of the myriad historical processes that led to their creation and preservation, obscuring underlying laws. In the lucky cases when people are able to see these laws peeking through the clutter and try to capture them in idealized systems, the elements of these systems may be seen to apply to many of the objects belonging to the family resemblance clusters that were independently formed though simple observation of the correlational structure displayed by frequently encountered exemplars. In such cases, languages appear to assign the same verbal label to both. This is what leads to the ambiguity of *A penguin is a perfectly good bird*, one of whose readings is true, the other false. It also is what leads to such paradoxes as Armstrong *et al.*'s subjects who could assert both that odd numbers form an all-or-none category tolerating no intermediate degrees of membership, and that 13 is a better example of it than 23.

The fact that these systems are distinct is at the heart of Putnam (1975) and Kripke's (1972) well-known argument that natural kind terms are not defined by a set of conditions that pick out the members of the category in the world. Thus even though we think of "animal" as a necessary part of the definition of *cat*, if we were to discover that cats were in fact robots controlled from Mars, we would not conclude that *cat* no longer referred to the entities formerly called cats, or that it did refer to catlike entities on some other planet that really were animals. Rather, the label *cat* is rigidly assigned to a set of objects in the world. According to Putnam, people have a "stereotype" of such objects that helps them at tentative identification, but will defer to an expert in establishing category membership more definitively.

Schwartz (1979) points out that such intuitions about natural kind terms are driven by a belief that their members have an "underlying trait" in common. People act as if they believe in the existence of such a trait even if they are prepared to accept that their current belief of the nature of the trait is incorrect, even if they have no idea of the nature of the trait, indeed even if *no one* knows the nature of the trait. Schwartz's analysis suggests that people's intuitions are influenced by a metatheory, a kind of essentialism, that asserts that the varying forms that an object can assume are causally related in terms of their relation to a hidden trait or essence. These essences are clearly not family resemblance categories since it is possible, indeed typical, that they are not associated with *any* properties of the relevant objects at all, let alone a cluster of frequently co-occurring properties (that is, if Putnam and Kripke are correct, there is no property associated with the concept underlying "cat" or "gold" that cannot be relinquished by a person while he or she still believes the concept to apply to that category of objects). Rather, the hidden essences must be represented as abstract symbols within internally represented formal systems, defining slots for particular traits provided by folk or formal science, and allowing inferences to be made about heredity, growth, physical structure, change, and behavior. Subsequent research by Keil (1989) and Gelman (Gelman, *et al.*, 1994) has gathered evidence for essentialist thinking in preschool children and adults in nonliterate cultures. More generally, Medin (1989), Murphy (1993), Rips (1989), and Smith, Nisbett, and Langston (1992) have emphasized the importance of intuitive rule-like theories in the organization of people's conceptual categories.

In sum, natural kind terms like *cat* or *gold* are linked both to stereotypes, or family resemblance categories acquired by observing the correlational structure in sets of similar familiar objects, and abstract essences or hidden traits within an intuitive theory which unite objects' varying appearances and provide the infrastructure for bits of folk science and institutionalized science. (The Putnam–Kripke puzzles arise from thought-experiments in which these systems are separated.)

The human tendency to induce categories from clusters of similar objects they have encountered, to construct formal systems of rules applying to ideal objects, and to link entities of the two kinds with each other is probably the root of many apparent paradoxes in the study of concepts and often within the conceptual systems themselves. For example, exactly this duality can be found in the legal system in the distinction between reasoning by constitutionality and by precedent. Legal questions are commonly resolved by appealing to precedents, with more similar prior decisions carrying more weight. However when the constitutionality of a current decision is at issue, only a restricted set of principles is relevant, and similarity to earlier cases must be ignored.

First-order and higher-order systems

We have been highlighting the distinction between formal systems and correlational structures, but that does not mean one will commonly see either system in isolation. We have already noted that the two kinds of systems can cross-reference the same objects. Here we suggest that more complex kinds of interaction are also possible, and that the nature of these interactions can explain why the distinction may not appear clearcut in many cases.

Vanishing classical categories   Sometimes close scrutiny reveals a family resemblance structure even for categories that would seem to be classical through and through. Lakoff (1987) points out that even the set of "mothers" has a family resemblance structure. He is not even referring to stereotypes about children, church, and kitchen, but to the literal characterization of the concept "mother" itself. There are, he points out, surrogate mothers, adoptive mothers, eggdonor mothers, and foster mothers. Similarly, the notion of a "species" has unclear cases. There are populations dispersed over a wide area in which animal A might be able to mate with neighbor B, B can mate with neighbor C, but A cannot mate with C. Lakoff suggests that classical categories never exist in the world; they are artifacts of an outmoded Aristotelian mode of thinking.

Our account suggests a different analysis. Classical categories are implicitly defined by formal systems, but formal systems work only as *idealizations*. Real objects are never idealizations, by definition. Each is a nexus at which many influences converge. Therefore objects as they are found in the world should not directly fall into classical categories. Only as idealized within a single formal system do they function as members of classical categories. Often, *several* formal systems pick out the same class of individuals. Let us call them "first-order" systems. For example, the concept "mother" is used within several formal systems. In genetics, it corresponds to the contributor of half of an offspring's genes including those on the X chromosome in mammals. In evolutionary theory it corresponds to the producer of the larger of the two kinds of gametes in sexual reproduction. In the theory of reproductive physiology it is the site of prenatal growth and birth. In the ethology of mammals it is the adult that provides the greater minimal parental investment. In law it might be the spouse of the father, or the female guardian. In genealogy it is the immediate female ancestor.

This multiple ambiguity is usually invisible because the different notions of mother are generally the same individuals. These coinciding roles are put into register by other systems, which we call "second-order" systems. For example, theories within sociobiology predict that under certain general conditions the birth mother will also be the nurturance mother because of the effects of investing resources in individuals likely to share one's genes. Physiological considerations explain why it is the contributor of the larger of the two gametes that is likely to be the site of prenatal growth. The social anthropology of a society might dictate that the spouse of the father is the one who nurtures the offspring after birth.

These theories about theories, or second-order systems, systematically link entities within subordinate, first-order formal systems. And under the conditions in which the *second*-order systems apply, the category "mother" is classical in all of its usages. However, when the idealized conditions of the second-order system are *not* satisfied because of historical or other accidental contingencies, the different notions of "mother" are severed, and the entire superordinate set of mothers defines a family resemblance category. For example, with changes in reproductive technology, the contributor of half an offspring's genes may no longer be the birth mother. With changes in social systems allowing adoption, the birth mother may no longer be the mother legally responsible for nurturing and protecting the child. A family resemblance category is thereby formed containing members such as stepmother, surrogate mother, donor mother, and adoptive mother, for the same reason that family resemblance categories can arise in general: a law in formal system (in this case, the second-order system) no longer applies at a point in history; unrelated sets of local processes partially destroy category homogeneity. The difference between mothers and other family resemblance categories is that we have a formal system (the second-order system) applying and then ceasing to apply over roles within other (first-order) formal systems, rather that applying and then ceasing to apply over simple properties. Thus even within the full, family resemblance set of mothers in modern western society, there exists a classical category of "genetic mother" defined within the first-order formal system of genetics, a classical category "legal mother" within the legal system, a classical category "birth mother" within embryology, and so on.

A similar account can be provided for "species," which biologists recognize to be a multifaceted concept (Ridley, 1986; Maynard Smith, 1986; Dawkins, 1985; Mayr, 1982; Gould, 1983). The notion of "species" has at least the following interpretations: a phenetic sense as a cluster of morphological traits, an ecological sense as an occupier of a niche, a genealogical sense as the descendants of a common ancestor, a reproductive-physiological sense as a set of organisms that can produce fertile offspring, and a genetic sense as a common set of genetic structures. The different notions within these first-order theories are linked by various second-order theories. The theory of natural selection explains why a "phenetic species" is also a "genealogical species". Chromosomal genetics explains why populations with a common genetic structure are those that can produce fertile offspring. Population genetics explains why a cluster of morphological traits becomes uniform within a population of interbreeders. Physics and physiology explain why certain morphological traits are associated with certain ecological niches. However, some of these second-order theories apply only under the idealization of an interbreeding population in a stable local environment; when the idealization no longer can apply because of geographic barriers, dispersal, asexual reproduction, artificial selection, and so on, the second-order linkages fail. This gives rise to family resemblance categories such as the members of a "ring species" or a domesticated species, and other cases where the standard notion of species does not easily apply. However there still may be first-order theories in which some notion of a species is a useful category to make generalizations over, for example, when a population of widely spread organisms retains a unique derived morphological trait even if not all members can interbreed.

Complexities in the past tense system   The ability of classical and family resemblance categories to arise as second-order phenomena brings us full circle to the past tense system and can explain the *disanalogies* between the regular/ irregular distinction and the classical/prototype distinction. Skeptics could point out a number of counterexamples to our general claim: examples in which the regular system appears to have prototype effects. But in these cases the counterexamples can be shown to come from second-order systems rather than the first-order system of morphology that we have been describing.

First, the regular system is not a unified class but has three variants: *t, d, ed* (e.g., *walked, jogged, patted*). However, this is because the output of the regular rule, a stem affixed with *d*, is fed into a separate system, phonology, which adjusts the phonetic shape of the past tense form in ways that are general across the sound pattern of English, and independent of the past tense form itself (in any case these phonological adjustments are themselves perfectly rule-governed and hence define three classical categories; see Pinker and Prince, 1988). Second, as we noted earlier, some regular forms (e.g., *sneaked, dreamed*) are indeed graded in acceptability. However, this is because regularly affixed forms are fed into the (second-order) morphological paradigm system, in which regular and irregular forms must compete for a single paradigm slot and the gradedness of the irregular root can give rise to graded intuitions concerning the final output form of the product of the regular rule.

A disanalogy in the opposite direction comes from the irregular class. In fact, they are not just arbitrary statistical associations among phonological properties of the stem and past tense form, as a standard family resemblance category is and as the Rumelhart–McClelland model treats them. Rather, the associations are between a restricted set of properties of the stem (principally the number of syllables, rhyme, and alliteration), not just any phonological properties, and a constrained set of morphological processes, such as copying, changes of vowel quality, and affixation, not just any mapping between stem forms and past forms. Thus it is at least possible that the family resemblance structure of the irregulars may itself be a second-order associative structure defined over first-order, possibly classical mini-rules, not a first-order system defined over primitive phonological features. This has implications for the use of pattern associators to account for the representation of family resemblance categories. Even under our charitable suggestion that they may be useful for this task, the entities that are associated with one another are not always prim-itive features associated with simple binary units, but might themselves have to be complex rule-like structures or pointers to them.

Conclusions

It may be surprising to see so many parallels drawn between two phenomena that seem to be in such different domains. We are not claiming that past tense forms and conceptual categories are alike in all essential respects or that they are gen-erated by a single cognitive system. But often widespread similarities in remote domains makes the case for *some* common underlying principles compelling. English past tense forms come in two versions that are identical in function and at first glance only differ in size and degree of uniformity. On closer examination they turn out to represent two distinct systems that correspond point for point with classical and family resemblance categories, respectively. Moreover the two systems are linked with distinct psychological faculties, developmental courses, real-world causes, and computational architectures. A fundamental distinction must lie at the heart of this duality. Specifically, we suggest, human concepts can correspond to classical categories or to family resemblance categories. Classical categories are defined by formal rules and allow us to make inferences within idealized law-governed systems. Family resemblance categories are defined by correlations among features in sets of similar memorized exemplars, and allow us to make inferences about the observable products of history.

Notes

* The order of authors is arbitrary. We thank Ned Block, Paul Bloom, Ray Jackendoff, and Ed Smith for comments. This paper was prepared while the first author was a visitor at the MRC Cognitive Development Unit, University of London, and was supported by NIH grant HD 13831.
1 Note that the term means only "a pattern of resemblance such as one sees in a family"; it does not imply literal genealogical links.
2 There are also problems with the model's treatment of these phenomena; see Pinker and Prince (1988), Lachter and Bever (1988), and Sproat (1992).

References

Anderson, J.R. (1990). *The adaptive character of thought*. Hillsdale, NJ: Erlbaum.
Armstrong, S.L., Gleitman, L.R. and Gleitman, H. (1983). What some concepts might not be. *Cognition, 13,* 263–308.
Aronoff, M. (1976). *Word formation in generative grammar*. Cambridge, MA: MIT Press.
Bever, T. and Langendoen, T. (1963). (a) The formal justification and linguistic role of variables in phonology. (b) The description of the Indo-European E/O ablaut. (c) The E/O ablaut in Old English. *RLE Quarterly Progress Report* (summer). Cambridge, MA: MIT Research Laboratory of Electronics.
Bobick, A. (1987). 'Natural object categorization'. Unpublished doctoral dissertation, Department of Brain and Cognitive Sciences, MIT.
Brown, R. (1973). *A first language: The early stages*. Cambridge, MA: Harvard University Press.
Brown, R. (1977). Word from the language acquisition front. Invited address at the 48th Annual Meeting of the Eastern Psychological Association, Boston, April.
Bruner, J.S., Goodnow, J. and Austin, G. (1956). *A study of thinking*. New York: Wiley.
Bybee, J.L. (1985). *Morphology*. Philadelphia: Benjamins.
Bybee, J.L. (1991). Natural morphology: The organization of paradigms and language acquisition. In T. Huebner and C. Ferguson (Eds.), *Crosscurrents in second language acquisition and linguistic theories*. Amsterdam: Benjamins, pp. 67–92.
Bybee, J.L. and Moder, C.L. (1983). Morphological classes as natural categories. *Language, 59,* 251–270.
Bybee, J.L. and Slobin, D.I. (1982a). Rules and schemes in the development and use of the English past tense. *Language, 58,* 265–289.

Bybee, J.L. and Slobin, D.I. (1982b). Why small children cannot change language on their own: Suggestions from the English past tense. In A. Ahlqvist (Ed.), *Papers from the 5th International Conference on Historical Linguistics. (Current issues in linguistic theory Vol. 21, Amsterdam Studies in the theory and history of linguistic science IV.)* Philadelphia/Amsterdam: John Benjamins.

Campbell, A. (1959). *Old English grammar*. Oxford: Oxford University Press.

Cavalli-Sforza, L.L. and Feldman, M.W. (1981). *Cultural transmission and evolution: A quantitative approach*. Princeton, NJ: Princeton University Press.

Curme, G. (1935). *A grammar of the English language II*. Boston: Barnes and Noble.

Dawkins, R. (1985) *The blind watchmaker*. New York: Norton.

Ervin, S. (1964). Imitation and structural change in children's language. In E. Lenneberg (Ed.), *New directions in the study of language*. Cambridge, MA: MIT Press.

Fodor, J.A. (1981). The present status of the innateness controversy. In J.A. Fodor, *Representations*. Cambridge, MA: MIT Press.

Fodor, J.A., Garrett, M.F., Walker, E.C.T. and Parkes, C.H. (1980). Against definitions. *Cognition*, 8: 263–267.

Freyd, J.J. (1983). Shareability: The social psychology of epistemology. *Cognitive Science*, 7, 191–210.

Gelman, S.A., Coley, J.D. and Gottfried, G.M. (1994). Essentialist beliefs in children: The acquisition of concepts and theories. In L.A. Hirschfeld and S. Gelman (Eds.), *Mapping the mind: Domain specificity in cognition and culture*. New York: Cambridge University Press.

Gelman, S.A. and Markman, E. (1987). Young children's inductions from natural kinds: The role of categories and appearances. *Child Development*, 58, 1532–1540.

Gordon, P. (1985). Level-ordering in lexical development. *Cognition*, 21, 73–93.

Gould, S.J. (1983). What, if anything, is a zebra? In S.J. Gould, *Hen's teeth and horses' toes*. New York: Norton.

Hooper, J.B. (1976). *Introduction to natural generative phonology*. New York: Academic Press.

Hull, C.L. (1920). Quantitative aspects of the evolution of concepts. *Psychological Monographs*, 28, Whole No. 213.

Hunt, E. (1962). *Concept learning: An information processing problem*. New York: Wiley.

Hutchinson, G.E. (1959). Homage to Santa Rosalia, or why are there so many kinds of animals. *American Naturalist*, 93, 145–159.

Jespersen, O. (1942). *A modern English grammar on historical principles*, VI. Reprinted 1961: London: George Allen and Unwin Ltd.

Johnson, K. (1986). Fragmentation of strong verb ablaut in Old English. *Ohio State University Working Papers in Linguistics*, 34, 108–122.

Keil, F.C. (1989). *Concepts, kinds, and cognitive development*. Cambridge, MA: MIT Press.

Kelly, M.H. (1992). Darwin and psychological theories of classification. *Evolution and Cognition*, 2, 79–97.

Kim, J.J., Marcus, G.F., Pinker, S., Hollander, M. and Coppola, M. (1994) Sensitivity of children's inflection to morphological structure. *Journal of Child Language*, 21, 173–209.

Kim, J.J., Pinker, S., Prince, A. and Prasada, S. (1991). Why no mere mortal has ever flown out to center field. *Cognitive Science*, 15, 173–218.

Kiparsky, P. (1982a). From cyclical to lexical phonology. In H. van der Hulst and N. Smith (Eds.), *The structure of phonological representations*. Dordrecht, Netherlands: Foris.

Kiparsky, P. (1982b). Lexical phonology and morphology. In I.S. Yang (Ed.), *Linguistics in the morning calm.* Seoul: Hansin, pp. 3–91.

Konner, M. (1982). *The tangled wing.* New York: Harper and Row.

Kripke, S. (1972). Naming and necessity. In D. Davidson and G. Harman (Eds.), *Semantics of natural language.* Dordrecht: Reidel.

Kuczaj, S.A. (1977). The acquisition of regular and irregular past tense forms. *Journal of Verbal Learning and Verbal Behavior, 16,* 589–600.

Kuczaj, S.A. (1978). Children's judgments of grammatical and ungrammatical irregular past tense verbs. *Child Development, 49,* 319–326.

Kuczaj, S.A. (1981). More on children's initial failure to relate specific acquisitions. *Journal of Child Language, 8,* 485–487.

Lachter, J. and Bever, T.G. (1988). The relation between linguistic structure and associative theories of language learning – A constructive critique of some connectionist learning models. *Cognition, 28,* 195.

Lakoff, G. (1987). *Women, fire, and dangerous things: What categories reveal about the mind.* Chicago: University of Chicago Press.

McClelland, J.L. and Rumelhart, D.E. (1985). Distributed memory and the representation of general and specific information. *Journal of Experimental Psychology: General, 114,* 159–188.

McClelland, J.L., Rumelhart, D.E. and the PDP Research Group (1986). *Parallel Distributed Processing: Explorations in the microstructure of cognition. Vol. 2: Psychological and biological models.* Cambridge, MA: Bradford Books/MIT Press.

Macwhinney, B. and Leinbach, J. (1991). Implementations are not conceptualizations: Revising the verb learning model. *Cognition, 40,* 121–157.

Marcus, G.F. (1995). The acquisition of inflection in children and multilayered connectionist networks. *Cognition, 56,* 271–279.

Marcus, G.F., Brinkmann, U., Clahsen, H., Wiese, R. and Pinker, S. (1995). German inflection: The exception that proves the rule. *Cognitive Psychology, 29,* 189–256.

Marcus, G., Pinker, S., Ullman, M., Hollander, M., Rosen, T.J. and Xu, F. (1992). *Overregularization in language acquisition.* Monographs of the Society for Research in Child Development, 57 (4, Serial No. 228).

Maynard Smith, J. (1986). *The problems of biology.* Oxford: Oxford University Press.

Mayr, E. (1982). *The growth of biological thought.* Cambridge, MA: Harvard University Press.

Medin, D.L. (1989). Concepts and conceptual structure. *American Psychologist, 44,* 1469–1481.

Mencken, H. (1936). *The American language.* New York: Knopf.

Murphy, G.L. (1993). A rational theory of concepts. In G.H. Bower (Ed.), *The psychology of learning and motivation. Vol. 29.* New York: Academic Press.

Osherson, D.N. and Smith, E.E. (1981). On the adequacy of prototype theory as a theory of concepts. *Cognition, 15,* 35–58.

Pinker, S. (1984). *Language learnability and language development.* Cambridge, MA: Harvard University Press.

Pinker, S. (1991). Rules of language. *Science, 253,* 530–535.

Pinker, S. and Mehler, J. (Eds.) (1988). *Connections and symbols.* Cambridge, MA: MIT Press/Bradford Books.

Pinker, S. and Prince, A. (1988). On language and connectionism: Analysis of a Parallel Distributed Processing model of language acquisition. *Cognition, 28:* 73–193.

Pinker, S. and Prince, A. (1994). Regular and irregular morphology and the psychological status of rules of grammar. In S.D. Lima, R.L. Corrigan and G.K. Iverson (Eds.), *The reality of linguistic rules*. Philadelphia: John Benjamins.

Plunkett, K. and Marchman, V. (1991). U-shaped learning and frequency effects in a multi-layered perceptron: Implications for child language acquisition. *Cognition*, 38, 43–102.

Plunkett, K. and Marchman, V. (1993). From rote learning to system building. *Cognition*, 48, 21–69.

Prasada, S. and Pinker, S. (1993). Generalizations of regular and irregular morphology. *Language and Cognitive Processes*, 8, 1–56.

Prokosch, E. (1939). *A comparative Germanic grammar*. Philadelphia: Linguistic Society of America.

Putnam, H. (1975). The meaning of "meaning." In K. Gunderson (Ed.), *Language, mind, and knowledge*. Minneapolis: University of Minnesota Press.

Quine, W.V.O. (1969). Natural kinds. In W.V.O. Quine, *Natural kinds and other essays*. New York: Columbia University Press.

Rey, G. (1983). Concepts and stereotypes. *Cognition*, 15, 237–262.

Ridley, M. (1986). *The problems of evolution*. Oxford: Oxford University Press.

Rips, L.J. (1989). Similarity, typicality, and categorization. In S. Vosniadou and A. Ortony (Eds.), *Similarity and analogical reasoning*. New York: Cambridge University Press.

Rosch, E. (1973). On the internal structure of perceptual and semantic categories. In T. E. Moore (Ed.), *Cognitive development and the acquisition of language*. New York: Academic Press.

Rosch, E. (1978). Principles of categorization. In E. Rosch and B.B. Lloyd (Eds.), *Cognition and categorization*. Hillsdale, NJ: Erlbaum.

Rosch, E. (1988). Coherences and categorization: A historical view. In F. Kessel (Ed.), *The development of language and of language researchers: Papers presented to Roger Brown*. Hillsdale, NJ: Erlbaum.

Rosch, E. and Mervis, C.B. (1975). Family resemblances: Studies in the internal representation of categories. *Cognitive Psychology*, 7, 573–605.

Rumelhart, D.E. and McClelland, J.L. (1986). On learning the past tenses of English verbs. In J.L. McClelland, D.E. Rumelhart and the PDP Research Group, *Parallel Distributed Processing: Explorations in the microstructure of cognition. Vol. 2: Psychological and biological models*. Cambridge, MA: Bradford Books/MIT Press.

Schwartz, S.P. (1979). Natural kind terms. *Cognition*, 7, 301–315.

Shepard, R.N. (1987). Toward a universal law of generalization for psychological science. *Science*, 237, 1317–1323.

Slobin, D.I. (1971). On the learning of morphological rules: A reply to Palermo and Eberhart. In D.I. Slobin (Ed.), *The ontogenesis of grammar: A theoretical symposium*. New York: Academic Press.

Smith, E.E. and Medin, D.L. (1981). *Categories and concepts*. Cambridge, MA: Harvard University Press.

Smith, E.E., Medin, D.L. and Rips, L.J. (1984). A psychological approach to concepts: Comments on Rey's "Concepts and Stereotypes." *Cognition*, 17, 265–274.

Smith, E.E., Nisbett, R. and Langston, C. (1992). The case for rules in reasoning. *Cognitive Science*, 16, 1–40.

Smolensky, P. (1988). On the proper treatment of connectionism. *Behavioural and Brain Sciences*, 11, 1–74.

Sober, E. (1984). *The nature of selection*. Cambridge, MA: MIT Press.

Sproat, R. (1992). *Morphology and computation*. Cambridge, MA: MIT Press.

Stromswold, K.J. (1990). Learnability and the acquisition of auxiliaries. Unpublished doctoral dissertation, Department of Brain and Cognitive Sciences, MIT.

Ullman, M. (1993). The computation and neural localization of inflectional morphology. Unpublished doctoral dissertation, Department of Brain and Cognitive Sciences, MIT.

Whittlesea, B.W.A. (1989). Selective attention, variable processing, and distributed representation: Preserving particular experiences of general structures. In R.G. Morris (Ed.), *Parallel Distributed Processing: Implications for psychology and neuroscience*. New York: Oxford University Press.

Williams, G.C. (1966). *Adaptation and natural selection: A critique of some current evolutionary thought*. Princeton: Princeton University Press.

Winston, P.H., Binford, T.O., Katz, B. and Lowry, M. (1983). Learning physical descriptions from functional definitions, examples, and precedents. MIT Artificial Intelligence Laboratory Memo 679.

Wittgenstein, L. (1953). *Philosophical investigations*. New York: Macmillan.

Xu, F. and Pinker, S. (1995). Weird past tense forms. *Journal of Child Language, 22,* 531–556.

2 The modularity of language
Some empirical considerations

Yosef Grodzinsky

Abstract

This paper presents several empirical arguments supporting a modular view of language. It begins by formulating certain questions that arise in the context of the modularity of language, and proceeds to demonstrate possible answers to each. It provides an example of an argument for a modular view of syntactic knowledge, and also gives reasons for believing in the functional and neuro-anatomical distinctness of the syntactic processing device. All these points are supposed to underscore the view that the modularity debate is exclusively empirical.

Introduction

The scholarly and popular press are constantly flooded with debates over the nature of cognitive processes. The amazing media success of the PDP community has managed to ignite people's imagination, and even my mother (let alone my freshmen students) goes around muttering the magical words *parallel distributed processing* and *neural networks* as if they were mantras, keys to ultimate understanding of human nature.

The fundamental question is, of course, how many independent mental faculties there are. The PDP approach, with all its different versions and nuances, claims, after all, that at some level of description all mental processes are alike. Proponents of the modularist approach maintain the opposite, arguing that our mental life is governed by a number of independent principles. There may be areas of agreement between these two approaches: some hold the view that the mind consists of modularly organized neural nets. The disagreement, then, is around the appropriate level of description of the cognitive system, which might lead to profound understanding of its true nature. In this respect, the conflict between the two approaches is genuine, leading to a debate which has captured the imagination of many.

Still, fascinating as this debate may seem to the public at some general level, the question of modularity of language (and most importantly – the combinatorial properties thereof) boils down to the following rather concrete forms:

1   Is the number of (independent) grammatical principles we know greater than, or equal to one, and are they distinct from other knowledge we possess?

2   Is the number of (independent) algorithms implementing these in use greater than, or equal to one, and are they distinct from other algorithms we use?

3   Is the number of (distinct) brain loci subserving linguistic activity greater than, or equal to one, and are they distinct from other brain regions?

As stated, these questions are not subject to philosophical meditation; they are matters of contingent truth. They are, in short, all *bona fide* scientific questions, to be decided on factual evidence. Each embeds two questions within it – regarding the distinctness of language from other mental faculties, and about internal structure. Moreover, the answer to all is <*Greater than one, yes*>, at least as far as our current understanding goes. In this brief note I will try to give an empirical argument or two for each.

1 The modularity of grammatical knowledge

What would it take to demonstrate the modularity of grammatical principles? And is there an a priori need to do that? Very many sheets of paper, and a lot of mental energy have been dedicated to this issue. The huge variety of human ability *ipso facto* leads to modularity as the null hypothesis. Nevertheless, empirical demonstrations are necessary. What, then, would count as an argument? To show modularity, as Dan Osherson (1981) put it succinctly years ago, is to show that two pieces of cognition are neither reducible to one another, nor can they be made to follow from an independent, yet single, (set of) principles. In what follows, I will present several types of arguments given by linguists in support of the modularity of grammatical knowledge.

1.1 Grammar and other cognitive domains

1.1.1 The modularity of language and mathematics: general arguments in brief

Grammatical theory is by now a reasonably developed and rich set of claims, accounting for a wide array of linguistic facts. It is believed to apply to the language domain only. Could it, perhaps, be extended to other cognitive domains? Two such areas immediately come to mind, as both seem to require certain abilities to carry out combinatorial operations: mathematics and music. Some of the discussions regarding the relation between language and mathematics have reached "pro-modularist" conclusions (cf., for instance, Chomsky, 1991, 1995). The arguments against a unified account of these two domains are of several types. First, when one looks at the way grammatical principles are formulated, one notices that they are predicated over abstract (yet real) linguistic categories. One can hardly imagine how these would reduce to categories of a different sort, generalizable to, say, some branch(es) of mathematics. These things simply look very different, as far as our current understanding and imagination go. As a quick example (slightly different in content yet similar in form), consider Chomsky's point regarding the relationship between linguistic concepts of spatial objects, and their properties as specified by geometric description. Imagine a coin hanging in the middle of a box. We would say of it that it is *inside* the box. Yet, geometrically speaking, this is false, as the geometric concept "box" refers only to its surface, not to the space it encloses. Were the coin to be outside the box, our linguistic and geometric concepts would match, whereas in the reverse case, there is a mismatch. Our linguistic conceptions of the *inside/outside* relations, he concludes, differ quite radically from those specified by geometry. In fact they are different in a way that is, in all likelihood, irreconcilable, namely, a theory reducing one to the other (or generalizing over both) does not seem forthcoming. Osherson's requirements, then, are rather straightforwardly met.

1.1.2 The modularity of grammar and music: some considerations

Similar discussion (with different conclusions) regarding the relation between language and music can be found in Bernstein (1971) and Lerdahl and Jackendoff (1980). The latter authors, in fact, have come up with a detailed theory that may have discovered what they call a "deep parallel" between language and music. Yet, it is important to emphasize that the proposals have been at best tentative. Lerdahl and Jackendoff are quick to acknowledge that their theory, if true, holds of tonal music only, whereas, for reasons that are not well understood, other musical types (e.g., certain Indian and Macedonian tunes) fall outside its scope, even though they are *bona fide* musical styles, created, performed, memorized and liked by human beings with equal musical abilities.

Finally, it is important to remember that even if all these claims were true, and the theoretical construct proposed by linguists would turn out to characterize human mathematical, musical, and linguistic abilities, opponents of modularity would still be hard pressed to show how the same body of theoretical claims holds of the rest of the richness of our mental life.

1.1.3 The modularity of language knowledge: arguments from congenital pathology

A second type of argument comes from neurological dissections between language and other cognitive faculties. There are well-known cases indicating distinctness of the linguistic system from other cognitive systems, whether congenital or acquired. There are dissociations between language and other cognitive capacities and even cases of severe cognitive impairment accompanied, strangely enough, with an exceptional talent for languages (Smith,

Tsimpli, and Ouhalla, 1993). Yamada (1990) and Bellugi *et al.* (1992), for instance, have documented remarkable disturbances to cognitive functioning, ranging from Williams syndrome to severe retardation, with apparently intact linguistic skills, pointing once again to the fact that there is more than one cognitive faculty, and that language is indeed distinct.

1.2 The modular structure of syntax: an example

Finally, there are claims regarding the *internal* modular structure of the grammar. This kind of question would appear more interesting to linguists, as it carries a lot of empirical content. An example of this type of argument regards, for instance, the autonomy of syntax from semantics – a much debated issue in the past three decades (see Higginbotham, 1987, for relatively recent discussion).

Consider, then, an easy, concrete example of a syntactic case. It is well known that the relationship between reflexives and their antecedents is local. This can be seen in the contrast in grammaticality in (1):

(1) a. John likes himself
   b. *John asked Sue to touch himself

In (1b) the antecedent, *John*, is too far in some (structural) sense, and the ungrammaticality follows. The theory of syntax indeed contains a locality requirement (part of what is called Binding Theory), which also accounts for other facts, for instance the one in (2):

(2) *Which man believes Mary likes himself

Here, too, the antecedent, *which man*, is too far to be linked to the reflexive. If properly formulated, the Binding Theory should rule out this example as well. Yet the surprising example in (3) seems a direct slap in the face to this account:

(3) a. Which man does Mary believe likes himself
   b. *Which man does Mary believe likes herself

Consider (3a). Not only is this example grammatical, contrary to prediction, but also, its similarity to (2) is very striking: it contains the same elements, it is a question, the distance between the reflexive and its antecedent is the same, and still, the example is grammatical. Moreover, (3b) shows the opposite: what is perceived to be local, namely Mary, turns out to be the wrong antecedent for the reflexive, and ungrammaticality results. There appears to be something fundamentally wrong with our approach. The oddity of (3) becomes even stronger when we look at the declarative counterparts of the questions in (2)–(3a), with the antecedents bolded to emphasize their position:

(4) a. **Which man** does Mary believe likes himself
   b. *__Which man__ believes Mary likes himself
   c. Mary believes that **the man** likes himself
   d. *__The man__ believes Mary likes himself

We see that of all these, (4b,d) violate the locality requirement. Something else is necessary for our theory to work. For that, we need to look at the facts from a different perspective.

(2) and (3a) are questions. As such, they are derived by a movement rule (a grammatical transformation), that takes the question expression and moves it from its underlying position, which we see in (5):

(5) a. Mary believes [**which man**] likes himself
   b. [**which man**] believes Mary likes himself

Looking at these representations, it turns out that the position of the antecedent in (5a) puts it in a local relation to the reflexive, unlike (5b), which remains distant even in underlying structure. Could this difference be exploited to account for the contrast in grammaticality between (2) and (3a)? It could, but on two conditions: first, that we agree that the locality requirement on antecedent/reflexive relations can apply not only to surface forms, but also to underlying representations. But second, and most important, we must agree that there is a grammatical operation, call it a transformation or a movement rule, that – independent of the locality requirement – can somehow change the position of constituents and relate, for instance, (5a) to (4a). Otherwise, the whole story would not work.

This grammatical operation is perhaps the best known part of the theory of syntax, and naturally, has motivation that goes beyond the facts above. What is most important to us, in the present context, is that the application of this type of rule is *independent* of the application of the locality constraint, and that it is only their *interaction* that yields an adequate account of the observed array of fact. And while the presentation here is, obviously, sketchy and far from being complete and precise, it brings about the desired conclusion: In the grammar there are several independent types of grammatical principles, whose interaction is required to explain the linguistic facts. The claim for internal modularity is thus established, again motivated by the factual record.

2 Modularity of language processing

2.1 *Modularity of knowledge vs. processing*

Thus far, I have talked about the modular organization of linguistic knowledge, namely, structural modularity, and showed the way we go about looking for data to argue that grammatical knowledge is organized in separate stores, each having its own independent principles. But there is another interpretation of the notion of modularity, namely, the modularity of the language processing device – the medium in which effective procedures carry out linguistic analysis. This is a different, yet related, concept. The concern here is to show that the actual machine implementing linguistic knowledge in use – the language processor which is involved in real-time computation of the structure and interpretation of incoming (and perhaps outgoing) sentences – this machine is modular. As before, this device is believed, first of all, to be dedicated to linguistic analysis only, and to nothing else, and second, to be composed of several separate modules, in which interaction of different information types is extremely limited. The working hypothesis is that the flow of information in this processing device is severely restricted, has a specific direction, and none of its subparts can interfere with the computation carried out by others, nor can it have access to their knowledge base. Put in simple language, "higher" processes – background knowledge, mood, and general level of awareness – can never interfere with their operation or have access to the knowledge stored in "lower" ones. Anyone can judge the grammaticality of strings, but most people cannot reflect on their judgments.

The language processing device, so the story goes (cf. Fodor, 1983), is characterized as modular by the three properties explicated above: it is domain specific (dedicated to language, and language alone); it is encapsulated (enabling conscious access to the products of grammatical analysis, but barring reflection on causes underlying this analysis); and it is impenetrable (blocking interference between "modules"). Attempts to demonstrate these properties usually rely on the precise measurement of processing times in various language tasks, yet it is important to emphasize that empirical studies of modularity need not be (and in fact, are not as we will see below) limited to this type of method. One component's inability to interfere with the operation of another, or lack of access to the inner workings thereof, refers to the sequencing of processes, which in many instances are reflected in processing times that experimentalists measure. Yet this is not a logical necessity. Demonstrations of intrinsic ordering of processes, and of their independence, may be done through other methodologies as well, error analysis for instance. Below we see both types of empirical arguments put forth to argue for "impenetrability" and "encapsulation".

2.2 Demonstrating "cognitive impenetrability": inaccessible semantic information during parsing

What does it take to demonstrate the impenetrability of a processing device? To show that, a kind of irrational behavior needs to be demonstrated. The logical structure of the argument is this: a system is said to be cognitively impenetrable if other cognitive processes can never interfere with its operation. What is sought, then, is a case where such interference can be motivated, because it would be beneficial to the organism in some sense: either it will save effort, or enhance performance on some task. So, if we know that the organism possesses some ability, and if we can argue that the use of this ability is unequivocally beneficial, then a failure to take advantage of something useful – namely, a lack of interference – indicates irrational behavior: the organism could have used a cognitive resource to its own benefit, and it did not. Finally, assuming that organisms do the best they can, the only explanation to our observation would be that there is an architectural barrier that blocks certain cognitive processes from influencing others: The system possesses the relevant resource, but was unable to use it at the time we probed it, namely, while other processes are taking place. These latter processes are cognitively impenetrable.

The significance of such a structural barrier cannot be underestimated: as speakers, we have immense capabilities. We understand sentences at an incredible speed, sometimes under the most difficult of conditions – noise, distraction, stress; and yet, our language processing device is quite reliable. Prima facie it seems, then, fit to its job. Discovering limits on this system, of the type just described, would be rather surprising, and would be most indicative as to the device's internal structure.

Hickok, Canseco-Gonzales, Zurif and Grimshaw (1992) obtained evidence to that effect. Like many before them (cf., for instance, Swinney, 1979; Shapiro, Zurif and Grimshaw, 1990; and many others), they were concerned with properties of lexical access, and their interaction with structure building operations during sentence comprehension. So here is the question: in the process of assigning a syntactic analysis to an incoming string (i.e., building an annotated phrase marker, or tree structure), does the syntactic analyzer – the human parser – consult with all the information there is around, so as to carry out its task most precisely and efficiently? If, for instance, it turns out that the system possesses a piece of information that can enhance parsing, or reduce effort, and that time and again, this piece is not used, cognitive impenetrability would be demonstrated, and this is what Hickok *et al.* sought to investigate.

Consider the sentences in (6). Their grammaticality indicates that the verb *remind* has more than one argument structure – that it can take more than one type of complement:

(6) a. She reminded me [PP of my long lost cousin]
    b. She reminded me [IP to go see my beloved aunt]
    c. She reminded me [CP that my long lost cousin was in town]

Each of these complements not only takes on a different meaning, but also, has a different syntactic structure: in the first case, the complement to the verb *remind* takes a prepositional phrase; the second (6b) is a bit more complicated: it takes an infinitival clause (Inflection Phrase), but importantly, the subject of the infinitive is missing, and has to be inherited from the object of *remind*: it is related to *me* – I am the one who has to go see the cousin. Finally, in the third case (6c), the verb *remind* takes a full sentence with its complementizer *that*, hence a Complementizer Phrase.

This multiple argument structure (or subcategorization frame) is not unusual in natural language: there are very many verbs that have this property (cf. Grimshaw, 1990; Levin, 1993 for recent discussions). This information, being idiosyncratic to each verb, is obviously stored in the mental lexicon. Can it be used at any stage of language processing, to the advantage of the language user, or rather, is this information privileged, accessible only in given points in time, and forcing the user to labor unnecessarily on certain occasions?

Consider a temporary (local) ambiguity that arises in questions involving the verb *remind*. In sentences like those in (6), at the point the verb appears, there is no way to know which frame will follow. Only after (at least part of) the complement appears can the user confidently assign a unique structural analysis to the incoming string. The user – torn between the drive to do anything to parse the sentence in a speedy and efficient manner, and the drive for precision and lack of error – must wait until more information will flow in, and enable a safe assignment. And waiting, as we know, may have detrimental effects on the comprehension device, and finally, on communication. A similar situation is evident in the sentences in (7), where even a relatively long string prior to the verb does not reveal any clues regarding the structure that needs to be built subsequently. Any of the complements in (6) will do:

(7) a. **Which man did she remind** . . . me of (answer: my long lost cousin)
  b. **Which man did she remind** . . . to go see my beloved aunt (answer: me)
  c. **Which man did she remind** . . . me to go see (answer: my long lost cousin)

There are, however, other cases, in which information in left context – that part of the string that is prior to the verb – allows the hearer to safely rule out some of the possibilities (and at times, even be left only with one). Consider, for instance, a case in which the question is about some (abstract or concrete) object:

(8) a. **Which rock did she remind** . . . me of (possible answer: the Rock of Gibraltar)
  b. **Which rock did she remind** . . . to go see my long lost cousin (nonsense)
  c. **Which rock did she remind** . . . me to go see (answer: the Rock of Gibraltar)

The possibility in (8b) can be ruled out safely: the verb *remind* takes only animate (perhaps even human) objects – its remindees; a rock is not human, hence, a frame taking an infinitival clause whose subject had been extracted and questioned about cannot possibly be the correct choice of complement here, because this subject must be linked to the object of *remind*. An efficient machine would obviously use the information regarding the animacy of the questioned element in order to rule out continuations such as (8b), and focus on more likely analyses, (8c), and perhaps the remotely possible (8a).

Nevertheless, this does not happen. The language parsing device is not optimally efficient. The evidence Hickok *et al.* obtained indicates that, at the time the verb is accessed, and further structure is projected, animacy information is ignored, contrary to what such efficiency considerations would dictate. The system appears to project multiple structure, some of which is suppressed after analysis proceeded further downstream, and encountered the actual complement. Using the well-known priming technique, they found that speakers' expectations – as measured by the words they prime right after the verb *remind* as compared to other points during comprehension – indicate that even nonsense options like (8b) are temporarily entertained by speakers, despite the fact that use of the available lexical information could have ruled it out, and potentially eased processing. This finding, coupled with many others to the same effect, is rather suggestive: barring other interpretations, it indicates that structure-building operations are blind to lexical content. Namely, at the point where possible complements are arrayed, semantic features of particular words are not used to zero-in on the correct structure to be projected, even though the use of this information may have made processing easier, faster, and more precise. So, either the system deliberately ignores available information – thus exhibiting irrational behavior – or, more likely, the flow of information within it is restricted, perhaps due to the complexity of incorporating semantic considerations into account while building structure. Either way, the evidence suggests impenetrability.

3 Neuropsychological arguments: inaccessible grammar during interpretation in aphasia

We showed how a later, "higher" component of the language processor does not intervene in the action of a "lower", earlier-operating one. Here, evidence for the reverse will be given: a later process fails to use information stored in data structures of an earlier one. This is what Fodor (1983) calls informational encapsulation. Here is the logical structure of the argument: Find a case where, for optimal performance, a system must call upon a certain data structure, which it is known to possess. Show that this does not happen, and that in effect, the measured performance is worse than it could have been. A rational system would seek to perform as well as it can, and exploit any piece of information it has to process sentences most rapidly and accurately. Hence the necessary conclusion that will follow will be that at the point in the processing sequence where this piece of knowledge is necessary, access to it is blocked, hence information encapsulation.

To demonstrate that, we want to show language mishaps that could have been avoided, and are ostensibly linked to a failure to use available information. The evidence below is of this type. It presents a performance pattern of agrammatic Broca's aphasics that indicates that they make comprehension errors of types that could be avoided, had their interpretive system had access into the grammar they possess at an interpretive stage. It will be shown that they have the knowledge to get around their deficit, yet they do not. Thus the reason for this failure will be attributed to their inability to access certain data structures at the right time. So, on the basis of error analysis of aphasic performance, I will argue that certain grammatical information is impenetrable to interpretive processes of a particular kind.

Consider the comprehension deficit in agrammatic Broca's aphasia, and methods for its discovery. One version of a comprehension experiment with these patients presents them with a sentence, and with a set of pictures, each consisting, typically, of a character performing some action on another. Their task is to choose the picture that matches the sentence they heard. They usually get two pictures – one representing the correct interpretation, and the other with the thematic roles reversed. As we are interested in their syntactic abilities, we remove semantic and other contextual cues from which they can infer the correct answer and compensate for potential syntactic deficits. We present them with a set of theoretically selected syntactic types, with several tokens of each. This way we can measure their overall syntactic ability.

Take a look, now, at the following complex array of data, reflecting aphasic performances recorded in several experiments. The array groups data in cells where performance level is pitted against chance, with each of the cells distinguishing itself statistically from the others. *Above chance* performance means normal, or near-normal comprehension; *at-chance* indicates guessing behavior; and *below-chance* indicates systematic reversal of thematic roles. These three types of performance (collected from a large number of experiments) constitute part of the data base we have on the comprehension deficit in this syndrome (for much more complex data sets regarding the same syndrome, see Ansell and Flowers, 1982; Caplan and Futter, 1986; Grodzinsky, Pierce and Marakovitz, 1991; Grodzinsky, 1995a; Hickok and Avrutin, 1995; Saddy, 1995; Balogh and Grodzinsky, 1996; among many others).

(9) *above chance*
    a. The girl pushed the boy
    b. The girl who pushed the boy was tall
    c. Which girl pushed the boy

(10) *chance*
    a. The boy was pushed *t* by the girl
    b. The boy who the girl pushed *t* was tall
    c. Which boy did the girl push *t*

(11) *below chance*
    a. The girl was admired *t* by the boy

So we have a peculiar pattern of performance, in which the factor that determines performance is ostensibly syntactic. The contrast between active (9a)
and passive (10a) suggests that a grammatical movement rule (present in
passives, but not actives) is involved; the asymmetry between performance on
subject relative clauses and questions (9b–c) which are properly understood,
and object relative clauses and questions (10b–c) which are at chance, further
suggests that a movement rule, generalizing over passives, as well as these cases
(i.e., Move-α), is at issue. The case in (11a), where the patients perform below
chance on passives of psychological predicates (although they are above chance
in their active counterparts, not listed here), distinguishes itself from the other
passive in (10a), indicating that it is not just a matter of canonical ordering
or constituent NPs around the verb. The symbol "*t*" stands for a trace of movement, marking the position from which extraction of an NP had occurred –
the first one in every movement-derived string among those we have here.
Data from other languages leads to similar conclusions (see Hagiwara, 1993
for Japanese; Beretta, Hurford, Patterson and Pinango, 1996 for Spanish;
Grodzinsky, 1995b for a theory that generalizes over these data as well).

The Trace-Deletion Hypothesis (Grodzinsky, 1986, 1990, 1995a) claims that
traces of syntactic movement are deleted from the annotated syntactic representations of agrammatic aphasic patients. So, we can distinguish the
sentences in (9) from those in (10)–(11), since the latter two are derived transformationally. But this is not quite enough. Just distinguishing the cases that
elicited good performance from those eliciting errors does not tell the whole
story. We must also account for the patients' performance relative to chance
in each of the cells in (9)–(11). Namely, we must give a precise account that
derives the exact performance levels we specified above. In particular, we must
distinguish not only (9) from (10), but also, the transformationally derived
(10)–(11) from one another, and obviously, this cannot be done by mere reference to Move-α, because they both have the same status with respect to this
rule, as indicated above by the trace contained in the annotated representation of both. If we seek to be precise, we must specify the exact nature of the
aphasic patients' representation of these sentences, in a manner that would
give rise to the deviant performance pattern we observed. Since, as we can
obviously see, this pattern represents only a partial breakdown of the language
system, we can safely assume that a large part of the language processing device
is spared for these patients. Yet, on the other hand, the performance we find
is still abnormal. We have to invoke at least some unusual principles that guide
the patients' behavior, and it will be exactly these principles and their interaction with the spared grammatical abilities that will later be the driving force
of the argument for modularity.

Technical details aside, the best available account of these findings is the
following. The patients cannot represent relations between transformationally

derived NPs and their traces, due to the deletion of the latter. Traces are crucial for correct recovery of thematic roles. An NP dislocated by the rule Move-α cannot, therefore, be assigned a thematic role. Yet such assignment is precisely what the experiments are after. The patients, recall, are always required to indicate "who did something to Whom". The postulated deficit – trace deletion, however, has the consequence that transformationally derived NPs do not have thematic roles. The comprehension of a sentence requires every NP to have such a role. So, the agrammatics use, at this point, a non-linguistic, heuristic strategy, which kicks in, to "salvage", as it were, these NPs. Crucially, since the strategy comes in to help the grammar, it is *not* (and cannot be) based on grammatical principles. Rather, it is formulated on the basis of general knowledge, gained inductively by experience, which is based, in its turn, on frequency of occurrence of certain linear orderings of elements in language use. Thus, in an SVO language like English, the first NP in a sentence is most commonly an agent of action, and if this is the NP that lacks a thematic role, it will be exactly the one to fall under the scope of the heuristic strategy, which will thereby assign it with the thematic role of agent. So, we end up with a representation in which grammatical analysis correctly assigns an agent role to the NP in the *by*-phrase, as you can see in (12), by the spared linguistic ability; the subject NP, lacking its link to the position from which it had been moved by a transformation, is assigned an agent role, too, yet by the heuristic strategy:

(12)   Normal assignment

                 theme   agent

                 $[_{NP1}$the boy] was pushed by t $[_{NP2}$the girl]

                 agent   agent

                    Agrammatic assignment

This results in a representation that contains two agents, rather than an agent and a theme, and given that, the aphasic is forced into guessing, giving chance performance on this type of construction. This, however, is not the case for the sentences that are not derived by a transformation. Moreover, the inverse, below chance performance in (11) is also predicted by this account, because of the particular thematic properties of the verb there, making the agrammatic representation to consist not of equal competing agent roles, but rather, a role of experiencer in the *by*-phrase, "lower" on a syntactically moti-vated measure (hierarchy) than the strategically assigned agent in the subject, as can be seen in (13):

(13)   Normal assignment

                 theme   experiencer

                 $[_{NP1}$the boy] was admired by t $[_{NP2}$the girl]

                 agent   experiencer

                    Agrammatic assignment

Systematic reversal in interpretation follows, as is indeed observed (see Grodzinsky, 1995b for experiment and analysis). So, we can see that the heuristic strategy, putatively invoked to help the patients' impaired processing machine, actually trips them at times, and leads to errors. So, this is a way (in fact the only way) to account for the peculiar performance pattern of the aphasic patients.

The account of agrammatic comprehension involves the interaction of grammatical and non-grammatical knowledge sources. What I will show now is that the operation of the non-grammatical knowledge is carried out in a manner that ignores the grammar altogether. Moreover, were grammatical knowledge that the patient still possesses to be consulted, then at least in some critical cases, the heuristic strategy would have withheld its operation, and wisely so, because such a move would improve performance.

Consider the case of passive, just illustrated. Let us see what kinds of information pertinent to the solution of the problem – correct interpretation – are available to the patient's cognitive system. Here they are, written as premises in a deduction:

(14) P1: The verb has two thematic roles: <agent, theme> (lexicon)
      P2: The string to be analyzed has two NPs (representation)
      P3: NP2 = agent (grammatically based assignment)

If the flow of information in the system were unrestricted, the patients would have had access to all this information. From it, they should be able to deduce this:

(15) NP1 = theme

For optimal performance, application of the inference should suppress the use of the strategy, because this strategy sticks the role of agent to the relevant NP, leading to aberrant performance. However, patients do not suppress the strategy, assigning instead the agent role to NP1. Assuming our patients to be rational and do the best they can, we are left with two possibilities: either their deductive abilities are lost, or one (or more) of the premises are inaccessible to them at the right time. Our knowledge of agrammatic aphasics indicates that their deductive abilities are well preserved. Had these abilities been impaired, the patients' daily functioning would be hindered. This, however, seems not to be the case. It follows, then, that the problem lies with the premises in (14). But which one is missing at the point where the strategy applies?

P3 must be available, because the patients assign an agent theta-role to NP2. Similarly, P2 must be available: the patients know that the strings contain two NPs. It follows that P1 is unavailable – in other words, that knowledge of the thematic properties of predicators is missing. But here a contradiction follows: we have assumed that most of the thematic representation patients have is constructed by their use of thematic knowledge. In fact, there is independent evidence that agrammatic aphasics have retained their lexicon (Shapiro and Levin, 1990). Yet now we are saying that thematic knowledge is unavailable. Our patients possess lexical knowledge, and do not possess it at the same time.

The way out of this paradox is natural: not all information is available at any given stage of sentence processing. Namely, we assume that although the thematic properties of predicators are available to the parser at the time it constructs a syntactic analysis for the sentence, this knowledge is unavailable to processes that are outside the parser. In other words, the strategy has access to the output of the parser (in our case a thematically incomplete representation), but it cannot look at the grammatical knowledge (principles, rules, and so forth) that the parser uses. This conclusion is further supported by the observation that the Theta Criterion is violated in agrammatic comprehension, even though in judging the grammaticality of sentences, patients show that they actually possess this grammatical principle. It follows that the strategy lies outside the jurisdiction of the Theta Criterion and cannot use it.

In sum, then, the heuristic strategy comes into play only after the parser has completed its work, because the strategy's domain of application is defined syntactically and without a full syntactic analysis a phrase complying with this definition cannot be identified. This satisfies the requirement of cognitive impenetrability. On the other hand, the application of the strategy is completely blind to lower-level grammatical knowledge; if the strategy had access to this knowledge, its operation would improve the patients' performance. This satisfies the requirement of informational encapsulation.

4 An afterthought

What is it about the modular approach that buys it so many enemies? Why is it that, whenever there is an opportunity to find structure within a cognitive system, there are many who seek to deny that, and would rather seek evidence for the view that all mental processes are alike? Human behavior, after all, is highly rich and complex, and any effort to understand the engines that drive it must break these engines into their component parts. Yet many labor tirelessly to prove that there is little, if any internal structure in the knowledge base that governs our mental life and action. This I find rather curious. Why would anyone make efforts to deny the obvious – that our mental life can be broken down into sophisticated component parts? I do not know. Perhaps there is something comforting in the thought that as creations in this world we are, after all, not very complex.

Note

Supported by NIH Grant DCD00081 to the Aphasia Research Center, Department of Neurology, Boston University School of Medicine, and by a grant from the Office of the Chief Scientist, Israel Ministry of Health. The author wishes to thank Danny Fox and Edgar Zurif for their invaluable help. Address all regular mail correspondence to the author at the Department of Psychology, Tel Aviv University.

References

Ansell, B. and Flowers, C. (1982). Aphasic adults' use of heuristic and structural linguistic cues for analysis. *Brain and Language*, *16*, 61–72.

Balogh, J. and Grodzinsky, Y. (1996). Varieties of passive in agrammatism. Paper presented at the Academy of Aphasia, London.

Bellugi, U., Bihrle, A., Neville, H., Doherty, S. and Jernigan, T. (1992). Language, cognition, and brain organization in a neurodevelopmental disorder. In M. Gunnar and C. Nelson (eds.), *Developmental behavioral neuroscience: The Minnesota Symposia on Child Psychology*. Hillsdale, NJ: Erlbaum.

Beretta, A., Hurford, C., Patterson, J. and Pinango, M. (1996). The proper description of comprehension deficits in agrammatic aphasia. *Natural Language and Linguistic Theory*, *14*, 725–748.

Bernstein, L. (1971). *The unanswered question*. Cambridge, MA: Harvard University Press.

Caplan, D. and Futter, C. (1986). Assignment of thematic roles by an agrammatic aphasic patient. *Brain and Language*, *27*, 117–135.

Chomsky, N. (1977). *Questions of form and interpretation*. Amsterdam: North Holland.

Chomsky, N. (1991). Linguistics and cognitive science: problems and mysteries. In A. Kasher (ed.), *The chomskyan turn*. Cambridge, MA: Blackwell.

Chomsky, N. (1995). Language and nature. *Mind*, *104*, 413.

Fodor, J.A. (1983). *The modularity of mind*. Cambridge, MA: MIT Press.

Grimshaw, J. (1990). *Argument structure*. Cambridge, MA: MIT Press.

Grodzinsky, Y. (1986). Language deficits and the theory of syntax. *Brain and Language*, *27*, 135–159.

Grodzinsky, Y. (1990). *Theoretical perspectives on language deficits*. Cambridge, MA: MIT Press.

Grodzinsky, Y. (1995a). A restrictive theory of agrammatic comprehension. *Brain and Language*, *51*, 26–51.

Grodzinsky, Y. (1995b). Trace-deletion, Θ-roles, and cognitive strategies. *Brain and Language*, *51*, 469–497.

Grodzinsky, Y., Pierce, A. and Marakovitz, S. (1991). Neuropsychological reasons for a transformational derivation of syntactic passive. *Natural Language and Linguistic Theory*, *9*, 431–453.

Hagiwara, H. (1993). The breakdown of Japanese passives and role assignment principle by Broca's aphasics. *Brain and Language*, *45*(3), 318–339.

Hickok, G. and Avrutin, S. (1995). Comprehension of Wh-questions by two agrammatic Broca aphasics. *Brain and Language*, *50*, 10–26.

Hickok, G., Canseco-Gonzales, E., Zurif, E. and Grimshaw, J. (1992). Modularity in locating *wh*-gaps. *Journal of Psycholinguistic Research*, *21*, 545–561.

Higginbotham, J. (1987). The autonomy of syntax and semantics. In J. Garfield (ed.), *Modularity in knowledge representation and natural language understanding*. Cambridge, MA: MIT Press.

Lerdahl, F. and Jackendoff, R. (1980). *A generative theory of tonal music*. Cambridge, MA: MIT Press.

Levin, B. (1993). *English verb classes and alternations*. Chicago: Chicago University Press.

May, R. (1985). *Logical form: its structure and derivation*. Cambridge, MA: MIT Press.

Osherson, D. (1981). Modularity as an issue for cognitive science. *Cognition*, *10*, 241–242.

Saddy, J. (1995). Variables and events in the syntax of agrammatic speech. *Brain and Language*, *50*, 135–150.

Shapiro, L. and Levin, B. (1990). Verb processing during sentence comprehension in aphasia. *Brain and Language*, *38*, 21–47.

Shapiro, L., Zurif, E. and Grimshaw, J. (1990). Verb processing during sentence comprehension: contextual impenetrability. *Journal of Psycholinguistic Research*, *18*, 223–243.

Smith, N., Tsimpli, I. and Ouhalla, J. (1993). Learning the impossible: the acquisition of possible and impossible language by a polyglot savant. *Lingua*, *91*, 279–347.

Swinney, D. (1979). Lexical access during sentence comprehension: (Re)consideration of context effects. *Journal of Verbal Learning and Verbal Behavior*, *18*, 645–659.

Swinney, D., Zurif, E. and Nicol, J. (1989). The effects of focal brain damage on sentence processing: an examination of the neurological organization of a mental module. *Journal of Cognitive Neuroscience*, *1*, 25–37.

Yamada, J. (1990). *Laura*. Cambridge, MA: MIT Press.

3 The perspective of situated and self-organizing cognition in cognitive psychology

Wolfgang Tschacher and Christian Scheier

Abstract

We discuss a theoretical framework of cognitive psychology that allows for an understanding of the adaptivity, goal-directedness, and flexibility of behavior. Goals and intentions as explanatory principles were banned from academic psychology under the influence of behaviorism. With the advent of the information processing view of cognitive psychology, this taboo has been overcome, but scientific understanding of intentionality is still lacking. At present a computational view of cognition and action dominates throughout psychology. Such current syntactical models are usually descriptive and make strong assumptions concerning internal representations; they imply a manipulation of symbols and categories which are supposed to correspond to entities in the world. Other recent theories in cognitive psychology are oriented more toward motivational constructs; they are based on volition and intention as explanations for action regulation. These latter theories therefore encounter the problem of teleology, because they rely on semantic homunculi in the mind which allocate attention, retrieve information from memory stores, and develop intentions, enabling the individual to act.

In our view, two approaches may be helpful to achieve a coherent new theoretical framework for cognitive psychology. First, synergetics and self-organization research provide principles of pattern formation and adaptivity which can be applied to complex systems such as the mind. Second, "New Artificial Intelligence" (Embodied Cognitive Science) and the situated cognition approach have criticized classical AI research for being in quite a similar kind of impasse as cognitive psychology is. Consequently, the approach of "situated and self-organizing cognition" claims that emergent patterns in cognition regulate action in an adaptive manner. Cognition is situated by control parameters ("valences" which express environmental constraints). Optimality of patterns is achieved by synergetic dynamics in the valence-driven mind.

1 Problems of cognitive psychology and action psychology

The current state of affairs in cognitive psychology is characterized roughly by two approaches.

The first approach is the view of *information processing* which goes back to the "cognitive turn" psychology took in the 1960s (Miller *et al.*, 1960). At the heart of the information processing view is the notion of computation of mental symbols which represent real-world entities (Fodor, 1975). The mechanisms of cognition are supposed to be implemented as cybernetic control of hierarchical feedback loops (Carver and Scheier, 1982). Motivational variables and intervening variables (like self-efficacy expectations: Bandura, 1986) result from perceived discrepancies of actual state and goal state. Computer science and classical AI have been important driving forces for the introduction of the information processing framework in psychology.

The second approach is that of *action theory*, which has a long-standing tradition in psychology. The concept of action defined as goal-directed and planned behavior is deeply rooted in psychological introspection and philosophy (Aristotle's "causa finalis"). Early psychological theories of willed action (Ach, 1910; Lewin, 1926) are elaborated in today's volitional psychology (Heckhausen and Kuhl, 1985). Volition research focuses on the cognitive and motivational analysis of intentions as determinants of action control (Heckhausen *et al.*, 1987).

The two approaches rest on opposing premises. Cognitive information processing derives from a technical notion of a computational model of the mind (Anderson, 1983; Langley, 1983). This view is syntactic and cybernetic in nature. In action theory, on the other hand, motivational variables (wishes on the emotional side, intentions on the cognitive side) as a means of self-regulation are primary. This is more compatible with folk psychology (see A. Clark, this volume) in that it assumes behavior to be self-controlled and intentional. Thus, the action approach is basically semantic. Both approaches share the assumption of mental models and mental representations of the world, upon which the mind is supposed to act. Only after the various stages of mental processing have been passed can the stage of realizing action finally be entered.

Both approaches encounter serious problems which have prompted us to look for alternative paths of conceptualization. Which problems are these? As the two approaches described above are diverse, we shall start with discussing each separately. For the sake of clarity, we will not explicitly address the efforts which have been made to combine the two approaches (e.g. Kuhl, 1992, who claims that "a functional treatment of *self* within a computational theory of mind is possible").

The problems of the computational view have been discussed extensively by many authors in AI (see below) and in psychology (e.g. Kolers and Smythe, 1984). It has been shown, for example, that at least the initial stages of attentional processes are massively parallel rather than serial (Neisser, 1976). Recognition of patterns is not easily understood as a process reducible to bitwise processing of information. This point has already been made in gestalt psychology (Wertheimer, 1912; Helson, 1933), which put forward a holistic theory stating that an array of features is not just the sum of the features of all components but a different entity, a "gestalt". In other words, there may be emergent properties in perception and, generally, in cognition, which can hardly be accounted for by a computational approach.

In simulations of computational models of cognition several shortcomings become apparent. This may be one of the reasons why most of the criticisms of the computational approach have been formulated in AI, whereas there is no comparable debate in psychology (for exceptions, see e.g. Haken and Stadler, 1990; Thelen and Smith, 1994). For example, one problem that emerged in AI research concerns *learning* in tasks that demand unsupervised learning (see below). More generally, the computational view does not handle *change* and the dynamics of cognition very well. This point is addressed by connectionist AI where learning is studied in the context of neural networks. We will discuss this approach in more detail below.

Additionally, we may also look at the other side of the coin of dynamics, at *stability*. It is vitally important that cognitive entities remain stable under quite diverse conditions. This is evident in perception where objects are perceived as invariant even if they are changed, distorted, occluded, transposed, etc. In social cognition, belief systems and attitudes are maintained in different environments and under different circumstances. Generally, a concept may be applied meaningfully to different sets which have not one component in common. Concepts, therefore, are not simply linear compositions of elements but must have higher level qualities which can be evoked in a non-symbolic way. This topic is treated in several chapters of this volume. Thus, stability in the face of various transformations is an important attribute of cognition.

In conclusion, it seems that basic *dynamical* attributes of cognition – learning and stability – which are fundamentals of any cognitive processing, are not readily understood by computational theory (see also Vallacher and Kaufman, 1996).

Many of these criticisms do not apply to the action theoretical approach. On the contrary, those phenomena that are hardest to define in computational terms are the premises of action theory. The setting and pursuit of goals by a self-determined agent is prerequisite to the very definition of action. The main problem here is that we are dealing with concepts that are teleological right from the start, so that an old debate arises: how can goals (i.e. *future* states of an individual) cause intentions and wishes that determine the individual's behavior in the *present*? Obviously, this formulation may be an adequate description of anybody's introspection but is not a scientific explanation.

Action theory claims its intentionalistic terminology can explain behavior. This situation resembles pre-Darwinian biology: the giraffe has a long neck because it intends to eat from trees. But we may accept the terminology of action theory as a sort of abbreviated, *descriptive* code for mechanisms that have yet to be explained, non-intentionalistically and in detail. In section 4, we "intend" to do just this.

Another assumption of most theories of cognitive psychology has recently come under vigorous attack, namely the assumption of mental representations. The computational view of representation is based on the premise that there is a "language of the mind" (Fodor, 1975); the world is mapped into the mind in a logical (propositional) or analogous (mental models) fashion. Thus the world is represented by mental tokens (categories) and the categories are processed according to computational syntactical rules. But research on categorization and on memory has shown that this is probably not the whole story. Human categories do not have the "classical" properties of set-theoretical categories where membership is defined by singly necessary and jointly sufficient conditions (Rosch and Lloyd, 1978; see also Pinker and Prince, this volume). As we have already stated above, categories are dynamical entities that are diffuse *and* stable in a way that is appropriate under the given constraints of a social and cultural environment. Furthermore, the rules by which thinking connects categories and concepts are often not identical with the rules of probability and logic (see e.g. the conjunction fallacy in decision making, Kahneman *et al.*, 1982). This again shows that computation is not a sufficient explanation of human cognition.

How can these problems be overcome?

Cognitive psychology presents a rationalistic picture of cognition: action is seen as behavior that progresses systematically from wishes to intentions, according to a plan, schema or script. Decision is determined by "value × expectation" considerations. There are hierarchies of feedback loops. In short, in the foreground of this view we deal with a fixed cognitive architecture applying fixed formal algorithms to symbols that represent the world in an unambiguous manner.

But what we know from observation and self-observation seems quite different: there usually is a flow of thought, ideas, intentions, emotions. All mental events are incessantly changing even in the absence of environmental change (although we are not concerned here with the neurological substrate of cognition, this applies also to brain activity). Creative and adaptive ideas and actions may come out of a broad "stream of consciousness" which is perceived as being beyond control and planning. We doubt that there is as much a priori structure in our cognitions and actions as the cognitivists tell us.

Therefore we suggest that cognition should be conceptualized differently: we will not take structure for granted but start from the flow of thought. Dynamical pattern formation can serve as an alternative to pre-wired computation. Thus, we can ask the opposite question: how does cognitive architecture emerge from cognitive dynamics?

Several attempts have been made in psychology to investigate alternatives to the predominant computational theory of mind. We have already mentioned gestalt psychology. Gestalt theory gave way to behavioristic theory (i.e. anti-cognitive information processing) in the middle of this century, but specialized species of gestalt-like conceptualizations still exist. One of them dwells in the ecological approach to perception, which was put forward by Gibson (1979) and Kugler and Turvey (1987). Gibson, who had been a student of Lewin, developed an "ecological theory of perception". Its central term is *affordance*, a concept that links ecological stimuli directly to the perceiver. Usually (when enough ambient information is available, i.e. outside the tachistoscopic lab), perception consists of a direct "pick up" of relevant information.

In philosophy, affordances reflect the property of "Zuhandenheit" (readiness-to-hand) (Heidegger, 1962/1927). In a "hermeneutical cycle", perception may be seen as interpretation or as understanding of objects based upon some pre-knowledge, which has its roots in culture and phylogeny. Therefore, all symbol processing is based on a history of antecedents because it is embodied; expressed in terms of the recent debate, symbol processing is always situated.

This point is elaborated in psychology, among others, by Greeno's situativity theory. Situativity is seen as a general characteristic of cognition (Greeno and Moore, 1993; Law, 1993), which puts the focus more on environment–organism coupling than on cognition "inside the mind". As this debate – situated action vs. computation – is a core topic of cognitive science, we shall elaborate on it in the next section.

2 The problems of classical AI

There seems to be consensus within a large part of the research community in AI that classical systems are brittle, that they lack integrated learning and generalization capabilities, and that they cannot perform in real time. This makes them ill-suited for real world applications. We will not discuss these problems in detail as they are well known. We would rather focus on the under-lying reasons for these problems because they were instrumental in the Embodied Cognitive Science approach (Pfeifer and Scheier, in press).

The frame problem

The frame problem was originally pointed out by McCarthy and Hayes (1969). It has more recently attracted a lot of interest (e.g. Pylyshyn, 1987). The central issue concerns how to model *change* (Janlert, 1987): given a model of a continuously changing environment, how can the model be kept in tune with the real world? Assuming that the model consists of a set of logical proposi-tions (which essentially applies to any representation in classical AI) any proposition can change at any time. For example, consider propositional repre-sentations such as: INSIDE(ROBOT, ROOM) or ON(BATTERY, WAGON). Assume that there is a set of such representations of the environment stored in a robot's memory. There is a battery and a time bomb on a wagon. The task of the robot is to remove the battery from the room and recharge it in a safe place. The problem here is one of determining the implications of an action. For example, the action of moving the wagon has the "side effect" that the bomb will also be moved. Unfortunately, the robot does not know that this is relevant. What is entirely obvious to a human observer has to be made explicit for a robot.

The first idea is to have the robot take possible "side effects" into account. There are potentially very many. Checking them all takes a lot of time and most are entirely irrelevant. Another solution might be to try to distinguish between relevant and irrelevant inferences. But in order to do this one has to consider them all anyway, which implies that this approach does not have a significant advantage over the former one.

The frame problem really is about the system–environment interaction. The question is how models of a changing environment can be kept in tune with the environment. This is not a problem of logic, but rather one of modeling.

In the real world it is not necessary to build a representation of the situation in the first place: one can simply look at it, thereby disburdening oneself of cumbersome updating processes. Moreover, we can point at things when talking about them (see also "situatedness" below).

The frame problem is a fundamental one and is intrinsic to every modeling approach. As soon as there is a model of a changing environment, there is a frame problem. An important goal of intelligent systems design in Embodied Cognitive Science is to minimize the implications of the frame problem. One of the ways to achieve this is to minimize the amount of modeling in the first place.

The symbol grounding problem

The symbol grounding problem refers to the question of how symbols relate to the real world. In classical AI the meaning of symbols is typically defined in a purely syntactic way by how symbols relate to other symbols and how they are processed by some interpreter (Newell and Simon, 1976; Quillian, 1968). The relation of the symbols to the outside world is rarely discussed explicitly. In other words, we are dealing with closed systems. This position pertains not only to AI but to computer science in general. Except in real-time applications, the relation of symbols (e.g. in database applications) to the outside world is never elaborated, it is assumed as somehow given, the – typically implicit – assumption that designers and potential users will know what the symbols mean (e.g. the price of a product). Interestingly enough this idea is also predominant in linguistics: it is taken for granted that there is some kind of correspondence between the symbols or sentences and the outside world. The study of meaning then relates to the translation of sentences into some kind of logic-based representation where the semantics is clearly defined (Winograd and Flores, 1987, p. 18). This position is acceptable in the area of natural language since there is always a human interpreter and it can be safely expected that he or she is capable of establishing the appropriate relations to some outside world: the mapping is "grounded" in the human's experience of his or her interaction with the real world.

However, once we remove the human interpreter from the loop, as in the case of autonomous agents, we have to take into account that the system needs to interact with the environment on its own. Thus, the meaning of the symbols must be grounded in the system's own interaction with the real world. Symbol systems in which symbols only refer to other symbols are not grounded because the connection to the outside world is missing. The symbols have meaning only to a designer or a user, not to the system itself.

It is interesting to note that for a long time the symbol grounding problem did not attract much attention in AI or cognitive science – and it has never been an issue in computer science in general. Only the renewed interest in autonomous robots has pushed it to the foreground. This problem has been discussed in detail by Harnad (1990). It can be argued that the symbol grounding problem is really an artifact of symbolic systems and "disappears" if a different approach is used.

The problem of situatedness

The concept of situatedness has recently attracted a lot of interest and led to heated debates about the nature of intelligence and the place of symbol processing systems in studying intelligence. For example, a complete issue of the journal *Cognitive Science* is dedicated to "situatedness" (*Cognitive Science 17*, 1993). "Situatedness" roughly means the following. First, it implies that the world is viewed entirely from the perspective of the agent (not from the observer's perspective – see the "frame-of-reference" problem below). Second, a situated agent capitalizes on the system–environment interaction. Its behavior is largely based on the current situation rather than on detailed plans. Third, a situated agent brings its own experience to bear on the current situation; depending on its experience, it will behave differently. In other words, it changes over time. As it turns out, situated agents, i.e. agents having the property of situatedness, are much better at performing in real time because while exploiting the system–environment interaction they minimize the amount of central processing.

The perspective of situatedness contrasts with traditional AI where the approach has been – and still is – to equip the agents with detailed models of their environment. These models form the basis for planning processes which in turn are used for deciding on a particular action. But plan-based systems quickly run into combinatorial problems, i.e. the frame problem. If the real world changes, one of the main problems is keeping the models in tune with the environment. Inspection of the problem of taking action in the real world shows that it is neither necessary nor desirable to develop very comprehensive and detailed models (e.g. Suchman, 1987; Winograd and Flores, 1987). The more comprehensive and detailed the models, the harder the agent will be struck by the frame problem.

Typically, only a small part of an agent's environment is relevant for its action. In addition, instead of performing extensive inference operations on internal models or representations, the agent can interact with the current situation. The real world is, in a sense, part of the "knowledge" the agent requires in order to act (we put "knowledge" in quotes to indicate that this is not the

Figure 3.1 Simon's ant on the beach
Source: Simon, 1969

standard way of using this term in AI; the standard way refers to knowledge structures that are represented internally). The agent can merely "look at it" through the sensors.

Traditional AI systems are not situated and there is no reason why they should be for there is always a human interpreter in the loop. However, if we are interested in building (or understanding) systems that act directly in the real world, they must be situated. Otherwise, given the properties of the real world, the system will not be able to perform intelligently, i.e. in real time, taking only the relevant aspects of the situation into account.

The frame-of-reference problem

Whenever we are involved in designing an intelligent system, we have to be aware of the frame-of-reference problem. Our outline of the problem is based on Clancey's extensive treatment (Clancey, 1991). He argued that if we want to build models using computers or robots, we must appropriately conceptualize the relation among the observer, the designer (or the modeler), the artifact, and the environment. This problem is called the frame-of-reference problem.

The first thing we must understand is that behavior is always the result of a system–environment interaction. In order to clarify this point, let us refer to the example of Simon's ant on the beach (Figure 3.1; Simon, 1969). Let us assume that an ant starts moving on the right-hand side of a beach and its anthill is somewhere on the left. The direction it travels is roughly from right to left. The path the ant might take will be arduous because the beach is full of pebbles, rocks, puddles, and other obstacles. But this complexity may, in fact, be only an apparent one. It would be a frame-of-reference mistake to conclude from the – apparent – complexity of the trajectory that the internal mechanisms that are responsible for generating the behavior of the ant also have to be complex. The mechanisms that drive the ant's behavior may be very simple, implementing "rules" that we would describe as follows: "if obstacle sensor on left is activated, turn right" (and vice versa). In interaction with the environment, the apparent complexity of the trajectory emerges. The "rules" are patterns in the neural structures of the ant (how simple patterns may originate in a neural system, which is complex even in the ant, will be discussed in section 4).

Note that the seeming complexity of behavior emerges from the interaction and not from the environment alone: it would be just as erroneous to claim that the complexity of the trajectory is due to the complexity of the environment. The complexity of the environment is only a prerequisite. If we were to increase the size of the ant, say, by a factor of 100, and let it start in the same location with exactly the same behavioral rules as before, it would go more or less in a straight line! What appeared to the normal ant as obstacles would no longer be recognized as such by the giant ant. Its antennae would not be sensitive enough to detect the irregularities on the beach.

Or take a human sitting on the beach. Introducing other humans will make the environment much more complex and interesting as this offers the potential for highly sophisticated interactions (talking, playing, kissing, etc.). Now replace our first human by an ant. To the ant it is entirely irrelevant whether an object in the environment is a human or any other moving object: it does not have the sensors and brain system to experience the complexity.

Starting in the early 1980s, many of the problems of classical AI have been claimed to be solvable using the principles of connectionism. For example, neural networks are not brittle when confronted with new learning input as are propositional systems. They show "graceful degradation" when information is incomplete or noisy. Moreover, certain classes of learning algorithms, namely the non-supervised learning schemes (e.g. Kohonen feature maps, Hopfield nets), are compatible with the self-organization view advocated later in this chapter. They can be shown to form patterns and achieve pattern recognition based on the local interactions of subsymbolic components.

Nevertheless, they do not resolve the more fundamental problems mentioned in this section; neural networks still face the frame-of-reference problem. For example, the activation of output nodes in the standard back-propagation networks must be interpreted by a human observer – thus, there is always an observer in the loop. Also, neural networks *always* learn; they do not (have to) distinguish between relevant and irrelevant input stimuli. All items of the learning sets are relevant because the observer typically has made a careful preselection of the input data.

We suggest that neural networks are viable tools if they are embedded in a complete system that interacts autonomously with its environment. Only in this way can neural networks circumpass the frame-of-reference problem. There is no longer any need for an observer to interpret the activations of the nodes in the networks, rather the network is grounded in the physical body and the interactions with the real world (Harnad, 1990). This point, which is at the core of Embodied Cognitive Science, will be discussed in more detail below.

3 The Embodied Cognitive Science approach: complete autonomous agents

Embodied Cognitive Science has emerged as an alternative to classical AI, as an attempt to overcome the problems of the traditional approach. The core idea is to study the interaction of an agent (human, animal or robot) with the environment or real world, rather than investigating well-defined problems in virtual or block worlds. In other words, the focus is on the situated activity of an agent in its environment. Intelligence is seen in the interaction, not within the system.

This approach has several implications. We shall focus on three of them: embodiment, completeness, and ecological niches.

Embodiment

Interaction with an environment implies that *embodied* systems have to be constructed. Embodiment is a prequisite of situated cognition. Only if a system is in direct relation with its environment, i.e. only if it has a body of some sort, is it able to act in a situated way.

In terms of intelligent systems design and modeling the idea of embodiment has led to a remarkable increase of work with *mobile robots* or *autonomous agents*. Mobile robots constitute the optimal tool for Embodied Cognitive Science, because on the one hand they allow for a synthetic approach (the hallmark of AI), and on the other hand can be used to study issues of situated cognition implemented in interaction with the real world. Let us look at one example.

Brooks' subsumption architecture was the first approach towards Embodied Cognitive Science, or behavior-based robotics (Brooks, 1986a, b). It is a method of decomposing the control architecture of a robot into a set of task-achieving "behaviors" or competencies. The usual approach of conceptualizing intelligence is based on functional decomposition: first, there is sensing (i.e. perception), then internal processing (e.g. world modeling, planning, decision making), and finally some actions are executed (e.g. moving forward, grasping an object). This leads to the sense–think–act cycle of the traditional information processing approach. It is sometimes also called horizontal decomposition since each module follows the other sequentially (see Figure 3.2). In contrast with the traditional approach, subsumption architecture builds control architectures by incrementally adding task-achieving behaviors on top of each other. Implementations of such behaviors are called layers. Higher level layers (e.g. WANDER) build and rely on lower level ones (e.g. AVOID). Higher layers can subsume lower layers. Hence, instead of having a single sequence of information flow – from perception to world modeling to action – there are multiple paths which are parallelly active. Each of these paths (or

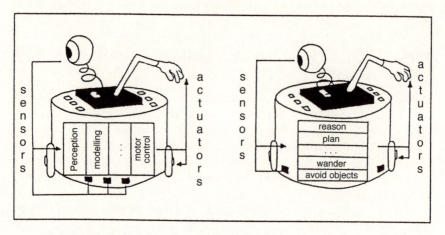

Figure 3.2 Horizontal and vertical decomposition
Left: the traditional decomposition of a control architecture into a
sequence of horizontally layered functional modules. Right: vertical
decomposition based on task-achieving behaviors in the subsumption
approach

Source: Pfeifer and Scheier, in press

layers) is concerned with only a small subtask of the robot's overall task such
as avoiding walls, circling around targets, moving to a charging station, etc.
These layers can function relatively independently. They do not have to await
instructions or results produced by other layers. In short, the subsumption
approach realizes the direct couplings between sensors and actuators, with only
limited internal processing, and can therefore tackle the frame problem mentioned above.

Complete systems

In 1961 the Japanese psychologist Masanao Toda proposed studying "Fungus
Eaters" as an alternative to the traditional methods of academic psychology
(Toda, 1982). Rather than performing ever more restricted and well-controlled
experiments on isolated faculties (memory, language, learning, perception,
emotion, etc.) and narrow tasks (memorizing nonsense syllables, letter perception on degraded stimuli, etc.) we should study "complete" systems, though
perhaps simple ones. This idea is fundamental to the research agenda of Embodied Cognitive Science. "Complete" in this context means that the systems
are capable of behaving autonomously in an environment without a human
intermediary. Such systems have to incorporate capabilities for classification,
navigation, object manipulation, and for "deciding" what to do. The integration of these capabilities into a system that is capable of behaving on its own,
so the argument went, will yield more insights into the nature of mind or

intelligence than looking at fragments of the unbelievably complex human mind. The "Fungus Eater" approach can be seen as a precursor of a more ecologically minded psychology (e.g. Neisser, 1976, 1982; Neisser and Winograd, 1988).

The "Fungus Eater" is an autonomous agent sent to a distant planet to collect uranium ore. The more ore it collects, the more it will be rewarded. It feeds on a certain type of fungus which grows on this planet. The "Fungus Eater" has an internal fungus store and means of locomotion (legs), means for decision making (brain), and collection (arms). Any kind of activity, including "thinking", requires energy. If the level of fungus in the store drops to zero the "Fungus Eater" is dead. The "Fungus Eater" is also equipped with sensors, one for vision and one for detecting uranium ore (e.g. a Geiger counter).

The scenario described by Toda is interesting in a number of respects. The "Fungus Eaters" must be autonomous: they are simply too far away to be controlled remotely. They must be self-sufficient as there are no humans to replace the batteries and to repair the robots, and they must be adaptive because the territory in which they function is largely unknown. The goal of Embodied Cognitive Science is to bring Toda's Gedanken experiments to scientific grounds by building synthetic robot models of various aspects of intelligence and adaptive behavior. Let us finally look at another implication of the situated and embodied perspective on cognition: the fact that there cannot be universality in intelligence systems.

Ecological niches and universality

If we look at biological agents, i.e. animals, we find that they require an environment for survival that is suited to satisfy their needs. Such an environment is called an "ecological niche". Wilson (1975) gives the following definition: "the range of each environmental variable such as temperature, humidity, and food items, within which a species can exist and reproduce" (p. 317).

In nature, there is no such thing as a "universal animal". Animals (and humans) are always "designed" by evolution for a particular niche. Agents behave in the real world. As pointed out, they always require certain conditions for their survival. A robot always requires some kind of energy source. It must be equipped with sensors and effectors in order to perform its task in a particular environment, or more precisely, in a particular "ecological niche". If the robot has to work at night, it may not be a good idea to equip it only with a vision sensor: an infrared device might be necessary. So, the idea of an ecological niche holds for robots as well. It follows that there can be no universal robot, a constraint deriving from the fact that it has to perform in the real world.

This contrasts sharply to computation. Computation is universal: Turing machines are the only machines that need to be studied. This is, of course, only possible because computation, by definition, "takes place" in a virtual world. And universality only applies in this virtual world. Computers are sometimes said to be universal. This is true only when focusing on computation. If we look at computers as being real machines, they depend very much on their environment. They require a supply of electricity, must be handled by their users with care, must not be exposed to excessive heat, etc. In this sense, computers, just like any other artifact, are designed for a particular ecological niche. Of course, some robots can perform several tasks and exist in more varied environments compared to others, so their niche is broader, but nonetheless still there.

The fact that agents in the real world are not universal but have to function in a particular niche, sounds like a severe restriction. However, there is a lot of leverage to be gained, too. Because the ecological niche is restricted, has its own laws and characteristics, its types of objects and agents, its temperature profile (i.e. how temperature changes over time), its lighting conditions, etc., there is no need to provide for everything in the agent itself. Assume that in a particular niche only large objects are relevant. Then there is no need for a high-resolution sensor for distinguishing very small objects. If the niche is flat, wheels are sufficient. Often, learning problems that at the purely computational level seem intractable, converge in real time if the constraints of the econiche are exploited. For example, it might be the case that all objects of interest have a bilateral symmetry, which implies that learning can be unilateral. This makes life much easier. However, as always, there is a tradeoff: the more constraints we exploit in our designs, the less universal the agent will be.

The goal of Embodied Cognitive Science is to build autonomous, self-sufficient, situated, embodied agents designed for a particular ecological niche. We shall not go into any further detail here because this would be far beyond the scope of this chapter (for reviews of Embodied Cognitive Science research, see Pfeifer and Scheier, in press; Steels and Brooks, 1995).

4 Synopsis: situated and self-organizing cognition

In this last section, we will – based on our considerations so far – outline a framework for a cognitive "architecture" that dispenses with an architect, but still has the capacity to account for organized and rational action. In the theoretical framework to be presented below, cognition and goal-oriented action are viewed as emergent properties of a self-organized cognitive system.

Which phenomena have to be addressed by such a framework? Let us first – in another "Gedanken experiment" – picture the mind as a bundle of innumerable rudimentary cognitive items, a set of fleeting cognitive and emotional micro-events, a "stream of consciousness". In terms of dynamics, we address a system spanning a very high-dimensional phase space. Daringly, we may name this bundle a "cognitive–emotional system", CES for short. There would initially be no coherence and pre-wired structure in this system, just the microscopic chaos of the local behavior of the cognitive components (to be defined later). We might find "associations", i.e. some local interaction between components which happen to be in some (temporal or spatial) vicinity (all spatial terms are to be understood based on the notion of phase space of dynamical systems theory, i.e. as an abstract space which is usually not the Euclidean space; Abraham and Shaw, 1992).

We would have to expect this system's behavior to be very complex, with almost as many degrees of freedom as the number of items or dimensions it consists of. Obviously, such a system is not a good choice for a model of the mind. What would be lacking?

(*a*) *Pattern*   A CES would have to devise a way in which its components can be structured and organized. Components must be grouped, sorted, combined, etc. on a large scale, depending on their relevance for different tasks and demands. Thus, if some situation requires all the cognitive items that pertain to, say, writing an essay, then other items adequate for repairing a bicycle should be relatively less active. Of course, an outside designer/interpreter or an internal homunculus is not allowed to provide for pattern.

(*b*) *Stability*   As soon as some cognitive–emotional pattern is established it should be stable over time, random or irrelevant changes in the environment and in the CES must not result in immediate restructuring. The stable state of a dynamical system ("attractor") may be defined as a state whose neighbors in phase space remain in the former's vicinity. Asymptotic (global) stability means that (all) perturbations to an attractor are damped out with time. As long as a pattern within the CES is stable, the activity of "writing an essay" is not (at least not necessarily) transformed into "repairing a bicycle" should, for example, a bicycle happen to pass by the window of my study.

(*c*) *Optimality*   Writing essays or repairing bicycles may temporarily be inadequate actions for an individual. Thus, not only should a CES have the potential to form patterns with some asymptotic stability, but the patterns and their stability should also be useful in a given situation. There must be a function that "tells" the CES how to shape its patterns in order for it to be optimally adapted to an environment.

Self-organization

We propose that an answer to these demands may lie in the phenomenon of self-organization which is modeled comprehensively by synergetics (Haken, 1983). Self-organization is ubiquitous in complex systems which are in a far-from-equilibrium state (Prigogine and Stengers, 1984). Archetypal physical systems like the Bénard instability and the laser are well-known examples of such systems; these systems are capable of pattern formation not imposed by an external designer.

The Bénard instability can be demonstrated in a layer of fluid (Kratky, 1992). When the fluid is heated from below while the medium at its upper surface is kept at a constant lower temperature, a heat flux permeates the fluid system.

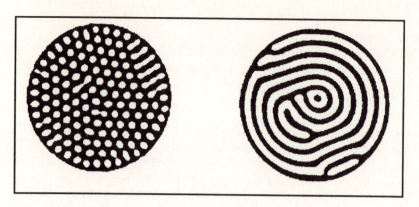

Figure 3.3 Bénard hexagonal and roll patterns seen from above
Source: after Bestehorn *et al.*, 1993

As soon as the heat flux reaches a critical value, highly coordinated patterns of convection appear in the fluid. In addition to local interactions among fluid molecules, a much stronger long-range interaction is imposed. Patterns take the shape of rolls or of hexagonal cells, depending on the form of the container and the site of the heat application (Figure 3.3). Upon a further increase of heat flux (i.e. of the difference in temperature above and below the fluid) patterns change first to oscillating rolls and later to nonperiodic patterns showing deterministic chaos. The Bénard instability and equivalent atmospheric systems can be modeled quite well by equations of only three degrees of freedom (Lorenz, 1963).

In summary, what is remarkable about this behavior is the emergence of a highly ordered macroscopic pattern out of the random microscopic movements of fluid molecules, i.e. of many degrees of freedom. Furthermore, the capacity of the system to transport heat is increased when its control parameter grows; loosely speaking, the system adapts to its non-equilibrium environment by "trying to reduce" the gradient of temperature. All three attributes listed above – pattern formation, stability, and optimality – can be found in the dynamics of the Bénard instability and other self-organizing natural systems.

A general model of self-organizing systems is illustrated in Figure 3.4. This model has three constituents. Control parameters are variables of the system's environment that denote the system's departure from thermodynamic equilibrium (i.e. the temperature gradient in case of the Bénard instability). Control parameters "drive" the complex system (the particles of the fluid); after a phase transition this driving produces patterns (quantified by order parameters). Thus the complex system (endowed with many degrees of freedom at the start) has become a two-level system: it may now be described completely at a macroscopic level by the few degrees of freedom of order parameters (in our example, by specifying the regular convection patterns). The two levels of the system

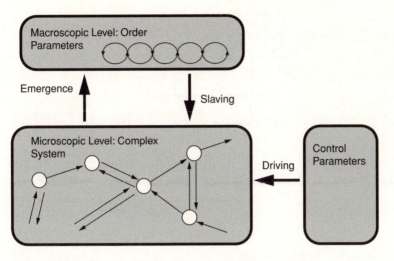

Figure 3.4 General model of a self-organizing system (schematic)

are linked recursively; order parameters emerge from the microscopic dynamics, and in turn structure ("enslave") the motion of the system's many microscopic components.

Application to cognition

Our suggestion is to apply what has been said about self-organizing systems in general to the cognitive–emotional system (CES) mentioned above. If the prerequisites for self-organization are met by the CES, this should yield an outline of a self-organizational theory of cognition (Haken and Stadler, 1990; Tschacher, 1997). A good theory of pattern formation is useful also as a theory of pattern recognition (cf. Arbib and Rizzolatti, this volume).

At the beginning of this section we addressed the conceptualization of the microscopic level of a CES. The cognitive components may be seen as "behavior kernels" (Tschacher, 1997), i.e. hypothetical cognitive micro-items not directly accessible to introspection and experiment. If we tentatively cross the mind–body language border, the micro components may be identified as the activation of neuronal cell assemblies which translate, for instance, into time-dependent EEG potentials over brain tissue (for a synergetic theory of brain dynamics see Haken, 1995). But we shall refrain from raising the eternal issue of the mind–body interface here.

Conscious cognition (thinking, memory, intention), at any rate, is to be located at the macroscopic level of our model; we view cognition as an order parameter of the CES, a pattern of the cognitive system. In Embodied Cognitive Science, cognition may be designed accordingly as attractors in the phase space of a robot. The SMC 2 model of situated categorization (Scheier and Lambrinos,

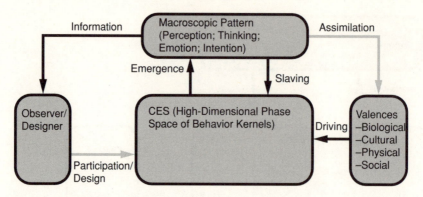

Figure 3.5 Schematic model of cognition as self-organized dynamics

1996) consists of a number of neural networks which are connected to the input (a CCD camera) and to the effectors of the robot (arm-gripper system). It turns out to be feasible to operationalize the synchronization of these networks as being equivalent to macroscopic pattern formation of a CES. This synchronization can be assessed using principal-component analysis and related measures.

Consequently, cognition does not result from mere associations of single cognitive items, i.e. in terms of AI cognition is not propositional. Cognition emerges from a multitude of synchronized items whose activity is selected in the CES owing to the control parameters in its environment. We previously posited that control parameters evoke order parameters in such a way as to reduce the environmental nonequilibrium. Optimality and fitness are thereby increased.

It is important to note that our basic construct, the complex system CES, is free from any intentionality. There is no volition, wish, or motivational variable in the CES *per se*. Behavior kernels are just the potential elements of what – after synchronization via self-organization – may evolve into perception, thought, emotion, intention, plan, and consequently, action. The CES represents only the prerequisites to think and act. All intentionality results from the interaction of the CES with its environment, which we conceptualize as a driving of the CES by control parameters. The equivalence to Embodied Cognitive Science, where intelligence arises from situatedness, may gradually become apparent.

The application of synergetics to cognition is symbolized by Figure 3.5. The model of Figure 3.4 has been completed in two respects. First, an "Observer/ Designer" who receives information and participates in a system he or she observes or designs was added. Second, the loop between the cognitive system and its environment was closed by providing for "Assimilation". We will elaborate both aspects in the following section.

Systems theory allows for a formulation of concepts suitable for a wide range of further applications. Particularly, a definition of "complex system" can be tailored to the needs of *social theories*, as we may conceptualize variables of social interaction as the components of the system-under-study (Tschacher *et al.*, 1992). One may then empirically test the occurrence of pattern formation and nonlinear phenomena against a different systems background, for example social groups and therapeutic dyads (Tschacher and Brunner, 1995; Tschacher and Grawe, 1996).

Situatedness and motivation

The interaction of cognitive order parameters with the environment is the decisive point where synergetics turns into a situated theory; it will be shown how closely synergetic psychology and Embodied Cognitive Science are linked. We are first led to the question of what the concept of "control parameter" refers to in the case of CESs and what "nonequilibrium" means in cognition.

In psychology, energizing and incentive variables are treated under the heading of *motivation*. Several motivational theories have conceptualized motivation as reduction of libidinous tensions and disequilibria (as in Freudian psychology) or, in a more cognitive fashion, as attempts to reestablish cognitive balance and reduce dissonance (e.g. theories of social psychologists such as Heider (1958) and Festinger (1964)). In the latter's work, cognitive approaches go back again to Lewinian field theory (as does Gibson's concept of affordance mentioned in section 1).

Lewin's (1926) motivational construct of "Aufforderungscharakter" or *valence* comes very close to our general idea of motivation being the driving of a CES by nonequilibrium control parameters. The difference lies mainly in the general theoretical frame: Lewin's field theory is based on the concept of forces ("vector psychology") as basic causes of psychological dynamics; valence then results from the tension in a psychological field. We opt for the synergetic approach, however, which is centered on dissipation and "thermodynamic" nonequilibrium instead of forces. The progress achieved by this approach is that nonequilibrium dynamics (synergetics) can account for the formation of pattern and of attractors, whereas forces can only explain change. Thus, field theory must leave open the basic question of pattern formation and optimality (and for this reason cannot provide an answer to the symbol grounding problem). Nevertheless, the analogy to Lewinian thought is striking, so that we use and redefine the term "valence" to denote a control parameter of a CES (see Figure 3.5).

In Figure 3.5 valences are located outside of the cognitive system CES. We recognize the sources of valence in the biological, social, cultural, and physical environment of the CES (seen this way, the body is "environment" to cognition). The cognitive–emotional state of an individual is therefore continuously embedded in biological nonequilibrium (e.g. hypothalamic activity leading to "hunger" cognition/emotion), cultural and social nonequilibrium (e.g.

working atmosphere in an organization may facilitate or impede creativity), physical nonequilibrium (e.g. affordances built into housing and architecture, enabling certain "standing patterns of behavior" while discouraging others (Barker, 1968)).

In reacting to the frame-of-reference problem, Embodied Cognitive Science argues for a wide definition of the cognitive system. Representation and memory, for example, also encompass the cultural setting and sensorimotor loops of an autonomous agent: culture and motor behavior can be seen as parts of cognition. Thus, there seems to be a discrepancy with our model which locates valences outside the CES. However, this discrepancy is superficial and easily resolved: valences are defined in such a way as to transfer pragmatic information (about various kinds of nonequilibrium) to the CES. A pebble is not a valence, but the pebble's being an obstacle to an ant is (as well as its posing a challenge to a child!). Therefore valences are *interfaces* between pebbles and agents. We consider it to be of minor importance whether we view "pebble-valence" inside cognition or as environment to cognition. We stress that a CES becomes *situated by valences*, and to us it seems purely a matter of terminology whether valences are seen as cognition or as constraints for cognition. Dynamical systems theory (e.g. Thompson and Stewart, 1993) is liberal when it comes to defining systems; what is conceptualized as part of, or environment to, a dynamical system-under-study is mainly a matter of convenience and convention. "System" is not an ontological concept and should by no means be treated as such.

Evolutionary situatedness

Embodied Cognitive Science designs agents for specific ecological niches. In biological agents, it is obvious that the interaction of CES and valences is based on a long history of coevolution (i.e. joint and mutual evolution of CES and valences). For example, in human infants (but not in infant dolphins) there is a *preparedness* for visual cliffs, and for small, black, eight-legged animals: certain behavior kernels seem to exist from birth as predesigned candidates for being selected by certain valences in the physical environment.

The fit of system and control parameters/valences may take different forms:

(a) In the Bénard instability the fluid is chosen accordingly (gasoline would not work as well because of its viscosity and inflammability).
(b) In robotics, designers provide autonomous agents with predesigned value systems to adapt them for their niches.
(c) In the case of animals like the human individual, phylogeny has provided constraints for cognition by a highly prestructured (though not pre-wired!) neuronal substrate.

In the case (c) of "natural" coevolution, the fit of system and control parameters is accounted for by the loop "valence–CES–pattern–valence" of Figure 3.5.

This loop of coevolution deals with the symbol grounding problem; it has made the cognitive system capable of adaptation on a phylogenetic time scale. This time scale is much larger than the one of cognition in the here-and-now. In principle, however, the mechanism of coevolution is analogous to cognition seen as selection of order parameters in the here-and-now. Accordingly, Haken (1983) speaks of a "Darwinism of microscopic modes". Therefore, long-term coevolution is the platform on which self-organization occurs. Or rather, coevolution sets the stage for its own core method, namely self-organization (for a treatment of "endosystems" – systems that modify their environment to modify themselves – see Rössler, 1987; Atmanspacher and Dalenoort, 1994; Tschacher, 1997).

This is different in the two other examples given, (a) Bénard and (b) robot, where the observer or designer determines the systems' components and/or valences in a meaningful way. The functioning and pattern formation in these systems depend on the participation of the observer or designer. We therefore have to introduce yet another loop (observer–CES–pattern–observer) into Figure 3.5. This accounts for the frame-of-reference problem of Embodied Cognitive Science (Clancey, 1991), and more generally, for the observer-dependence of any observation. It seems that our descriptions can never be entirely free of a homunculus. Scientific explanation is always more or less threatened by infinite regress. The interactions related to this principle of uncertainty are given by gray arrows in Figure 3.5.

This point leads us to a caveat for robot design. The fundament of adaptivity in natural organisms is laid by coevolution. The adaptivity of cognition and action, with which this chapter mainly deals, is grounded upon this fundament. Valences and cognition/action thus refer to each other because of their common history. If we design a robot to act autonomously in an environment, however, we shall have to design its value system (the valences) and its hardware substrate (e.g. the types and positions of sensors that cause a specific preparedness), at least to a certain extent. We should keep in mind, though, that the value systems and hardware should have the flexibility to evolve with the environment, because Embodied Cognitive Science knows well that pre-wired implementations lead to impasses as they confine the evolution of the system. Therefore, with pre-installed values and preparednesses an autonomous agent may have but few options to develop intelligent behavior; a competing computational expert system may consequently have an advantage right from the start (its designer did his or her best to create an optimal knowledge base). It is not easy for a synthetic approach like AI to beware of the homunculus of the designer.

The lesson of situated and self-organizing cognition at this point would be to provide an autonomous robot with many degrees of freedom, but just enough structure to get along and *organize itself*. We should heed Brooks' warning that it took evolution the longest to reach the simplest level of intelligence. The evolution of insect-level intelligence lasted 3 billion years, the subsequent evolution of human intelligence "only another 500 million years" (Brooks, 1991). A fascinating empirical question is how much faster AI might be.

The frame problem, the symbol grounding problem, and the frame-of-reference problem of AI are highly relevant for psychology in that they show that intelligence and adaptive cognition cannot be computed and implemented directly. The lesson of Embodied Cognitive Science for action psychology is that one-sidedness leads to pseudo explanations. Embodied Cognitive Science suggests that intelligence is perhaps unlikely, but may evolve from the interaction of several environments with and in a situated cognitive system. Since we know that intelligent cognition exists, we may suppose it is a result of evolutions at different time scales; it dwells at the interface of these evolutions.

References

Abraham, R.H.; Shaw, C.D. (1992) *Dynamics – The Geometry of Behavior*, Redwood City CA, Addison-Wesley.

Ach, N. (1910) *Über den Willensakt und das Temperament*, Leipzig, Quelle und Meyer.

Anderson, J.R. (1983) *The Architecture of Cognition*, Cambridge MA, Harvard University Press.

Atmanspacher, H.; Dalenoort, G.J. (eds.) (1994) *Inside Versus Outside*, Berlin, Springer.

Bandura, A. (1986) *Social Foundations of Thought and Action*, Englewood Cliffs NJ, Prentice-Hall.

Barker, R.G. (1968) *Ecological Psychology*, Stanford CA, Stanford University Press.

Bestehorn, M.; Fantz, M.; Friedrich, R.; Haken, H. (1993) Hexagonal and Spiral Patterns of Thermal Convection, *Physics Letters A*, vol. 174, pp. 48–52.

Brooks, R.A. (1986a) Intelligence without Representation, *Artificial Intelligence*, vol. 47, pp. 139–159.

Brooks, R.A. (1986b) A Robust Layered Control System for a Mobile Robot, *IEEE Journal of Robotics and Automation*, vol. 2, pp. 14–23.

Brooks, R. (1991) Integrated Systems based on Behavior, *SIGART Bulletin*, vol. 2, pp. 46–50.

Carver, C.S.; Scheier, M.F. (1982) Control Theory: A Useful Conceptual Framework for Personality-Social, Clinical, and Health Psychology, *Psychological Bulletin*, vol. 92, pp. 111–135.

Clancey, W.J. (1991) The Frame-of-Reference Problem in the Design of Intelligent Machines, in van Lehn, K. (ed.), *Architectures for Intelligence*, Hillsdale NJ, Erlbaum.

Festinger, L. (1964) *Conflict, Decision, and Dissonance*, Stanford CA, Stanford University Press.

Fodor, J.A. (1975) *The Language of Thought*, New York, Crowell.

Gibson, J.J. (1979) *The Ecological Approach to Visual Perception*, Boston MA, Houghton Mifflin.

Greeno, J.G.; Moore, J.L. (1993) Situativity and Symbols: Response to Vera and Simon, *Cognitive Science*, vol. 17, pp. 49–59.

Haken, H. (1983) *Synergetics – An Introduction*, Berlin, Springer.

Haken, H. (1995) *Principles of Brain Functioning*, Berlin, Springer.

Haken, H.; Stadler, M. (eds.) (1990) *Synergetics of Cognition*, Berlin, Springer.

Harnad, S. (1990) The Symbol Grounding Problem, *Physica D*, vol. 42, pp. 335–346.

Heckhausen, H.; Gollwitzer, P.M.; Weinert, F.E. (eds.) (1987) *Jenseits des Rubikon: Der Wille in den Humanwissenschaften*, Berlin, Springer.

Heckhausen, H.; Kuhl, J. (1985) From Wishes to Action: The Dead Ends and Short Cuts on the Long Way to Action, in M. Frese and J. Sabini (eds.), *Goal Directed Behavior: The Concept of Action in Psychology*, Hillsdale NJ, Erlbaum, pp. 134–160.

Heidegger, M. (1962) *Being and Time* (Original: *Sein und Zeit*, 1927), New York, Harper and Row.

Heider, F. (1958) *The Psychology of Interpersonal Relations*, New York, Wiley.

Helson, H. (1933) The Fundamental Propositions of Gestalt Psychology, *Psychological Review*, vol. 40, pp. 13–32.

Janlert, L.E. (1987) Modeling Change – the Frame Problem, in Z.W. Pylyshyn (ed.), *The Robot's Dilemma. The Frame Problem in Artificial Intelligence*, Norwood NJ, Ablex, pp. 1–40.

Kahneman, D.; Slovic, P.; Tversky, A. (eds.) (1982) *Judgement under Uncertainty: Heuristics and Biases*, Cambridge, Cambridge University Press.

Kolers, P.A.; Smythe, W.E. (1984) Symbol Manipulation: Alternatives to the Computational View of Mind, *Journal of Verbal Learning and Verbal Behavior*, vol. 23, pp. 289–314.

Kratky, K. (1992) Chaos and Disorder, in W. Tschacher, G. Schiepek and E.J. Brunner (eds.), *Self-Organization and Clinical Psychology*, Berlin, Springer, pp. 88–101.

Kugler, P.N., Turvey, M.T. (1987) *Information, Natural Law, and the Self-Assembly of Rhythmic Movement*, Hillsdale NJ, Erlbaum.

Kuhl, J. (1992) A Theory of Self-Regulation: Action versus State Orientation, Self-Discrimination, and Some Applications, *Applied Psychology*, vol. 41, pp. 97–129.

Langley, P. (1983) Exploring the Space of Cognitive Architectures, *Behavior Research Methods and Instrumentation*, vol. 15, pp. 289–299.

Law, L.-G. (1993) *Symbolic Processing vs. Situated Action: A Dialectical Synthesis?*, Research report, no. 24, Universität München: Lehrstuhl für Empirische Pädagogik und Pädagogische Psychologie.

Lewin, K. (1926) Vorsatz, Wille und Bedürfnis, *Psychologische Forschung*, vol. 7, pp. 330–385.

Lorenz, E.N. (1963) Deterministic Non-Periodic Flow, *Journal for the Atmospheric Sciences*, vol. 20, pp. 130–141.

McCarthy, J.; Hayes, P.J. (1969) Some Philosophical Problems from the Standpoint of Artificial Intelligence, in B. Meltzer and D. Michie (eds.), *Machine Intelligence*, vol. 4, pp. 463–502.

Miller, G.A.; Galanter, E.; Pribram, K.H. (1960) *Plans and the Structure of Behavior*, New York, Holt, Rinehart, and Winston.

Neisser, U. (1976) *Cognition and Reality (Principles and Implications of Cognitive Psychology)*, San Francisco CA, Freeman.

Neisser, U. (1982) *Memory Observed: Remembering in Natural Contexts*, San Francisco CA, Freeman.

Neisser, U.; Winograd, E. (eds.) (1988) *Remembering Reconsidered: Ecological and Traditional Approaches to the Study of Memory*, Cambridge, Cambridge University Press.

Newell, A.; Simon, H.A. (1976) Computer Science as Empirical Inquiry: Symbols and Search, *Communications of the ACM*, vol. 19, pp. 113–126.

Pfeifer, R.; Scheier, C. (in press) *Understanding Intelligence*, Cambridge MA, MIT Press.

Prigogine, L.; Stengers, I. (1984) *Order out of Chaos: Man's New Dialogue with Nature*, New York, Bantam Books.

Pylyshyn, Z.W. (ed.) (1987) *The Robot's Dilemma. The Frame Problem in Artificial Intelligence*, Norwood NJ, Ablex.

Quillian, R. (1968) Semantic Memory, in Minsky, M. (ed.), *Semantic Information Processing*, Cambridge MA, MIT Press.

Rosch, E.; Lloyd, B.B. (eds.) (1978) *Cognition and Categorization*, Hillsdale NJ, Erlbaum.

Rössler, O.E. (1987) Endophysics, in J.L. Casti and A. Karlqvist (eds.), *Real Brains, Artificial Minds*, New York, Elsevier, pp. 25–46.

Scheier, C.; Lambrinos, D. (1996) Categorization in a Real-World Agent Using Haptic Exploration and Active Perception, in P. Maes, M. Mataric, J.-A. Meyer, J. Pollack and S. Wilson (eds.), *From Animals to Animats*, Cambridge MA, MIT Press, pp. 65–75.

Simon, H.A. (1969) (second ed.) *The Sciences of the Artificial*, Cambridge MA, MIT Press.

Steels, L.; Brooks, R. (eds.) (1995) *The Artificial Life Route to Artificial Intelligence: Building Embodied, Situated Agents*, Hillsdale NJ, Erlbaum.

Suchman, L.A. (1987) *Plans and Situated Actions – The Problem of Human–Machine Communication*, Cambridge MA, Cambridge University Press.

Thelen, E.; Smith, L.B. (1994) *A Dynamic Systems Approach to the Development of Cognition and Action*, Cambridge MA, MIT Press.

Thompson, J.M.T.; Stewart, H.B. (1993) A Tutorial Glossary of Geometrical Dynamics, *International Journal of Bifurcation and Chaos*, vol. 3, pp. 223–239.

Toda, M. (1982) *Man, Robot, and Society*, The Hague, Nijhoff.

Tschacher, W. (1997) *Die Anwendung der Selbstorganisationstheorie und der Theorie dynamischer Systeme auf Probleme der Psychologie*, Göttingen, Hogrefe.

Tschacher, W.; Brunner, E.J. (1995) Empirische Studien zur Dynamik von Gruppen aus der Sicht der Selbstorganisationstheorie, *Zeitschrift für Sozialpsychologie*, vol. 26, pp. 78–91.

Tschacher, W.; Brunner, E.J.; Schiepek, G. (1992) Self-Organization in Social Groups, in W. Tschacher, G. Schiepek and E.J. Brunner (eds.), *Self-Organization and Clinical Psychology*, Berlin, Springer, pp. 341–366.

Tschacher, W.; Grawe, K. (1996) Selbstorganisation in Therapie-prozessen – Die Hypothese und empirische Prüfung der "Reduktion von Freiheitsgraden" bei der Entstehung von Therapiesystemen, *Zeitschrift für Klinische Psychologie*, vol. 25, pp. 55–60.

Vallacher, R.R.; Kaufman, J. (1996) Dynamics of Action Identification. Volatility and Structure in the Mental Representation of Behavior, in P.M. Gollwitzer and J.A. Bargh (eds.), *The Psychology of Action*, New York, Guilford, pp. 260–282.

Wertheimer, M. (1912) Experimentelle Studien über das Sehen von Bewegungen, *Zeitschrift für Psychologie*, vol. 61, pp. 165–292.

Wilson, E.O. (1975) *Sociobiology* (abridged edition), Cambridge MA, Harvard University Press.

Winograd, T.; Flores, F. (1987) *Understanding Computers and Cognition: A New Foundation for Design*, Wokingham, Addison-Wesley.

4 Complex systems methods in cognitive systems and the representation of environmental information

Philip Van Loocke

Abstract

The hypothesis that higher level cognition is organized in a modular way is explored. Emphasis is put on features that are present in modules that represent biological and environmental information. It is proposed that methods from complex systems theory may provide useful tools for cognitive subsystems that process this type of information. Such methods may furnish recoding techniques leading to representations that are of relevance when developing biological concepts. Complex systems methods that are related to quantum theory are considered.

1 Introduction: cognition and modularity

In recent years, many cognitive scientists have proposed that human pre-processing operates in a modular way. Immediately after a pattern is realized at the level of the senses, it is analyzed in specialized modules. In the well-known view of Fodor (1983), these modules have a strong genetic basis, and processing occurs in an "informationally encapsulated" way, which means that there is no communication between processes going on in different modules. Further, processing at this stage is bottom-up: higher level cognition has no influence on pre-processing. This view has been amply discussed, and many specifications as well as modifications have been put forward. For instance, it appears that, at relatively early processing stages, attention binds features detected in different modules, so that their independence is not absolute (Treisman, 1988). As another example, Kosslyn and Sussman (1995) argue that there is no such thing as "immaculate perception". Instead imagery acts top-down and interacts with information that is prepared by bottom-up pre-processing. Nevertheless, most authors agree that a Fodorian view on pre-processing is fruitful at least to some approximation.

The cognitive science community is much more divided about the stages after pre-processing. Fodor postulates that pre-processing is followed by a non-modular cognitive stage. To the extent that different sub-processes can be discerned, they can exchange information, and profoundly influence each other.

Furthermore, they basically use one "language of thought". Similarly, Pylyshyn (1980) argues that a single language of thought suffices to generate such different processes as imagery and verbal reasoning. Facing this view is the stance of Kosslyn (1987) and Paivio (1986), according to which higher cognition depends on clearly different subsystems that use different codes. In particular, imagery and verbal thought would depend on such different codes. A related view can be found in Gardner (1983), who argues that intelligence is "multiple", and that different people may have different abilities for mathematics, language, or music. A similar approach couched in terms of neural networks has been proposed by M. Arbib (1989). Recently, A. Clark, in his connectionist-friendly discussion of the acquisition of expertise, has developed a forceful argument for the point that the strategy "*modularize whenever possible*" seems most compatible with empirical evidence (Clark, 1993, p. 85).

In his recent work, Pinker advocates a strong version of the modularity hypothesis (e.g. Pinker, 1994). Along with a linguistic module, the human brain is proposed to contain at least fifteen specialized higher level modules, each of which is supported with some form of innate organization. Among them is a module that specializes in "intuitive mechanics, such as knowledge of motions, forces, and deformations that objects undergo" (Pinker, 1994, p. 420). Another module develops an intuitive biology. Still another one generates mental maps for large territories. A further module is specialized in habitat selection, and recognizes safe, information-rich, productive environments, and so on. The existence of such modules can be defended with arguments from an experimental psychological context as well as with arguments that stem from biological anthropology; in particular, Pinker refers to Barkow, Cosmides and Tooby and their compendium *The adapted mind* (1995). This chapter will take as its point of departure that higher level cognition is modular at least to some extent.

In the next section, fairly universal human patterns of reaction to characteristics of the natural environment that are related to survival are considered. Then, the recoding problem that appears when cognitive systems are modeled by connectionist nets is formulated (section 3). The remaining sections (4–9) explain how codes developed in a complex systems context may help in recoding for modules that specialize in processing biological information. Some weight will be given to principles that stem from quantum theory.

2 Modules for intuitive biology and for processing landscapes

Because of its importance for the subject of this chapter, I will be more specific about higher level modularity with respect to intuitive biology and with respect to landscape processing. First, consider the hypothetical functional module for intuitive biology. At first sight, it may sound far-fetched to postulate such a subsystem in the brain, especially if it is suggested that some of its structure is inherited genetically. However, from the standpoint of biological anthropology, this is less strange. After all, humans as well as their predecessors evolved in a biological environment. Following Pinker (1994, pp. 422–424), biological entities have four characteristics not shared by non-biological objects:

(a) Organisms (at least sexually reproducing organisms) belong to species within which interbreeding is possible. This requires that not all kinds of hybrid animals can occur in nature, and results in relatively constant within-species structure and behavior.
(b) Related species stem from a common ancestor. The less related, the further one has to go back in time in order to find a lineage from which two species split off. These historical relations in terms of lineage splitting entail that organisms can be divided in hierarchically organized classes, and that in general an animal belongs to a single class only at a given level of the hierarchy.
(c) Due to their biochemical structure and their self-organizing nature, organisms have typical dynamical properties: they grow in typical ways and may move.
(d) A genotype is never met; rather, different phenotypes of a species are present in nature. A genotype can be considered as the "hidden essence" of a phenotype.

These characteristics appear to be reflected in human knowledge about biological entities in a universal way. Studies in cultural anthropology show that primitive cultures classify plants and animals at the genus level (of Linnean taxonomy – since a local ecology usually contains only one species for a given genus, this level corresponds to the species level as well), and that higher level categories are present too (like quadruped animals, birds, fishes, etc.). These classes are exclusive, in contradistinction, for instance, with classes to which man-made objects belong. For example, a piano can belong to the class "furniture" as well as to the class "musical instrument", but a sparrow does not belong to the class "bird" and some other class like "fish". This is tightly related to the characteristics (a) and (b) mentioned above. Property (c) has been illustrated in Spelke's ontogenetic work (Spelke *et al.*, 1992). Babies as young as three to six months expect other types of movements from inanimate objects like balls than from animate entities like people. Finally, Keil (1989) has illustrated point (d) in ontogenetic and cultural anthropological contexts. When a child is shown two animals, and when it is told that the latter one will be painted and operated to look like the former, it still claims that the manipulated animal will not have become a member of the same genus as the former. Similar findings are obtained for illiterate cultures, suggesting that biological entities have "hidden essences" that cannot be transformed by simple manipulation. Even if neurobiology is far from giving us any detailed information on this point, converging evidence in ontogenetic psychology and cultural anthropology on universality and ontogenetic primacy suggests that specialized modules for intuitive biology are present in the human brain.

A similar point can be made with respect to landscape processing. Recent research in the field of environmental aesthetics can be classified in two approaches (Orians and Heerwagen, 1995). A first method examines the preference of humans for different biomes, and tests in particular if landscapes in which humans evolved are preferred over others. In one important study, Balling and Falk (1982) took subjects from six age groups. It appeared that at 8 years old children showed a preference to live in and to visit savannah landscapes. Since these children never had been in a savannah, this evidence is suggestive of an innate bias for this type of landscape. From 15 years on, children started to like deciduous forest, coniferous forest and savannah to the same extent; these landscapes were still preferred over rain forests and deserts. The widening of the preferences of older children has been explained by the continued exposure to landscapes different from savannahs (Orians and Heerwagen, 1995). Among savannah landscapes, it is possible to differentiate between high quality habitats, and wetter and dryer landscapes. Trees have different characteristic shapes in each type of savannah. Orians and Heerwagen (1995) focussed on one particular tree (*Acacia tortilis*), and presented its three characteristic shapes to persons from Australia, the USA and Argentina. All of them appeared to prefer the shape characteristic of the high quality savannah habitat (which is a shape with a spreading multilayered canopy and with a trunk that branches close to the ground). Other converging evidence for a preference for (high quality) savannah-like landscapes comes from an analysis of the design of parks and gardens (Orians, 1986).

The second approach is more analytic. It proposes that landscapes in which particular features appear allow easier survival for humans. Though these features may be present in particular in savannah landscapes, they may apply in principle to other landscapes as well. Kaplan (1995) identifies four main variables that determine landscape attractiveness: coherence, complexity, legibility and mystery. A landscape has coherence if it is composed of a modest number of distinctive regions; these regions must be relatively uniform within themselves, and clearly different from each other. Such a landscape can be contrasted with an irregular region that is filled with randomly arranged rocks. The latter may be high in complexity, which means that there is a high number of different objects in the landscape. A landscape has legibility when it is open enough to allow visual access, and when it contains distinct and varied objects to serve as landmarks. Finally, mystery means that a landscape holds the promise of unveiling thus far obscured elements when entered. Mystery and legibility appear to correlate fairly linear with attractiveness. Coherence, and in particular complexity, are variables that reach a saturation value. Landscapes that become too high in complexity may even decrease in attractivity, as has been suggested by Wohlwill (1968).

Kaplan's theory has been anticipated by Appleton (1975). After studying landscape paintings, Appleton proposed his prospect and refuge theory. Though these variables do not map exactly onto the four factors identified by Kaplan, prospect means that a landscape promises future opportunities, for food gathering among others. Promise is often correlated with legibility; also mystery may contain a dimension of promise. If a landscape offers opportunities for refuge, it must have a certain degree of complexity.

The appeal of natural landscapes in comparison with buildings, and of city parts with vegetation in comparison with parts without, has been well documented (Kaplan, 1995). This appeal is not restricted to feelings of an aesthetic kind. Ulrich (1986) found that subjects show lower distress responses when exposed to natural landscapes than when exposed to buildings. In hospitals, flowers may improve mental health and rate of recovery (Watson and Burlingame, 1960). In people's perception of their neighborhoods, the impact of flowers is very significant (Vernez-Moudon and Heerwagen, 1990), and so on.

Most landscape preferences are produced without conscious reasoning. For instance, people cannot rely on introspection to give the four factors identified by Kaplan. Hence, landscape appreciation is not produced by a central, consciousness-generating controller. The overall picture that emerges from these lines of research is more compatible with the existence of functional modules that operate outside the reach of consciousness and that have different types of specialization.

3 Representations in modules and the recoding problem

In their recent work, Clark and Thornton (1997) analyze the capacity of connectionist methods to generate useful representations. They find that the ordinary, straightforward backpropagation approach often does not work in a satisfying way. Consider, for instance, a feedforward network that is trained to master the parity problem. Then, the network is trained with a set of input–output patterns. In case of a network with eight input units, two instances of such patterns may be (00110110,0) and (01000000,1); the input part of the former pattern must lead to 0 at the output since it contains an even number of 1's; the second one has to generates a 1 on the output unit since it has an odd number of 1's. In this example, the total number of possible input patterns is 2^8. Suppose that the network is trained with a proper subset of the set of possible training patterns. Then, backpropagation is able to set connections in such a way that correct mappings are generated for all training items.

The input–output pairs that did not occur in the training set can be used as test patterns. If the pattern 11000000 did not occur as an input vector in the training set, and if the network generates a 0 at the output unit on presentation of this pattern, then it generalizes correctly. However, it appears that, in general, backpropagation networks generalize very poorly on this kind of task. This means that, as far as this task is concerned, backpropagation is able to produce networks that behave like look-up tables, but it adds nothing to the properties of such tables. The reason for this disappointing generalization performance is the complex partition that the network has to generate in the space of input patterns: input patterns differing by a single bit only must systematically be mapped onto opposite output values. When such complicated tasks are given to connectionist nets, they require a number of training stimuli of such magnitude that generalization is only marginally possible. Hence, in many intended applications of connectionist networks, a variation of a "poverty of stimulus" situation occurs. This means that the number of training examples effectively used is too low to obtain a properly generalizing network.

This type of problem led Clark and Thornton (1997) to the assumption that to use networks properly, input stimuli often have to be recoded to make a problem tractable. The most straightforward solution would suggest that a pre-processing network, or a subset of the units of the network, transforms the input space in such a way that inputs of the same class belong to more homogeneous regions. The remaining units would subsequently differentiate between the different classes. However, the problem of finding a suitable recoding transformation is a complex one, since the space of possible recoding transformations is as large as the space of Turing machines.

Clark (1993) considers three strategies to tackle the recoding problem. In the first strategy, an experimenter analyzes a problem, and uses his knowledge to configure a network that is composed by subnetworks. Each of these subnets is trained separately, and the global configuration of the networks is used to solve the problem at hand. This strategy usually works only if the experimenter injects much knowledge in the system and if he or she is lucky. An example of this situation is presented by Norris (1990), who uses a cascade of networks to model the performance of idiot savants in a task of telling the day of the week corresponding with a numerically specified date (e.g. which day of the week will 8–9–3088 be?). In two other strategies, the experimenter does not need to divide the network into separately trained subnetworks which are reassembled after training. They can be found in Elman's work on the mastering of grammar by connectionist systems (Elman, 1993).

In Elman's experiments, a network is trained with a database of sentences that obey a simplified grammar. The words of every sentence are shown sequentially. The task of the network is to produce the next word with correct grammatical features. The net has context units serving as a short-term memory which stores relevant features of previous words. Words and grammatical information are represented in a distributed way. After the network has been trained, it appears to be able to generate words that complete test-sentences in a grammatically sound way.

However, this applies only if ordinary backpropagation is replaced by alternative training regimes which serve as an implicit recoding strategy. The first way to accomplish this is to rearrange the training stimuli in such a way that the network receives only easy sentences during a first training phase. During the second training phase, a mixture of easy and more difficult sentences is presented. According to this recoding strategy, the experimenter gives the network a head start not by partitioning it or by giving weights a priori values, but by arranging the training set in a way suited to the learning procedure of the network.

The second strategy verified by Elman proposes different developmental phases for the network. If the number of time steps, during which the context units provide feedback to the hidden units, is small initially and is allowed to increase gradually, the network appears to be able to master the training set in a gradual way. This solution is attractive in that it has some ontogenetic plausibility. Infants "start small" in comparison with adults as far as fully myelized neural pathways are concerned. It adds some plausibility to the stance that hereditary schedules for neural development play a role in cognitive development.

Clark and Thornton (1997) put emphasis on the importance of the environment. It is not possible for an uninformed neural net to code an arbitrarily structured set of sequential patterns. If the brain manipulates language in a proper way, then this is a fortunate, but not an accidental fact: language evolved in such a way as to be recodable by brain tissue. We can differentiate between two positions in this context: (i) given the characteristics of efficient language, the brain evolved a module that could realize these characteristics, and (ii) given the recoding capacities of the brain, language evolved in such a way that it could maximally exploit these recoding capacities. Position (i) is compatible with the view that different cognitive capacities are realized by modules that operate in a fairly specific way, whereas (ii) suggests that fairly uniform recoding principles of the brain may favor the creation of environments in which these principles are of maximal use. In phylogenetic evolution, both principles probably complemented each other: language may have evolved in a direction influenced by the nature of the brain, and the brain may have evolved in a direction partially determined by language. Current evolutionary cognitive theories suggest at least a partial validity of the view that asserts the existence of specialized modules. In the following sections, it is suggested that specific non-linguistic modules use recoding methods different from the ones mentioned in the present section.

4 Recoding and complex systems

Consider two modules A and B. Suppose that they have to communicate and to cooperate for a range of tasks. If they work with different codes, and if A communicates to B, then the code used by A must be cast in a form such that B can do something with it. In principle, there are different possible reasons why A and B may use different codes. One is that they have different specializations; another is that A is closer to perceptive processes in terms of neural pathways than B. Then, the code of B may be more abstract, or a more profound transformation of the codes used by input systems. In the latter case, a code transformation from A to B increases in usefulness if it suppresses noise that is present in a stimulus and that is not yet filtered at the stage in which A is addressed; also, the transformation becomes more useful if it brings about a further reduction of the complexity and of the independent degrees of freedom in the stimulus.

Suppose that the representations of module B are significantly more compact, so that the transformation to B entails a significant compression. Then, it is more efficient to store the information at the stage of B than at the stage of A. But this holds only to the extent that an inverse transformation allows the A-pattern to be recovered from the B-pattern whenever necessary. Compression is familiar in everyday computing applications. Files are stored efficiently in zip, jpeg, ps and other formats, and whenever required restored to their original format; in some cases, this means that the original is only approximated rather than exactly replicated. In case of a PC, the compressed file must be uncompressed in a file that can send its information to a screen. Cognitive systems do not literally have internal screens (although, according to some theorists, this is a good metaphor for part of our mental imagery: see Kosslyn, 1987). An influential theory, however, proposes a formally related scenario. When a module A communicates a pattern to B, the pattern may be stored in a recoded form in B. Now suppose that A communicates not only to B, but also to C, and that communication from B to C passes from B to A, and then from A to C. Then, if B needs to cooperate with C, the pattern that it has to send must be inversely transformed first to obtain the format used by A. Subsequently, the transformation from A to C may result in yet another code. This scenario is familiar in an influential cognitive theory on the function of consciousness (Baars, 1988; see also Dennett, 1991), in which consciousness is associated with a system A that coordinates communication between several modules that operate in different codes.

Apart from theories on consciousness, there are additional reasons to consider the situation in which A passes a pattern to a module B that stores it, and in which the recoded B-pattern must allow the original A-pattern to be restored in an approximated form. We have noted above that the biological environment is, in evolutionary terms, a very important environment for humans as well as for their predecessors. This environment changes continuously, since organisms have the property to grow and to be replaced after some time by other ones. In particular, seasonal and non-seasonal growth of plants and trees bear changes in the biological environment that have highly informative value for many organisms, including humans. In human evolutionary history, anticipating growth may have been vital. The capacity to anticipate growth may be seen as an important type of causality to be mastered by modules that specialize in processing biological information. In addition, information concerning growth is one of the factors that is useful when conceptual systems are generated. If one shape of a plant emerges from another after a season's growth, it must be closely associated with the former shape, even if it underwent remarkable changes.

Nature uses DNA codes in order to control growth. If a human brain produces inferences about growth in its environment, it does not extract DNA codes from visual information in order to internally simulate biological growth in its most concise way. Working on such a fine-grained level would surpass the capacities of the brain, and would be superfluous because DNA of plants and trees includes much information that was not vital for the survival of our evolutionary ancestors. The brain has to work with a code on a much higher level. I argue below that recent developments in complex systems theory give us indications of which types of codes are suitable for such a purpose.

Our considerations will lead us to the situation sketched above. A pattern in a code for representation in a module A is suitably transformed in a compressed code that is represented in a module B. Some developments in complex systems theory suggest that, though this compression may be substantial, the original pattern in A can be reconstructed from the B-pattern with a considerable amount of detail. In the approach that is explained in section 7, patterns can be made to grow. Though storage is more efficient in module B, growth has to occur in module A. The consequences of growth can be analyzed then in B, or in other modules (e.g. C) that receive information from A.

Some of the illustrations that appear in this chapter show growing patterns that could be perceived in nature, but I would like to make explicit that this is not intended as an implicit defence of a picture-in-the-head theory. The brain version of such a module A does not work with photographic pictures. However, due to the structure of the brain, it can be argued that the patterns that are present in such a module A are at least as fractal as the patterns that are present in the real world (MacCormac and Stamenov, 1996; Mandelbrot, 1982). Since we do not know what the detailed brain patterns at issue look like, the version of fractal growth developed will not be illustrated with such brain patterns, but with growing trees and a few other growing complex patterns.

5 Fractals and codes

The most famous codes that have been developed in a complex systems context are probably fractal codes. Among fractal methods, IFS codes take a prominent place (IFS stands for "Iterated Function System"). An IFS code consists of numbers that specify a set of affine transformations, more specifically contractions. Consider, for instance, the following set of five affine transformations (the values of these transformations are variations of values that can be found in Peitgen *et al.*, 1992):

$$x' = 0.195x - 0.488y + 0.464 \qquad x' = 0.462x + 0.414y + 0.251$$
$$y' = 0.344x + 0.443y + 0.495 \qquad y' = -0.252x + 0.361y + 0.57$$

$$x' = -0.58x - 0.07y + 0.597 \qquad x' = -0.035 + 0.07y + 0.488$$
$$y' = -0.45x - 0.111y + 0.097 \qquad y' = -0.469x - 0.022y + 0.507$$

$$x' = -0.637x + 0.856$$
$$y' = 0.501y + 0.251$$

Notice that the determinants of all matrices are smaller than one, which means that they are, indeed, contractions. These transformations generate an image

Figure 4.1 An example of a tree generated by an iterated function system

as follows. First, a point is selected randomly but in the neighborhood of the origin of the plane. This point is then transformed by only one of the above five transformations; the selection of the transformation that acts on the point occurs in accordance with a random process, but in such a way that the chance that a transformation is chosen is proportional to the determinant of its matrix. The resulting point is transformed again in accordance with the same probabilistic procedure, and so on. The set of points that are addressed in this way forms the image associated with the set of transformations. Much to the amazement of readers who are not familiar with fractals, this image is the one of Figure 4.1.

One may wonder if many real-world biological objects like trees, leaves and plants can be generated in such a way – if so, a dramatic compression could be achieved: instead of a complete intensity matrix, a handful of numbers specifying the transformations could code the images. One year ago, I asked a couple of students to scan a number of leaves, in order to examine if it was possible to determine which realistic leaves could be coded as an IFS fractal. With the help of genetic algorithms, we evolved codes that resulted in images more and more resembling the target image. In most cases, however, the genetic procedure appeared to converge to an IFS image with only moderate to poor resemblance to the target image. Fractals like the one of Figure 4.1 are easy to generate, but the inverse problem of finding the IFS code for a given image appears to be a rather hard one.

Nevertheless, fractal methods are used for image encoding. However, these methods heavily depend on a preceding segmentation. Only after an image is split into a few hundreds or thousands of small squares (or triangles) are parts obtained that are sufficiently simple to be encoded as an attractor of an IFS system. Due to this segmentation, the compression obtained is often of an order of magnitude that is comparable with more classical compression methods.

Furthermore, in the present context, it should be noted that images like Figure 4.1 are not obtained as a result of a growth process in which a small tree eventually results in the full-grown one. Rather, the image starts as a cloud with low density, and evolves through a cloud with higher density into a final more solid image. This shows that this code is not suited to reflect the biological causality to which we referred earlier.

There is another fractal method that does allow structures to grow; the so-called L-system method (after A. Lindemayer). An L-system is specified in terms of axioms. One axiom specifies a primitive element, and the other axioms dictate how this element is replaced. The objects by which the primitive element is replaced contain the primitive element themselves, so that they can again be replaced by the same objects, and so on. A large variety of typically brushwood-like images can be generated with this method. However, the growth of such systems is not really smooth; visual changes between successive iterations are often fairly drastic. Furthermore, L-systems are not used in practical applications, because the problem of how to approximate a given image by a fractal is even more difficult for L-systems than for IFS fractals. Section 7 proposes a new approach to growing fractals that attempts to avoid these problems.

6 A principle from quantum theory and connectionist models

Prior to section 7, an important element of the conceptual background of the method must be explained. It concerns the integration of a principle that is central in quantum theory with a connectionist system. In quantum theory, a system that is localized in a finite space has a discrete specter for its observables. Consider, for instance a linear harmonic oscillator. The eigenvalues of its energy operator are given by:

$$E_n = (n + (1/2)) \cdot h \cdot \omega_c$$

Suppose that the oscillator is in a state ψ. Then, the chance that the oscillator is observed in the n-th energy level is given by the square of the amplitude of the corresponding basis function in the decomposition in ψ. More generally, the squares of the amplitudes determine observation probabilities in quantum theory, but amplitudes themselves figure in the dynamical laws.

Consider a unit of a connectionist network. In the classical connectionist approach, such a unit has a single activation value. In a network that has been described earlier (Van Loocke, 1995; 1996a; 1996b), the state of a unit is characterized by a vector of values rather than by a single value. The k-th component of such a vector is called the amplitude of the unit in the k-th frequency. Suppose that a unit i communicates with another unit j. Then, the chance that i is observed to be active in the k-th frequency is determined by the square of the amplitude of i in the k-th frequency. If it is observed as active in that frequency, then the quantity used by j to adapt its activation value is the product of the amplitude of i in the k-th frequency and the weight between i and j. Unit j sums the quantities that it thus obtains from all units i, and subsequently adapts its amplitudes. As in quantum theory, observation probabilities are determined by squares of amplitudes, but amplitudes themselves determine how quantities change over time.

Suppose that the network has symmetric connections. It does not matter which learning rule is used, they may have been quenched according to Hopfield's rule, they may have evolved gradually according to the Boltzmann machine learning schedule, and so on. The main use of the integration of the aforementioned quantum principle is that the network has the following two properties:

(a) Suppose that different input patterns are initialized in different frequencies. Then, in every frequency, a content-addressable search for an attractor (e.g. a pattern to be recognized) takes place.
(b) Suppose that the same input is initialized in different frequencies. Then, the same pattern may be found in more than one frequency, or, if different attractors are compatible with the input, different attractors are retrieved in different frequencies. The interference between different frequencies is such that finding different attractors in different frequencies is stimulated.

Property (b) is cognitively interesting. Suppose we are dealing with a Hopfield net in which a number of patterns are stored. Suppose that an input is initialized in more than one frequency, and that the input is compatible with more than one stored memory. Then, notwithstanding the distributed nature of these patterns, the network will retrieve them in parallel. Amplitudes that belong to the same pattern are bound because they belong to the same frequency (see Van Loocke, 1995; 1996a; 1996b for illustrations).

7 Squared amplitudes and the growth of complex patterns

A similar inspiration stemming from quantum theory is useful to tackle the problems mentioned in section 5 in the context of complex systems. I will explain how the principle of probabilistic choice based on the square of variables leads to a new class of growing complex patterns. Consider a rectangular grid of pixels (the generalization to more than two dimensions is straightforward and will not be considered here). Suppose that a small core image is given. This core can be made to grow in the following way.

We differentiate between four types of outward boundary points. According to the present definition, an outward boundary point does not belong to the image, but at least one of its neighbors does. A point belongs to the upper outward boundary if it does not belong to the image but if its lower neighbor does; it belongs to the left outer boundary if it is not on the image and its right neighbor pixel is on it; similar definitions apply for the lower and right outward boundary. For every type of outward boundary, a small set of simple templates is selected. For every pixel on an outward boundary, one measures how well the templates associated with that boundary are realized in the image under construction. The squares of these measures determine the chance that the pixel is included in the image at the next time step (the squared measures are normalized so that a single pixel is chosen at every time step).

There are different ways to measure the extent to which a particular template is realized at an outward boundary point. A measure that appears to be particularly suited is the following one. One counts the number of pixels in the image under construction that are active in the template when the latter is centered at the pixel. Then, one counts the number of pixels that are present in the image under construction and that are situated in the square centered at the pixel and of the same magnitude as the template. If the former number is divided by the latter, the measure is obtained.

There are other measures that can be included in the construction procedure. For instance, in order to obtain trees with a broad shape but with relatively low density of branches and twigs, one can include measures for the number of unoccupied points in the neighborhood of an outward boundary point. We considered two alternative measures. The first one subtracts the number of occupied pixels in a small square centered at the point from the total number of pixels in the same square and divides the outcome by the former number. The second one divides the number of pixels in a small square by the number of pixels of the square that are occupied. The latter measure leads to complex forms with higher pixel density. Such measures can be calculated for different sizes of local squares. Whichever measure is used, best graphical results are obtained if the squares of these measures rather than the measures themselves are applied in the construction procedure. The reason for this is that squares increase differences in probability between points with different values for the measures.

The squares of the measures at issue determine probabilistically if a pixel on the outward boundary is included in the image on the next time step. We still have to specify how different measures are combined. Suppose that a single measure is calculated for the points on any outward boundary. Then, the chance that such a point is selected to be included in the image is proportional to the square of its (only) measure. This measure is the close analogue of the amplitude that has been considered in section 6. If we continue the analogy with quantum theory in the present case, and we call the present measures "amplitudes", then we can say that the collection of amplitudes that is defined over the outward boundaries serve as a wave function. At every time step, an image is enlarged with a particular pixel if the collapse of this wave function selects exactly this pixel.

Suppose now that two measures are associated with a point that belongs to an outward boundary. If we want to maintain the analogy with quantum theory, we are facing the problem that there are two alternative possibilities. If different

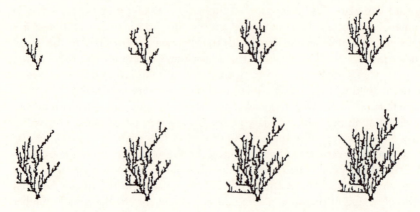

Figure 4.2 Evolution with templates of size 11 and first type of occupation measure; the image is shown after 200, 400, 600, 800, 1,000, 1,200, 1,600, and 2,000 updates

measures of the present algorithm are compared with amplitudes of different basis functions that belong to the same set of orthonormal basis vectors, then quantum theory suggests adding the squares of the amplitudes in order to obtain the measure that is sought. However, if the amplitudes are interpreted as referring to independent properties (such as position and spin in quantum theory), then quantum theory suggests taking the product of the squared amplitudes. The approach we took in practice was as follows. All measures in a pixel that stem from comparison with templates are squared and then summed. Next, also all measures in the pixel that refer to degrees of occupation are squared and summed. Then, both sums are multiplied. The determining argument for this choice is the assessment of its empirical consequences. This holds also for the general choice to use squared amplitudes instead of amplitudes. The variation of the present method that uses non-squared amplitudes usually produces amorphous, uninteresting circle-like or rectangle-like shapes.

Figure 4.2 gives an illustration of a growing tree using squared measures. Two templates were used for every boundary, except for lower boundary points (the latter were not used in the update procedure). Both had sides of 11 pixels. For the left boundary point, the number of pixels on the horizontal line to the right of this point, and on the skew line to the lower right point of the template were measured; similar templates were used for the upper and right boundary points. We used the first measure for the occupation degree with squares of sides with 11 pixels. Figure 4.2 shows the tree after 200, 400, 600, 800, 1,000, 1,200, 1,600 and 2,000 iterations. Figure 4.3 shows the evolving picture for the same conditions but with occupation measures calculated in accordance with the second method.

The wealth of growing complex forms that can be generated by this method is enormous, and certainly not limited to tree-like images. Opportunities for

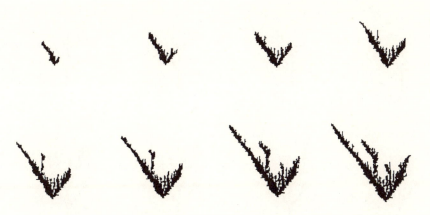

Figure 4.3 Evolution with templates of size 11 and second type of occupation measure; the image is shown after 200, 400, 600, 800, 1,000, 1,200, 1,400, and 1,600 updates

coloring such images abound. For instance, if the same color is used every time a member of the same outward boundary is selected, beautifully colored images result.

8 Reconstruction of given images

The algorithm described in section 7 allows the generation of a wealth of growing complex patterns. The property of growth is interesting in that it may be of help when biological causality has to be represented. What still needs to be specified is how this method offers us ways to determine possible previous stages of growth of a given, non-generic pattern, and how it would allow us to determine future stages of such a pattern. In order to be of use in a cognitive context, the least we should be able to determine for a given pattern are the main templates that guide its growth. Then, the information concerning these templates can be used to help classify the pattern, or to predict possible future states. Indeed, it is possible to specify an algorithm that is closely related to the one of the previous section and that is able to grow any connex pattern starting from one of its points. For each of the four outward boundaries, the templates that occur during this growth can be registered, and subsequently be used for further processing of the pattern.

For some patterns, the center of gravity is the best choice to start the growth process. If the process of growth is dominantly in one direction (for instance, upward in case of trees), we can take the point with the lowest coordinate in that direction (in case of a tree, we can take the bottom point). A set of small squares with different sizes is chosen. At any moment on the way to the reconstruction of the pattern, one can determine for every point that belongs to one of the outward boundaries of the preliminary image and that simultaneously

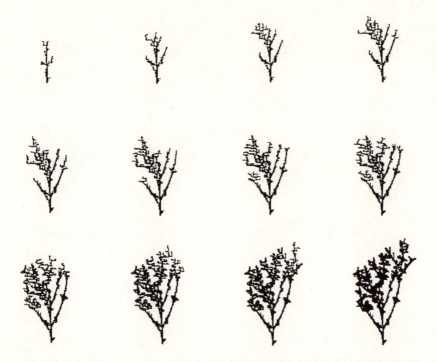

Figure 4.4 Reconstruction of a betula twig after 200, 400, 600, 800, 1,000, 1,200,
          1,400, 1,600, 2,000, 2,400, 2,800, and 3,200 iterations

belongs to the image that has to be reconstructed: (i) the templates that
surround the point in the preliminary image and that are of the size of the
selected squares, and (ii) the number of points of the original pattern that are
active in the squares at issue.

In the reconstruction process, the quantities obtained in (ii) are used to
calculate the occupation measures. The squares of these measures determine
the chance that the point is active in the next step in exactly the same way
as in the algorithm that was described in section 7. (For tree-like patterns, the
first type of occupation measure considered in section 7 proved to be most apt;
Figure 4.4 was made with occupation squares with sides of 11 points.) The
quantities obtained in (i) can be used after the reconstruction has been
completed, for instance to help classify the pattern. We illustrate the process
of reconstruction in Figure 4.4. The final image in the series of Figure 4.4 is
a scanned image of a betula twig. Its reconstruction is shown after 200, 400,
600, 800, 1,000, 1,200, 1,400, 1,600, 2,000, 2,400, 2,800 and 3,200 iterations.
Again, using squared amplitudes leads to much more fractal and "organic"
patterns than the variation of this algorithm that uses non-squared amplitudes.

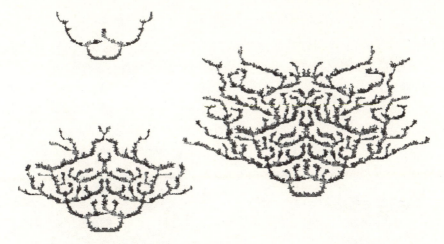

Figure 4.5 Growing form for cycling templates and selection probabilities in accordance with squares of measures

9 Complex growing forms with cycling templates

The aesthetic complexity of the forms considered so far can be enhanced by a number of simple modifications. One of them involves the introduction of cycling templates; we illustrate this with some simple examples. Suppose that, at every moment t, the templates for every outward boundary point

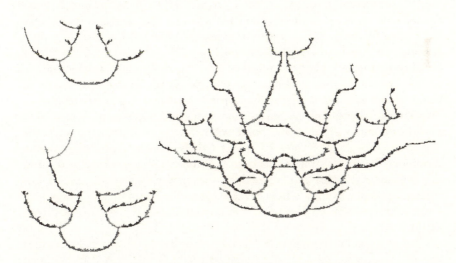

Figure 4.6 Growing form for cycling templates and selection probabilities in accordance with third powers of measures

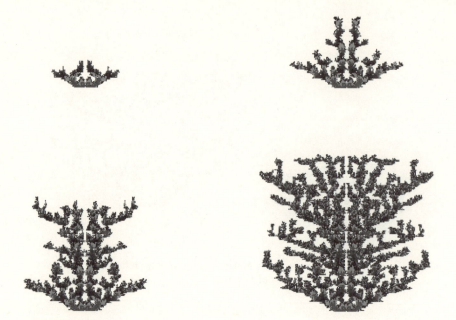

Figure 4.7 Growing form for cycling templates and selection probabilities in
accordance with first powers of measures

P consist of two small lines. If the coordinates of P are x and y, then the
coordinates of the pixels in the first template are $(x - int(a.cos(t/200)),$
$y - int(a.sin(t/200)))$, and the coordinates of the pixels in the second one
are $(x + int(a.cos(t/200)), y - int(a.sin(t/200)))$ (int is the integer function; a = 1, . . . ,10). A cycle is completed when t = t* = int$(200.\pi/2)$. This
means that the templates start with a horizontal orientation, and that they are
smoothly rotated until they become vertical at t = t*. After a first cycle of
template rotations, a second identical cycle starts, and so on.[1] Figure 4.5 shows
a typical growing form for selection probabilities in accordance with squares of
measures and with the first type of occupation measures. Symmetry relative to
the vertical axis was encouraged by multiplying the selection probability of a
boundary point by 5 when the point symmetric to the vertical axis already
belonged to the form. Figures 4.6 and 4.7 show growing forms for the same
conditions, except that the selection probabilities are in accordance with third
and first powers of measures, respectively. For powers higher than two, forms
diverge fast, and become aesthetically less interesting line structures. For powers
lower than two, the structure of the forms becomes fuzzy due to their high
density.

One variation on the theme of Figure 4.5 can be obtained as follows. After
the first cycle, a second cycle starts with templates defined in accordance with
$(x - int(a.cos(t/200)), y + int(a.sin(t/200)))$ and $(x + int(a.cos(t/200)),$
$y - int(a.sin(t/200)))$ (a = 1, . . . , 10). The templates of the second cycle

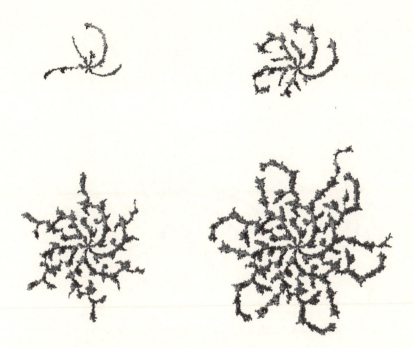

Figure 4.8 Growing form for repeated sequences of template cycles and supported by
a sixfold symmetry

are rotated 90 degrees relative to the ones of the first cycle. The third cycle
rotates the templates of the second cycle over 90 degrees, and similar for the
fourth cycle. When the fourth cycle is finished, the sequence of cycles is
repeated, and so on.

Also this procedure can be supported by symmetries. In case of the algorithm leading to Figure 4.8, a measure in a point was multiplied by 20 if the
point rotated over $2\pi/6$ in the left or in the right direction already belonged
to the form; and a measure was multiplied by 5 if the point with half the x-
and half the y-coordinate was already included in the form. Figure 4.8 shows
successive stages of the growing form; the largest image results after 12,000
points have been put. Figure 4.9 shows the same evolution, but this time the
number of points put during each cycle was doubled every time a sequence of
cycles was completed. This is a simple instance of the construction procedure
that is discussed in the next section.

10 A remark on decidability and complex patterns

I am tempted to make the following remark. Several authors have suggested
during the past few years that quantum theory or even quantum gravity is vital
to describe the brain, in particular when conscious processes are concerned.
Some of them have argued that important parts of our cognitive functioning

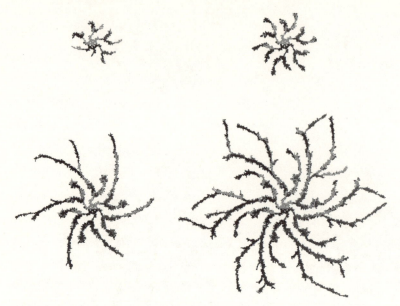

Figure 4.9 Growing form for the same conditions as in Figure 4.8 but with doubling number of points for each successive sequence of cycles

can be explained only if this is taken into account. Two of the most promi-nent authors in this respect are Penrose and Hameroff (e.g. Penrose, 1994; Hameroff, 1997). The developments described in the previous sections support the relevance of quantum processes for cognition to some extent. There are, however, clear differences between the present approach and the theory of Penrose. An important one is that the analogue of the collapse of the wave function in the above algorithm is a random process. In the view of Penrose and Hameroff, the reduction of the wave function is an "orchestrated" reduc-tion, which means that something so far hidden helps to steer the random process. This something, that is situated at the level of quantum gravity, has an important role in the generation of consciousness and in cognitive processes that depend on it. The present algorithm lacks such a hidden orchestrating mechanism.

The reason why I mention this point is that the hidden orchestrating mech-anism would allow a brain to go beyond the capacities of formal computation. In his explanation of concepts like undecidability, Penrose (1994) uses the tiling problem for polyominoes in order to construct an artificial universe with a deterministic, but non-computational evolution. The algorithm that is described in section 7 easily allows several prescriptions for non-computational evolutions to be found.

Consider sets of templates for the outer boundaries that lead to generic trees. The variation of the structure within a tree can be increased if the templates or the occupation measures that are used during its construction vary. Suppose that during a first epoch of N1 steps a set S1 is used; during the second epoch of N2 steps the construction is guided by S2; the third epoch is based again on S1, the fourth on S2, and so on. A one-parameter family of trees (with parameter a) can now be defined as follows. During the first epoch $n_1.a$ points are put in the pattern. The second epoch adds $n_2.a.a$ points, and so on, until the k-th epoch is reached, during which $n_k.a.a \ldots a$ (k times) points are added to the pattern (the numbers n_k are natural numbers). If all numbers n_i (i = 1 ... n) are equal to 1, this construction requires that every point on the image has the same generative power during every epoch, in that every point leads to a points during the next epoch. For different values of a, different trees will be realized, but the number of template alternations is the same for every tree belonging to the same family. Due to this fact, trees that belong to different families characterized by a polynomial of different order in general look different, so that the term "family" has also some visual justification. Now it is easy to formulate evolutionary rules for families of trees that are not computable. I will give one example.

Consider two families of different order (which means that the polynomials associated with each of them have different order). Include in an evolution schema for tree families the following prescription: "if the lowest order family contains k trees of exactly the same numerical complexity as the higher one, then the former family will survive and the latter one is eliminated". If "numerical complexity" is specified in the simplest possible way – in terms of the total number of points in the tree – then the inclusion of this prescription in an evolution scenario makes it non-computable. The reason for this is obvious: verifying the prescription would require solving a diophantine equation.

This type of problem can be straightforwardly formulated for L-systems, due to their successive branching nature. In the case of the present algorithm, however, there is no direct relation between the branches actually appearing in the image and the terms in the polynomial. Furthermore, for other template sets, the method of section 7 generates patterns that are fairly unlike trees, and in which no branches occur that would suggest at first sight the possibility of a diophantine problem. Nevertheless, the same undecidable evolutions can be formulated for these patterns too. In this sense, the range of complex forms for which undecidable diophantine problems can be formulated increases as a consequence of the present algorithm.

11 Discussion

Methods that can be useful for cognitive subsystems that process biological and environmental information were considered. The main argument of this chapter asserts that these methods are specific: they may help to grasp the type of causality inherent in intuitive biology or in environmental dynamics. For other modules, however, such as linguistic ones, these methods may be relatively useless. Emphasis is also placed on the importance of biological and natural environments in the evolutionary history of man. This is meant to imply that higher level modules processing such information are of equal importance to linguistic modules. The appreciation of this fact appears to be increasing, but seems not yet to be fully reflected in cognitive science research.

The environment on earth has changed drastically during the past centuries. At this time, natural environments are disappearing at an alarming rate. It is my conviction that lines of research congruent with the one that has been explained in the present chapter give us another argument for taking ecological responsibilities. If the new, artificial types of environment entail neglect of cognitive capacities that played a very important role in the evolutionary history of man, then man is risking the loss of an important part of himself. In order to assess how important this part has been, he may soon depend on theoretical guesses only, rather than on experiential introspection.

Acknowledgements

The author wishes to thank T. Valentine for his helpful comments on an earlier version of this chapter, and T. De Paepe, J. Ronsse, and F. Vandamme (Lab for Applied Epistemology, University of Ghent) for their valuable support during this work.

Note

1   The different shades of gray in Figures 4.5–4.9 refer to the different cycles during which the cells have been added. If one works with cycling templates rather than static ones, it becomes possible to complement the amplitudes with phase variables; this tightens the analogy with quantum theory. A first phase variable in a boundary cell P can be defined in terms of the moment in a cycle when the most recent neighbor of P was added to the form. A second phase can be defined in terms of the place in a cycle of the present time step. If these phases are allowed to interfere, constructive as well as destructive effects of interference are obtained. They can be used to control the degree of branching in a form and to constrain the places where branches occur; this has been elaborated in Van Loocke (1988).

References

Appleton, J. (1975), *The experience of landscape*, London: Wiley
Arbib, M. (1989), Modularity, schemas and neurons, a critique of Fodor, in P. Slezak, W. Albury (eds.), *Computers and minds*, Dordrecht: Kluwer, pp. 193–200
Baars, B. (1988), *A cognitive theory of consciousness*, Cambridge: Cambridge University Press
Balling, J., Falk, J. (1982), Development of visual preference for natural environments, *Environment and Behavior*, 14, 5–28
Barkow, J., Cosmides, L., Tooby, J. (1995), *The adapted mind*, Oxford: Oxford University Press
Clark, A. (1993), *Associative engines*, Cambridge MA: MIT Press
Clark, A., Thornton, C. (1997), Trading spaces: computation, representation, and the limits of uninformed learning, *Behavioral and Brain Sciences*, 20, 57–65
Dennett, D. (1991), *Consciousness explained*, Boston: Little and Brown

Elman, J. (1993), Learning and development in neural networks: the importance of starting small, *Cognition*, 48, 71–99

Fodor, J. (1983), *The modularity of mind*, Cambridge MA: MIT Press

Gardner, H. (1983), *Frames of mind: the theory of multiple intelligences*, London: Paladin

Hameroff, S. (1997), Models of classical and quantum computation in microtubules: implications for consciousness, in D. Lundh, B. Olsson, A. Narayanan (eds.), *Biocomputing and emergent computation*, Singapore: World Scientific Publishing, pp. 193–217

Kaplan, S. (1995), Environmental preference in a knowledge-seeking, knowledge-using organism, in J. Barkow, L. Cosmides, J. Tooby (eds.), *The adapted mind*, Oxford: Oxford University Press, pp. 581–598

Keil, F. (1989), *Concepts, kinds and development*, Cambridge MA, MIT Press

Kosslyn, S. (1987), Seeing and imaging in the cerebral hemispheres: computational approach, *Psychological Review*, 94 (2), 148–175

Kosslyn, S., Sussman, A. (1995), Roles of imagery in perception, or, there is no such thing as immaculate perception, in M. Gazzaniga (ed.), *The cognitive neurosciences*, Cambridge MA: MIT Press, pp. 1035–1042

MacCormac, E., Stamenov, M. (1996), *Fractals of brain, fractals of mind*, Amsterdam: John Benjamins

Mandelbrot, B. (1982), *The fractal geometry of nature*, San Francisco: Freeman

Norris, D. (1990), How to build a connectionist idiot (savant), *Cognition*, 35, 277–291

Orians, G. (1986), An ecological and evolutionary approach to landscape aesthetics, in E. Penning-Rowsell, D. Lowenthal (eds.), *Landscape meaning and values*, London: Allen and Unwin, pp. 3–25

Orians, G., Heerwagen, J. (1995), Evolved responses to landscapes, in J. Barkow, L. Cosmides, J. Tooby, *The adapted mind*, Oxford: Oxford University Press, pp. 555–579

Paivio, A. (1986), *Representations: a dual coding approach*, Oxford: Oxford University Press

Peitgen, H., Jurgens, H., Saupe, D. (1992), *Chaos and fractals*, New York: Springer-Verlag

Penrose, R. (1994), *Shadows of the mind*, Oxford: Oxford University Press

Pinker, S. (1994), *The language instinct*, London: Penguin Books

Pylyshyn, Z. (1980), *Computation and cognition: toward a foundation of cognitive science*, Cambridge MA: MIT Press

Spelke, E., Breinlinger, K., Macomber, J., Jacobson, K. (1992), Origins of knowledge, *Psychological Review*, 99, 605–632

Treisman, A. (1988), Preattentive patterns in vision, in Z. Pylyshyn (ed.), *Computational processes in human vision*, Norwood NJ: Ablex Publishing Corporation, pp. 341–369

Ulrich, R. (1986), Human response to vegetation and landscapes, *Landscape and Urban Planning*, 13, 29–44

Van Loocke, Ph. (1995), QNET: A quantum mechanical neural network. A new connectionist architecture and its relevance for variable binding and constraint satisfaction problems, *Cybernetica*, 38 (1), 85–106

Van Loocke, Ph. (1996a), The introduction of principles from elementary quantum theory in a Hopfield-style network and the solution of constraint satisfaction and variable binding problems, in C. Dagli, M. Akay, P. Chen, B. Fernandez, J. Ghosh (eds.), *Smart engineering systems: neural networks, fuzzy logic and evolutionary programming*, New York: ASME Press, pp. 129–136

Van Loocke, Ph. (1996b), The connectionist model QNET and its combination with genetic algorithms, in Ph. Van Loocke, Concepts: representation and evolution, *Philosophica*, 57, 76–91

Van Loocke, P. (1998), Algorithmic growth and the inclusion of principles from quantum theory in cellular automata, Paper presented at the 2nd International Conference on Anticipatory Systems, 10–14 August 1998, Liege, to be published in D. Dubois (ed.), Proceedings of the 2nd International Conference on Anticipatory Systems, Liege: Chaos Press.

Vernez-Moudon, A., Heerwagen, J. (1990), Residents' attitudes toward design diversity: Research report, Washington DC: National Endowment for the Arts

Watson, D., Burlingame, A. (1960), *Therapy through horticulture*, New York: Macmillan

Wohlwill, J. (1968), Amount of stimulus exploration and preference as differential functions of stimulus complexity, *Perception and Psychophysics*, 4, 307–312

5 Some psychological mechanisms of culture

Henry Plotkin

Abstract

There is a consensus amongst biologists interested in culture that one possible point of conceptual entry into this enormous and complex phenomenon is to consider cultural change as analogous to biological evolution. In this chapter this analogy is examined in the light of possible psychological mechanisms that allow humans to participate in culture. First, attention is paid to the general psychological mechanisms that make culture possible at all. The general stance adopted is that a viable theory of culture, including cultural change, can only be based upon adequate psychological theory, and that at least until the advent of extrasomatic storage human culture was strictly constrained by its psychological mechanisms. Knowing what these mechanisms are will help in reconstructing human history.

Introduction

There is a long history of interest in culture by psychologists, and a reciprocal interest in psychology by anthropologists whose specialism is culture. A significant example of the former is Freud (1913) as one instance of a number of books on cultural matters; prominent examples of the latter are Mead (1928) and Lévi-Strauss (1966). Freud's approach, typical of one school of thought, was to consider cultural practices as the social group's way of dealing with conflict in the same manner as neurosis is a result of conflict within the component parts and needs of the individual mind. Cultural phenomena such as taboos relating to food or the dead, and totemism, were all analyzed within the same psychodynamic framework that he used for understanding the individual mind. In essence, the approach was to view culture as an organism, the links between psychology and culture being made in terms of general organizational principles in an attempt to explain why any one culture has the characteristics that it does within particular circumstances. More recent approaches are very different from the culture-as-organism view. For example, Rosch (1973) considered the possibility of universal cognitive features whose appearance is invariant across cultures. This is much closer to what is attempted in this chapter, which is a brief consideration of (i) what might be the cognitive mech-anisms that are essential for the existence of culture, and (ii) an examination of a particular approach to culture by biologists that incorporates certain psycho-logically loaded conceptions. There is much overlap between these. The central premise of the chapter is Kitcher's (1987) assertion that a successful theory of culture must be rooted in and consonant with good psychological theory.

What is culture?

Literally hundreds of definitions of culture have been offered over the last 150 years, and these can be classified in a large number of ways (see Kroeber and Kluckholm, 1952; Keesing, 1974). In the face of such excess the appro-priate strategy is to settle on a definition that most suits one's own view. Given the focus of this chapter, this would be a definition most amenable to the analysis of mechanism. Goodenough's (1957) "culture consists of whatever it is one has to know or believe in order to operate in a manner acceptable to its members" is just such a vehicle. The point to note is that such a defini-tion does not center on the products of culture, be they artifacts or behavior. The emphasis is on knowledge, hence on the cognitive mechanisms that underpin the human capacity for acquiring and transmitting knowledge, and on acceptableness, and hence on the social forces that operate within human groups.

It should also be noted that culture is treated here as a species-specific attribute of humans. Although some other species, notably some primates, live in relatively complex groups and display a protocultural sharing of skills amongst some limited, usually small, numbers of the group, only humans display all the core characteristics of culture. These are identified by Tomasello *et al.* (1993) as (i) cultural traditions are acquired by all normal members of a social group; (ii) cultural knowledge and skills are present within social groups with remark-ably small degrees of variation; and (iii) "human cultural traditions often show an accumulation of modifications over generations (i.e. the ratchet effect)". The species-specific nature of culture means that any analysis of mechanism must focus on human psychology, with little help to be gained from studies of the psychological abilities of other species.

One of the most important aspects of culture is social construction (Searle, 1995 provides an excellent recent overview). A social construction is a highly complex belief system shared by all, or most, members of a group, which results in the creation of institutions and which guides and drives the behavior of the people in a group. Money is the obvious example. The western notion of justice based on fairness is another. The latter is not an immutable fact inexorably caused by our biochemistry and present in all humans. Some cultures have quite different social constructions of justice based on revenge, social status or religious precepts. The social construction of justice in western societies is what it is because members of our culture subscribe to the belief. It exists only because we think it so. Similarly with the construction of money. A one hundred guilder or ten dollar note has minuscule intrinsic worth. Its value resides in the agreed belief that it has value. Some biologists are skeptical about the existence of social constructions and suggest they are part of the mythology of the social sciences. This is a curious argument because it is manifestly the case that there is real causal force in social constructions. People live in the ways that they do, and die, because of them. Explaining culture *must* include an explanation of social construction, which exists in no other species.

We are not yet in a position, of course, to explain culture, which is a phenomenon of awesome complexity. But we are, I believe, moving to the stage where psychology can begin to offer a glimpse of the kinds of psychological mechanisms that cause culture. An outline of these is presented below.

Essential psychological mechanisms of culture

There is an obvious case that can be made for virtually every psychological trait and mechanism of humans, from sensation and perception through memory and reasoning and on to skilled motor performance, as being essential to our ability to create and enter into culture. But perception, memory and attention are traits, amongst many others, that are shared with other species, none of which have culture. Even though, say, attentional mechanisms are essential in the developing child for the process of enculturation, they are essential in a supporting role rather than as direct cause. A form of "substractive" reasoning, therefore, allows one to discard these aspects of human psychology shared with other species as either irrelevant to an explanation of culture, or as being only of secondary importance. If some set of traits, t_1–t_n, is shared with animals that do not have culture, then those traits cannot be essential for the existence of culture. What we are looking for is a combination of traits that are both human-specific and consonant with a definition of culture that emphasizes its cognitive-social dimensions of shared, acceptable knowledge within socially cohesive groups.

Consider again the matter of social constructions, which exist only because we *agree* to think that they exist. Agreement, it is suggested here, is of the essence. Whether readily entered into because of ritual interest, educated into, or coerced into, agreement is essential to shared knowledge. Knowledge can only be shared if there is agreement as to the where, what and how of that which is being shared. It cannot be denied that there are deep epistemological problems here that are grist to the mill of any philosopher. However, it also cannot be denied that people with normal colour vision agree that daffodils are yellow, even though there can be no certainty, indeed it is unlikely, that the sensation of yellowness is the same for all people. Indeed, even the colour blind will agree with those of normal vision on the colour of daffodils, their information on colour coming to them from more indirect sources. So while the philosopher may shudder at the complexities and uncertainties of what it means to agree on something as simple as the colour of a flower, it is a commonplace of everyday life that agreement exists. Mundane routines, like buying a loaf of bread, depend upon such agreement. That human culture exists at all is proof of the existence of agreement.

Agreement, then, is what must be explained, and in the following subsections three separate sets of psychological mechanisms are offered as the essential psychological ingredients of agreement.

Theory of mind

In a seminal paper, Premack and Woodruff (1978) posed the question whether the chimpanzee has a theory of mind. By theory of mind, they meant

> that the individual imputes mental states to himself and to others . . . a system of inference of this kind is properly viewed as a theory, first, because such states are not directly observable, and second, because the system can be used to make predictions, specifically about the behavior of other organisms.
>
> (p. 515)

Whether theory of mind, the attribution of mental states to self and others, occurs in chimpanzees, or any other species, remains a controversial issue (see Heyes, 1994 for a skeptical review). However, there is no question but that it occurs in all normal humans (Wimmer and Pemerl, 1983; Goldman, 1993; Gopnick, 1993; Leslie, 1994). There is accumulating evidence about the ontogenetic sequence as theory of mind develops in the human infant and child. Soon after birth infants show a marked sensitivity to the presence of eyes, and by 9 months there is good evidence of the existence of shared visual attention; by 12–14 months protodeclarative pointing (the use of an extended index finger and checking on the congruence between the pointing and the direction of gaze of an observer) has appeared; around 18–24 months the infant shows pretend play with others (hence showing appreciation that others can also have mental states), and begins to use the language of mental states (like wanting, thinking and knowing). Yet around 3 years of age the child thinks that what it knows is what all others know. Only at about 4 years old does the average human child enter the period of knowing not only that others have intentional mental states, but that they can be different from the mental states of itself, and indeed that such mental states might be false (see Baron-Cohen, 1995 for reviews).

Once a child has developed to the point of being able to attribute independent mental states to others, then it can begin to infer that on some occasions the attributed mental states of others are similar to its own. This assumed capacity for making a judgement about the degree of similarity of mental states, about the extent of agreement between the intentional mental states of self and others as well as just between others, is in fact quite close to one of the theories of theory of mind, which argues that the child has to do a lot of hard conceptual work – making inferences and constructing theories about the minds of others and testing their consequences and then revising their theory – before a mature theory of mind emerges (Gopnik, 1993).

Theory of mind, then, provides the platform or "stage" in the mind on which understanding of agreement is forged and then played, and which then makes social constructions possible. It is, however, only a stage or arena. Agreement needs more than a complex inference-making mechanism by which the mental states of self and others can be judged as being in some matching state. Driving the mechanism must be information.

Extragenetic transmission of information

There is a general debate amongst cognitive psychologists as to whether cognition is built upon general mechanisms of information processing or whether it is a product of a modular mind, each module sensitive to domain-specific problems and operating according to module-specific mechanisms (see Karmiloff-Smith, 1992 for a recent review of both positions). Even if the latter is correct and, in the most general sense, information for a theory of mind module must be coming in part from genes for the initial differentiation of it and all other modules, that argument can be side-stepped here. This is because it does not address the main problem, which is that given the existence of a theory of mind mechanism, whatever its provenance, the sources of information which feed into theory of mind and allow judgements of mental states being in agreement must be identified. One of the principal characteristics of culture, on which there are no dissenting voices, is the existence of extragenetic transmission of information. There are two distinctive possible kinds. The one is non-linguistic and the other is linguistic.

Non-linguistic information of interest to cultural theorists is most generally referred to as social learning, and embraces a variety of forms such as imitation, social facilitation and local enhancement (see Heyes and Galef, 1996 for a recent survey). Of these, imitation is most often cited as important for culture (Boyd and Richerson, 1985 for example). The ability to perform an act after seeing it done by another occurs early in humans (Meltzoff and Moore, 1977; 1983), and there is no reason to believe that it requires linguistic support. Somehow, and the mechanisms are not understood, information streaming in from one modality, usually vision, is transformed into an action, the sensory consequences of which, kinaesthetic and proprioceptive, are matched to the "inferred" input of the individual who is being imitated. Although it can be judged doubtful that human culture, ever since the evolution of language, is built in a significant way on such non-linguistic extragenetic mechanisms of information transmission, it is possible that the child's early experience of matching own to others' psychological states is significantly boosted through imitation. Since language most likely evolved over thousands or tens of thousands of years, it is also likely that the evolution of culture in humans was accomplished by a close interplay of such non-linguistic mechanisms with emerging language ability.

Language itself, of course, is widely recognized as an essential ingredient of culture. Quite apart from the massive quantities of information that can be transmitted via language, another role that it might play is in the formation of the understanding of shared mental states, i.e. of agreement between individuals. Many things happen during the acquisition of language, but one in particular may be crucial in this respect. This is the learning of words as having reference, as referring to specific objects in the world outside of the individual and those with whom they are communicating. When a child learns through a quite lengthy process that the word *cat* refers to a specific thing, it learns that others refer to that same object by the same word. Reference, like imitation, may be a stepping stone along the way to a wider understanding of agreed mental states whereby, eventually, entirely abstract notions, like justice, can be agreed upon. "Money, property, marriage, government and universities all exist by forms of human agreement that essentially involve the capacity to symbolize" (Searle, 1995, p. 228). The capacity to share meaning surely fuels the capacity to infer intentional mental states like knowing and believing that builds in each person the secure base for entering into culture as shared knowledge.

Social force

Two experiments are of relevance here. In a classic series of studies, Sherif (1936) exploited an optical illusion called the autokinetic effect. When someone fixates on a stationary point of light in a darkened room, after a time they will report that the light moves, and they can give an estimate of the amount of movement. Tested separately, people report a range of distances through which the light seems to move. Tested in a group and sharing their experiences, the judgement of all participants quickly settles on some shared standard or norm. Sherif argued that the formation of a common norm is a fundamental feature of social life across a wide range of judgements and beliefs. Subsequently, Jacobs and Campbell (1961) exploited this finding by initially putting together a social group made up entirely of planted subjects who were instructed to exaggerate greatly the apparent amount of movement of the light. Only one person in the group was a genuinely naive subject, and that person's judgement was markedly skewed in the direction of that of the planted subjects. Then, one by one, the phoney subjects were removed and replaced by genuine subjects during a series of repeated trials of exposure to a stationary point of light. Eventually the group was made up entirely of naive subjects, yet for some four or five "generations" after the removal of all the planted subjects, the "cultural tradition" of overstating the amount of perceived movement was maintained. The astonishing feature of the experiment is that the belief concerned an illusion – the light never moved, though the genuine subjects did not know this.

Powerful social forces of this kind have been variously called conformity, obedience and group cohesiveness by social psychologists. They are likely evolved psychological traits in a species the near entirety of whose evolution over several million years occurred with one constant feature – life was lived in small social groups, the coordinated activity of which was probably significant to the survival of the individuals making up the group. These social forces may directly contribute, as Sherif originally argued, to agreement; indirectly they may constitute a kind of contextual cement in which shared beliefs and judgements, including social constructions, are set.

There is no certainty as to how theory of mind, extragenetic transmission of information and social force combine as psychological mechanisms to give rise to culture; and it is certainly possible that there are other components of human psychology that are significant causal mechanisms of culture. What is offered above is illustrative of the kind of analysis that contemporary psychology offers in contrast to the approach by analogy used by Freud.

Cultural change and the concept of the meme

The use of analogy also figures large in a very different application of psychological mechanisms to the understanding of culture. Not long after Kroeber (1953) called for the incorporation of the understanding of culture into some appropriate biological theory as an important goal for a science of culture, Murdock (1956) suggested that cultural change could be understood in terms of selection theory. That is, in terms of the operation of the same processes that drive biological evolution, but embodied in mechanisms that are at least to some extent, if not entirely, separated from the genetic and phenotypic mechanisms of biological evolution. This is a theme repeated subsequently in a series of highly influential papers (Campbell, 1965; Cloak, 1975; Durham, 1976) and books (Dawkins, 1976; Pulliam and Dunford, 1980; Cavalli-Sforza and Feldman, 1981; Lumsden and Wilson, 1981; Boyd and Richerson, 1985). Attempts to identify the cultural analogues of genes and gene pools in the form of memes (Dawkins, 1976) or culturgens (Lumsden and Wilson, 1981) and meme pools (Dunn, 1970; Ryle, 1973; Durham, 1976) were necessary accompaniments to this work (see also Hull, 1982). The importance of these attempts is simple to understand: without identifiable units that can be counted and measured in various ways, we do not have a science of culture.

Recent general reviews (Plotkin, 1994; Cziko, 1995) provide more detailed accounts of selection theory. The bare bones of its application to cultural change is that cultural forms, entities or units, what Dawkins called memes, occur in variant forms. One reason for the variation is the occurrence of changes in memes, equivalent to genetic mutations, that are not directly caused by any selection processes; another is that changes are wrought on memes as they interact with one another. Selection results in memes being differentially propagated by copying and transmission systems which move the units about in space and may conserve them over time. The differential survival of memes resulting from such selection and transmission processes leads to changes in frequencies of memes in a cultural pool over time; the culture shows descent with modification. In other words, cultural change occurs because of cultural evolution.

These gene-culture co-evolutionary theories (for reviews see Laland, 1993; Laland, Kumm and Feldman, 1995), one form of which are dual inheritance theories (Boyd and Richerson, 1985), are concerned with the relationships between cultural and biological evolution, even if the emphasis generally has been on culture. The evolutionary analogy should not be taken to imply that variation is blind. Campbell and Cziko have adopted this stance, but it is simply not necessary to do so. It can be questioned whether any evolutionary change occurs by the way of blind processes, and that would apply as much to conceptual and cultural change as to biological evolution as conventionally understood. This is because mutation and variation is alway structurally constrained, the constraints arising from past selection histories.

For the purposes of this chapter, the concern of which is purely one of possible psychological mechanisms of culture and cultural change, the linkage with genes is ignored. Co-evolutionary theories have implicated a range of psychological mechanisms as constituting cultural selection devices and transmission processes involved in cultural evolution. In part the suggestions are governed, as they are in this chapter, by the theorists' views as to what is the most tractable approach to the problem of culture. Thus Boyd and Richerson (1985), for example, specifically reject Goodenough's definition based on knowledge and belief and instead define culture explicitly in terms of behavior and imitation. Whatever one's theoretical predilections, a complete theory of culture couched in these terms will have to identify the psychological mechanisms that are the basis of memes (the variants), selection processes (including the vehicles or interactors on which selection acts), and transmission processes. Each one of these warrants an extensive analysis on its own. Space constraints lead to a brief concentration here on identifying the meme.

Dawkins' (1976) own "unit of imitation", which is how he defined the meme, is exemplified by "tunes, ideas, catch-phrases, ways of making pots or of building arches" (p. 206), which is not a homogeneous grouping of entities. But the idea behind his formulation is a powerful one. Dawkins is important in developing the concept of the replicator as central to any evolutionary process. A replicator is any entity that can make copies of itself, the archetypal replicator being the gene. Memes too must be capable of making copies of themselves, and so perhaps tunes, ideas and ways of making pots are indeed memes because all can make copies of themselves by some process of imitation. Take as a more likely example of a "unit of imitation" the actions necessary for the construction of a stone tool. The behavior of a skilled stone tool-maker can be observed by another person and then copied, replicated, by the observer.

There are problems, though, in formulating the replicating unit of cultural evolution in this way. For one thing, many social scientists object to culture being analyzed in terms of actions and artifacts (Ingold, 1986 for example), even if some of the action involves speech or song. For another, it could be argued that behavior, which is what is being imitated, is not the replicator but the vehicle or interactor upon which selection acts, analogous to the pheno-type's role in biological evolution (Hull, 1982; Boyd and Richerson, 1985; Heyes and Plotkin, 1989). The replicator is properly identified as the neural networks and psychological mechanisms, in other words, the memories of the actions being imitated. This immediately runs into the difficulty of there being no understanding at all of the neurological basis of imitation, and no clear understanding or agreement on what psychological mechanisms are involved beyond the necessary informational transformations described earlier (see section on extragenetic transmission of information). It is extremely unlikely that the neural network states of the observer, after having successfully acquired the skill of how to fashion a stone tool, are copies, replicates, of the neural network states of the teacher. On the other hand, it is likely that once a func-tional understanding of imitation is gained by psychologists, the psychological mechanisms involved in producing a copied complex sequence of skilled actions will be the same in observer and teacher. But right now, we just do not know what these are.

The lesson to be learned, though, is that understanding what cultural repli-cators are will only come through understanding the psychological mechanisms that give rise to the behavior. They should not be identified with the behavior itself, and cannot be identified with the exact underlying neural network states. The loose linkage between neural network states and psychological mecha-nisms makes one wonder whether any form of strict eliminativism can ever be a viable scientific program. This means the emphasis must, for the moment, be placed on psychological mechanism not precise network states. However, this should not be taken to mean that there is room for folk psychological concepts. Psychological concepts of memory and higher-order structures bear little relationship to folk theory. This is Kitcher's (1987) point. We need good psychologial theory, at least to begin with. Theory pitched at the neuronal level is just as inadequate as that pitched at the folk level.

Imitation serves to warn of the difficulties of identifying memes, even when the notion of culture is hopelessly oversimplified to the transmission of simple, if skilled, acts. Culture, however, is not a matter of collective twitches. If we concentrate on the Goodenough definition of culture, then replicators are going to have to be sought amongst the psychological mechanisms that support beliefs and ideas, which must be some form of complex memory or higher-order knowl-edge structure; the transmission will be primarily linguistic; and the vehicles or interactors will be, at a minimum, the behaviors generated by beliefs and ideas, and possibly the performance (behavior) of social institutions such as courts of justice or government bodies, which are manifestations of social constructions. There is fearsome complexity that must be dealt with here.

Psychology takes us a little way in this complexity. Just as it is unlikely that a powerful theory of so complex a thing as culture will be built on simple imitated actions, so it is equally unlikely that a competent theory can be built on simple memory. For example, being told that a certain school has a good reputation for teaching science to girls is a non-complex, easily copied and transmitted piece of information. The name of the school, its location and its reputation are what is meant here by simple memories. Such memories, however, are the small change of culture. It is higher-order knowledge structures, variously referred to as schemas (Bartlett, 1932), frames (Minsky, 1975), scripts (Shank and Abelson, 1977), memory organization packets and thematic organization points (Shank, 1982) that are serious candidates as memes in cultural evolution. A higher-order knowledge structure of a school is some generic description of schools as places where children go for some part of each day and are taught by adults about language, maths, history and so on, and where they are exposed to large numbers of peers and learn how to live cooperatively with others. Every child growing up in our culture acquires the higher-order knowledge structure for schools, as well as structures relating to shops, games, sports, authority and many others. The transmission of such higher-order knowledge structures is the central feature of enculturation. Of course, every culture is characterized by different higher-order knowledge structures. The San people of the Kalahari do not acquire restaurant schemas and the English have no scripts relating to ancestral spirits. These structures are culturally transmitted at rates close to that of genetic transmission, that is, once in a normal lifetime. They are deep-level replicators that form the core structures from which are derived their more dynamic, surface-level replicators – the simple memories that inform us that this is a good school and that is a restaurant to be avoided – which are actively transformed and transmitted throughout our lives.

It is possible that there exists in all humans and every culture certain even deeper-level cognitive structures that form the fundamental architecture of cultural knowledge. These would be universal, innate, genetically determined and evolved structures of mind concerned with, for example, sharing resources, defending the social group, or reacting to strangers. From such a limited number of primitive, culturally universal meme structures might be built the deep-level, core, culture-specific memes of higher-order knowledge structures that characterize each culture; and clustered around these deep-level memes will be clouds of very large numbers of surface memes. There is as yet no evidence that such an architecture of memes actually exists. But it is congruent with current models of memory in terms of levels of processing, and it presents a complexity of explanatory structure that begins to do justice to the complexity of its subject matter.

Whatever eventually prove to be the appropriate units of cultural evolution, one thing is clear. The replicators and vehicles can only be sought amongst psychological mechanisms and the behaviors that they generate. No matter how complicated and presently ill-understood these mechanisms might be in terms of intentional mental states, social forces, language and semantics, simple memories and higher-order knowledge structures, memes and whatever supports and services them reside within the minds of the individuals making up culture. Whatever the characteristics of these mechanisms are, it is these that constrain culture, set its limits and determine its general nature. Until the invention of extrasomatic storage in the form of written scripts, human cultural practices were limited by the characteristics of human memory, which is a fallible and uncertain thing. These memories were, and still are, largely embedded in rituals and narratives in order better to preserve information, rather than in artifacts like tools. The advent of extrasomatic storage occurred only about six thousand years ago. It is only in the last one to two hundred years that there has been wider access to such stored information, which even now at the end of the twentieth century is not available to everyone. Six thousand years is a mere drop in evolutionary time and there could not have been significant evolutionary changes wrought in just a few thousand years. Strip away the rather flimsy trappings of twentieth-century mass media and the massive concentrations of populations, and whatever human culture is now in terms of causal mechanisms, it is what it has always been for hundreds of thousands of years. A science of culture, in other words, based upon psychological mechanisms as they exist now, should allow us to extrapolate back in time and understand something of the culture of humans in unrecorded time. Combining such understanding with archaeological and anthropological evidence should allow a more complete picture to emerge of human history.

The theme of this book is the structure of concepts and the relationship of that structure to the external world. What has been suggested in this chapter is that there is a three-way interaction of structures when culture is concerned. First, there are myriad specific features of the world (this school, this classroom, that teacher). Second, there are psychological mechanisms that allow generalization and communication of these via the processes of enculturation (all schools, all instruction). Third, our capacity for entering into culture, which may include the psychological traits advocated in this chapter as well as others in this book (notably those discussed in Chapters 3, 5 and 8), results in cultural institutions, themselves features of the world yet products of culture, such as broad-based educational establishments and laws concerning our relationships with these. Thus there is an intimate, complex and unfolding interaction, both within the course of individual lives and the wider history of human cultures, between conserved structures of the world and our concepts of them, driven by our extraordinary capacity for culture.

References

Baron-Cohen, S. (1995) *Mindblindness*. Cambridge, Mass., MIT Press.

Bartlett, F.C. (1932) *Remembering*. Cambridge, Cambridge University Press.

Boyd, R. and Richerson, P.J. (1985) *Culture and the Evolutionary Process*. Chicago, Chicago University Press.

Campbell, D.T. (1965) Variation and selective retention in sociocultural evolution. In H.R. Barringer, G.I. Blanksten and R.W. Mach (eds) *Social Change in Developing Areas: A Reinterpretation of Evolutionary Theory*. Cambridge, Mass., Shenkman, pp. 19–49.

Cavalli-Sforza, L.L. and Feldman, M.W. (1981) *Cultural Transmission and Evolution: A Quantitative Approach*. Princeton, Princeton University Press.

Cloak, F.T. (1975) Is a cultural ethology possible? *Human Ecology*, 3, 161–182.

Cziko, G. (1995) *Without Miracles: Universal Selection Theory and the Second Darwinian Revolution*. Cambridge, Mass., MIT Press.

Dawkins, R. (1976) *The Selfish Gene*. Oxford, Oxford University Press.

Dunn, F.L. (1970) Cultural evolution in the late Pleistocene and Holocene of Southeast Asia. *American Anthropologist*, 72, 1041–1054.

Durham, W.H. (1976) The adapted significance of cultural behavior. *Human Ecology*, 4, 89–121.

Freud, S. (1913) *Totem and Taboo*. New York, Norton.

Goldman, A.I. (1993) The psychology of folk psychology. *Behavioural and Brain Sciences*, 16, 15–28.

Goodenough, W.H. (1957) Cultural anthropology and linguistics. In P. Garin (ed.) *Report of the 7th Roundtable Meeting on Linguistics and Language Study*, Georgetown University Monograph Series on Language and Linguistics, 9, 167–173.

Gopnik, A. (1993) How we know our minds: the illusion of first-person knowledge of intentionality. *Behavioural and Brain Sciences*, 16, 1–14.

Heyes, C.M. (1994) Social cognition in primates. In N.J. Mackintosh (ed.) *Animal Learning and Cognition*. London, Academic Press, pp. 281–305.

Heyes, C.M. and Galef, B.G. (1996) *Social Learning in Animals: The Roots of Culture*. San Diego, Academic Press, pp. 281–305

Heyes, C.M. and Plotkin, H.C. (1989) Replicators and interactors in cultural evolution. In M. Ruse (ed.) *What the Philosophy of Biology Is*. Dordrecht, Kluwer, pp. 139–162.

Hull, D.L. (1982) The naked meme. In H.C. Plotkin (ed.) *Learning, Development and Culture: Essays in Evolutionary Epistemology*. Chichester, Wiley, pp. 273–327.

Ingold, T. (1986) *Evolution and Social Life*. Cambridge, Cambridge University Press.

Jacobs, R.C. and Campbell, D.T. (1961) The perpetuation of an arbitrary tradition through several generations of a laboratory microculture. *Journal of Abnormal and Social Psychology*, 62, 649–658.

Karmiloff-Smith, A. (1992) *Beyond Modularity: A Developmental Perspective on Cognitive Science*. Cambridge, Mass., MIT Press.

Keesing, R.M. (1974) Theories of culture. *Annual Review of Anthropology*, 3, 73–97.

Kitcher, P. (1987) Confessions of a curmudgeon. *Behavioural and Brain Sciences*, 10, 89–97.

Kroeber, A.L. (1953) Concluding review. In S. Tax, L.C. Eisely, I. Rousse and C.F. Voegellin (eds) *An Appraisal of Anthropology Today*. Chicago, Chicago University Press, pp. 357–376.

Kroeber, A.L. and Kluckholm, C. (1952) Culture: a critical review of the concepts and definitions. *Papers of the Peabody Museum of American Archaeology and Ethnology*, 47, 1–22.

Laland, K.L. (1993) The mathematical modelling of human culture and its implications for psychology and the human sciences. *British Journal of Psychology*, 84, 145–169.

Laland, K.L., Kumm, J. and Feldman, M.W. (1995) Gene-culture coevolutionary theory: a test-case. *Current Anthropology*, 36, 131–156.

Leslie, A.M. (1994) ToMM, ToBY, and agency: core architecture and domain-specificity. In L.A. Hirschfeld and S.A. Gelman (eds) *Mapping the Mind*. Cambridge, Cambridge University Press, pp. 119–148.

Lévi-Strauss, C. (1966) *The Savage Mind*. Chicago, Chicago University Press.

Lumsden, C. and Wilson, E.O. (1981) *Genes, Mind and Culture*. Cambridge, Mass., Harvard University Press.

Mead, M. (1928) *Coming of Age in Samoa*. New York, Mentor.

Meltzoff, A.M. and Moore, M.K. (1977) Imitation of facial and manual gestures by human neonates. *Science*, 198, 75–78.

Meltzoff, A.M. and Moore, M.K. (1983) Newborn infants imitate adult facial gestures. *Child Development*, 54, 702–709.

Minsky, M.L. (1975) A framework for representing knowledge. In P.H. Winston (ed.) *The Psychology of Computer Vision*. New York, McGraw-Hill, pp. 211–277.

Murdock, G.P. (1956) How culture changes. In H.L. Shapiro (ed.) *Man, Culture and Society*. Oxford, Oxford University Press, pp. 247–260.

Plotkin, H.C. (1994) *Darwin Machines*. Cambridge, Mass., Harvard University Press.

Premack, D. and Woodruff, G. (1978) Does the chimpanzee have a theory of mind? *Behavioural and Brain Sciences*, 1, 515–526.

Pulliam, H.R. and Dunford, C. (1980) *Programmed to Learn: An Essay on the Evolution of Culture*. New York, Columbia University Press.

Rosch, E. (1973) Natural categories. *Cognitive Psychology*, 4, 328–350.

Ryle, E.E. (1973) Genetic and cultural pools: some suggestions for a unified theory of biocultural evolution. *Human Ecology*, 1, 201–215.

Searle, J.R. (1995) *The Construction of Social Reality*. London, Allen Lane.

Shank, R.C. (1982) *Dynamic Memory*. New York, Cambridge University Press.

Shank, R.C. and Abelson, R. (1977) *Scripts, Plans, Goals and Understanding*. Hillsdale, NJ, Erlbaum.

Sherif, M. (1936) *The Psychology of Social Norms*. New York, Harper and Row.

Tomasello, M., Kruger, A.C. and Ratner, H.H. (1993) Cultural learning. *Behavioural and Brain Sciences*, 16, 495–511.

Wimmer, H. and Pemerl, J. (1983) Beliefs about beliefs: representation and constraining function of wrong beliefs in young children's understanding of deception. *Cognition*, 13, 103–128.

6 Neural expectations

A possible evolutionary path from manual skills to language

Michael A. Arbib and Giacomo Rizzolatti

Abstract

Any plausible account of language evolution must root language in forms of behavior that are "pragmatic" rather than "communicative" but must also offer a bridge from "doing" to "communicating about doing". Our key addition to the argument for a gestural basis for language (e.g., Hewes, 1973; Kimura, 1993; Armstrong *et al.*, 1995; MacNeilage, in press) is to assert the crucial role of an observation/execution matching system for grasping in monkeys which provides a representation of "expectations" which can both guide the monkey's own actions and enable it to comprehend the actions of other monkeys. We will argue that it is the addition of such an observation system that provides the necessary bridge from "doing" to "communicating about doing". This claim is bolstered by the finding that observation/execution system is located in monkey in an area that is considered the homolog of Broca's area in humans. We then offer a "case grammar" for grasping that suggests the continuity between praxis and language. However, we stress mechanisms that seem to distinguish language from other forms of praxis and analyze a number of human brain mechanisms, including those for consciousness, in that light.

Observation/execution matching systems in monkey and humans

The neurophysiological findings of Sakata, Rizzolatti and their co-workers (Taira *et al.*, 1990; Rizzolatti *et al.*, 1988; see Jeannerod *et al.*, 1995) indicate that parietal area AIP and ventral premotor area F5 in monkey form key elements in a cortical circuit which transforms visual information on intrinsic properties of objects into hand movements that allow the animal to interact appropriately with the objects. Motor information is then transferred to the primary motor cortex (F1 or M1), to which F5 is directly connected, as well as to various subcortical centers for movement execution (Figure 6.1).

The situation is in fact more complex, and "grasp execution" involves a variety of loops and a variety of other brain regions in addition to AIP and F5 (see Fagg and Arbib, 1996 for a computational model), but our task here

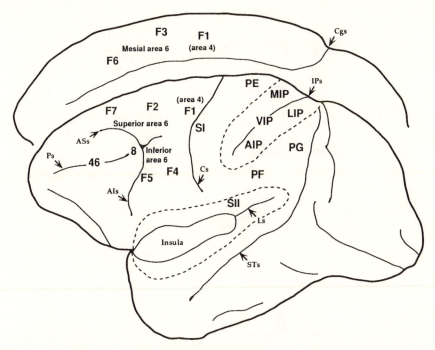

Figure 6.1 Lateral and mesial views of the monkey cerebral cortex
   Frontal cortical areas are classified according to Matelli *et al.* (1985). F5 is
   considered the monkey homolog of Broca's area (see Petrides and Pandya,
   1994). Abbreviations: AIP, anterior intraparietal area; AIs, inferior arcuate
   sulcus; ASs, superior arcuate sulcus; Cs, central sulcus; Cgs, cingulate
   sulcus; IPs, intraparietal sulcus; LIP, lateral intraparietal area; Ls, lateral
   sulcus; MIP, medial intraparietal area; Ps, principal sulcus; STs, superior
   temporal sulcus; and VIP, ventral intraparietal area. IPs and Ls have been
   opened to show hidden areas.

Source: modified from Jeannerod *et al.*, 1994

is to provide a conceptual framework that extends the above "execution system"
to include an "observation system", and then to discuss the possibility that the
combined system provides a substrate for the evolution of language.

   The key data are provided by the studies of Rizzolatti and his co-workers
(Di Pellegrino *et al.*, 1992; Rizzolatti *et al.*, 1996b; Gallese *et al.*, 1996) who
discovered "mirror neurons", a subset of the grasp-related premotor neurons of
F5, which discharge when the monkey observes meaningful hand movements
made by the experimenter, such as placing objects on or taking objects from
a table, grasping food, or manipulating objects. Mirror neurons, in order to be
visually triggered, require an interaction between the agent of the action and
the object of it. The simple presentation of objects, even when held by hand,
does not evoke the neuron discharge.

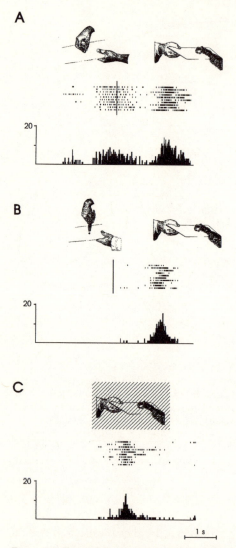

Figure 6.2 Example of a mirror neuron

A: the experimenter grasps a piece of food with his hand, then moves it toward the monkey, who, at the end of the trial, grasps it. The neuron discharges during observation of the grip, ceases to fire when the food is given to the monkey and discharges again when the monkey grasps it. B: the experimenter grasps the food with a tool. The subsequent sequence of events is as in A. C: the monkey grasps food in darkness. In A and B the rasters are aligned with the moment when the food is grasped by the experimenter (vertical line). In C the alignment is with the approximate beginning of the grasping movement. Each small vertical line in the rasters corresponds to a spike. Histogram bin width: 20 rns. Ordinates, spikes/bin; abscissae, time.

Source: from Rizzolatti *et al.*, 1996a

A

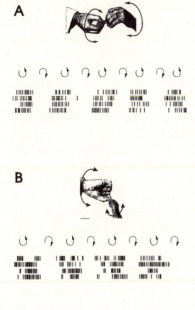

B

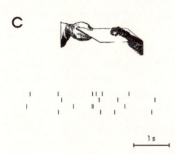

C

1 s

Figure 6.3 Example of a highly congruent mirror neuron
A: the monkey observes the experimenter who rotates his hands around a raisin in opposite directions alternating clockwise and counterclockwise movements. The response is present only in one rotation direction. B: the experimenter rotates a piece of food held by the monkey who opposes the experimenter movement making a wrist rotation movement in the opposite direction. C: monkey grasps food using a precision grip. Four continuous recordings are shown in each panel. Small arrows above the records indicate the direction of rotations.

Source: from Rizzolatti *et al.*, 1996a

An example of a mirror neuron is shown in Figure 6.2. In A, left side, the monkey observes the experimenter grasping a small piece of food. The tray on which the food is placed is then moved toward the monkey and the monkey grasps the food (right side of the figure). The neuron discharges both during grasping observation and during active grasping. B illustrates that when the food is grasped with a tool and not by hand the neuron remains silent. C shows that the neuron's discharge is also present without vision of hand or food during the monkey's own active movement.

The majority of mirror neurons are selective for one type of action (see Figure 6.3). Others respond to two actions, only few to many actions. Also in the latter case, however, the effective actions concern object-directed motor acts. For almost all mirror neurons there is a link between the effective observed movement and the effective executed movement. A series of control experiments ruled out possible interpretations of mirror neurons in terms of monkey's vision of its own hand, food expectancy, motor preparation for food retrieval or reward (Gallese *et al.*, 1996).

In conclusion, the properties of mirror neurons suggest that area F5 is endowed with an observation/execution matching system: when the monkey observes a motor act that resembles one in its movement repertoire, a neural code for this action is automatically retrieved. This code consists in the activation of a subset, the mirror neurons, of the F5 neurons which discharge when the observed act is executed by the monkey itself.

An observation/execution matching system in humans was demonstrated by Fadiga *et al.* (1995) using magnetic transcranial stimulation. The rationale of the experiment was the following: if the mere observation of a movement activates the premotor cortex (in a broad sense) in humans, as it does in monkey, then this activation should induce an enhancement of motor evoked potential recorded from the muscles that would be active if the action were executed by the observing individual. To test this hypothesis, normal human subjects were stimulated in four conditions: during detection of the dimming of a light, while they looked at 3-D objects, while they observed an experimenter grasping the same 3-D objects, and while they observed an experimenter tracing geometrical figures in the air with his arm.

The results showed an increase of the motor evoked potentials in the two conditions in which subjects observed movements. The activated muscles coincided with those used to perform the observed actions. For example, evoked potentials recorded from the opponens pollicis, a flexor muscle, increased in amplitude and duration during the observation of grasping movements, but not during the observation of tracing of geometrical figure with the arm, an action that involves mostly proximal muscles.

While these data indicate that an observation/execution matching system also exists in humans, they do not give information on the circuits underlying it. Data on this issue were provided by two recent PET experiments (Rizzolatti *et al.*, 1996b; Grafton *et al.*, 1996b). The two experiments differed in many aspects, but both had a condition in which subjects observed the experimenter grasping 3-D objects. In both studies, simple observation of the same objects was used as a control condition. (This condition also controlled for verbalization.) The data showed that grasp observation significantly activates the cortex of the left superior temporal sulcus (STS), of the left inferior parietal lobule and of the left inferior frontal gyrus (Brodmann's area 45).

In monkeys, neurons that become selectively active during the sight of hand actions were described by Perrett *et al.* (1990) in the region of the superior STS and, although in this case the evidence is rather anecdoctal, by Leinonen and Nyman (1979) in area 7b. Thus, the cortical areas active during action observation in humans and monkeys correspond very well. The homology, however, between Broca's area and F5 needs some discussion.

Monkey F5 as the homolog of Broca's area

A detailed discussion of the data relevant to the homology between Broca's area, as defined by electrical stimulation of Penfield and Roberts (1959), and F5, will be presented elsewhere. Here, we summarize the conclusions of that discussion.

In monkey, area F5 has a rough somatotopic organization. Hand movements are represented mostly in its dorsal part, while face, mouth and larynx movements are represented ventrally. The somatotopic representations, however, overlap to a considerable extent.

The caudal part of the human inferior frontal lobe gyrus, the site of Broca's area, is markedly enlarged with respect to the same region in the monkey. It is formed by two main cytoarchitectonic areas: areas 44 and 45. It is generally agreed that F5 is the most likely monkey homolog of human area 44 (Petrides and Pandya, 1994; see also Passingham, 1993). In contrast, the possible homolog of human area 45 is not clear, since area 45 in the monkey is mostly related to oculomotion (Bruce *et al.*, 1985; Bruce, 1988), a function not represented in human area 45.

A recent study of cytoarchitectonic organization of monkey premotor cortex shows that F5 is not homogeneous, but consists of various sectors (Matelli *et al.*, 1996). Mirror neurons are clustered in one of these sectors (mostly on the cortical convexity), while F5 neurons devoid of visual complex properties ("classical" F5 neurons) are concentrated in another sector located on the posterior bank of the arcuate sulcus (personal observations). This inhomogeneity indicates a beginning of segmentation of F5 into different areas and might suggest that a similar process occurred in humans. According to this view, the "classical" F5 would be located in humans on the posterior bank of the precentral sulcus and on the ventral bank of the inferior frontal sulcus, while the "mirror" zone would increase in humans and would occupy the cortical convexity ventral to the inferior frontal sulcus. Thus, both areas 44 and 45 would originate from an area homologous to F5.

Broca's area is most commonly characterized as an area for speech. A series of new data, mostly coming from brain imaging experiments, challenges this view and indicates that in Broca's area there is a representation of hand movements in addition to the bucco-laringeal one. Bonda *et al.* (1995), using PET techniques, showed that a sector of Broca's area becomes active during the execution of self-ordered hand movement sequences. Similarly, Parsons *et al.*

(1995) demonstrated a marked increase of activity in Broca's area during a task involving hand mental rotations. The data on activation of Broca's area during observation of grasping movements reported above (Rizzolatti *et al.*, 1996b; Grafton *et al.*, 1996b) are in good agreement with these observations.

Simple natural grasping hand movements typically fail to activate Broca's area (Grafton *et al.*, 1996b; Rizzolatti *et al.*, 1996b), possibly because of the simplicity and automaticity of the tested movements. Broca's area, however, may become active during hand grasping movements when the task requires particular accuracy and precision (Schlaug *et al.*, 1994). Mental imagery of hand grasping movements also activates Broca's area, mostly area 44 (Decety *et al.*, 1994; Grafton *et al.*, 1996b). Considering that mental imagery typically activates areas involved in task execution, this finding further supports the idea that the lack of activation of inferior frontal areas in the case of simple grasping movements depends essentially on the simplicity of the task employed. Note also that, whereas F5 activity is transient when it activates F1 during an actual movement, it must be "held" in F5 during an imagined movement. Finally, Broca's area is activated in patients who have recovered from subcortical infarctions when they are asked to use their previously paralyzed hand (Chollet *et al.*, 1991).

Further evidence in favor of Broca's area involvement in functions not related to speech comes from clinical studies of aphasic patients. Many of these patients have, in addition to language deficits, an impairment in pantomime recognition. Some patients makes errors in pantomime recognition of the semantic type. That is, they fail in trials in which the response choice includes items that are semantically related to the object acted upon during the mimed action. Since a similar pattern of errors is made also in the case of auditory verbal comprehension tests, some authors suggested that pantomime recognition and the verbal recognition deficit depend on the same basic symbolic disorder (Duffy and Watkins, 1984; see also Brain, 1961). Other patients, however, make errors of perceptual-motor type. When faced with foils in which objects are depicted that are either semantically similar to those represented in the pantomime or resemble them in terms of evoked actions, they indicate as correct the latter (Bell, 1994). The capacity to recognize pantomime appears, therefore, to be represented in Broca's area as a specific, not language-dependent, function. Summing up, there is convincing evidence that Broca's area, like F5, has a hand movement representation. This hand representation is activated during movements actively performed, during movement imagery, and during observations of gesture made by others. Furthermore, this activation appears to play a crucial role in understanding the meaning of pantomime. The importance of these findings for the study of language evolution will become evident in the following sections.

Action = movement + goal/expectation

What makes a movement into an action is that it is associated with a goal, and that initiation of the movement is accompanied by the creation of an expectation that the goal will be met. To the extent that the unfolding of the movement departs from that expectation, to that extent will an error be detected and the movement modified. In other words, an individual performing an action is able to predict its consequences and, therefore, the action representation and its consequences are associated. Thus a "grasp" involves not only a specific cortical activation pattern for the preshape and enclose movements, but also expectations concerning making appropriate contact with a specific object. We thus assert that an individual making an action "knows" what action he is performing to the extent that he predicts the consequences of his pattern of movement.

The data presented earlier show that a major evolutionary development has been established in primates: the individual can recognize ("understand") the actions made by others in the sense that the neural pattern elicited by their action is similar to that generated by him in doing the action. Three caveats should be noted:

(i) There is no claim that this mirroring is limited to primates. It is likely that an analogue of mirror systems exists in other mammals, especially those with a rich and flexible social organization.

(ii) The recognition of consequences may extend to actions beyond the animal's own repertoire, and may here involve mechanisms not much more complex than classical conditioning. For example, dogs can recognize the consequences of a human's use of a can opener (the sound of the can opener becomes associated with the subsequent presentation of the dog food from the can).

(iii) The present discussion is neutral as to consciousness. Here "prediction" means "creates a neural representation of a potential future state" rather than "is aware of this potential future state". Similarly "understanding" means "to be able to match an external (unknown) event to an internal (known) event", without any assumption as to who or what knows the internal event. We shall return to these distinctions below.

Arbib (1981) showed how to describe perceptual structures and distributed motor control in terms of functional units called *schemas* which may be combined to form new schemas as coordinated control programs linking simpler (perceptual and motor) schemas. Jeannerod *et al.* (1995) provide a recent application of schema theory to the study of neural mechanisms of grasping. This raises two opposing points to be explicitly addressed in the detailed modeling (not provided in this chapter) that will build upon the conceptual framework that we present in the next section:

(a) We hypothesize that the complete plan of an action (whether observed or "intended") should be encoded in the current brain state.

(b) However, we also need to model the processes whereby (i) a time varying pattern of inputs is segmented at some level, with the last "segment"

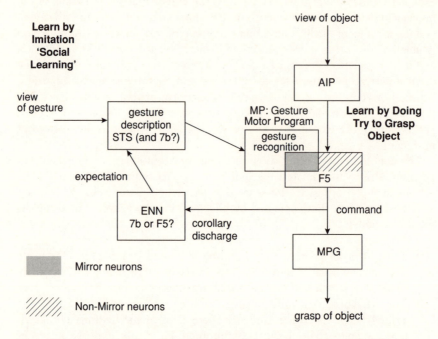

Figure 6.4 An integrated conceptual framework for analysis of the role of F5 in
        grasping
        The right hand, vertical, path is the *execution system* from "view of object"
        via AIP and F5 to "grasp of object" – it provides mechanisms for grasping
        a seen object. The loop on the left of the figure provides mechanisms for
        imitating observed gestures in such a way as to create expectations that
        enable the visual feedback loop to serve both for "social learning" (i.e.,
        learning an action through imitation of the actions of others) and also for
        (delayed) error correction during, for example, reaching towards a target.
        It combines the *observation matching system* from "view of gesture" via
        gesture description (STS) and gesture recognition (mirror neurons in F5
        and possibly 7b) to a representation of the "command" for such a gesture,
        and the *expectation system* from an F5 command via the expectation
        neural network ENN to MP, the motor program for generating a given
        gesture. The latter path may mediate a comparison between "expected
        gesture" and "observed gesture" in the case of the monkey's self-generated
        movement.

captured in a neural code, and (ii) a "neural plan" results in a pattern of
movement over time (e.g., by defining the motor schema which provides
the regnant control system to determine the, possibly feedback-dependent,
unfolding of movement).

Figure 6.4 presents our integrated conceptual framework for analysis of the
role of F5 in grasping. This combines mechanisms for (1) grasping a seen object
(the right hand path from "view of object" to "grasp of object"), and (2)

imitating observed gestures in such a way as to create expectations which, as we shall shortly see, not only play a role in "social learning" but also enable the visual feedback loop eventually to serve for (delayed) error correction during, for example, reaching towards a target (the loop on the left of the figure).

The Expectation Neural Network (ENN) is the "Direct Model" of Command → Response. When the animal gives a command (in the sense of brain regions issuing the neural signals that command a movement), ENN generates the expected neural code for the visual signal generated by the resulting gesture. We explicitly label the input to ENN, a copy of the motor command, as a corollary discharge. By contrast, the Motor Program MP provides an "Inverse Model" of Command → Response, by going from a desired response to a command that can generate it.

Our emphasis in this chapter is on a conceptual framework. It would be too daring at this stage of our neurophysiological knowledge to assign precise anatomical areas to the various stages forming the imitation loop. As a mere speculation one can propose two main possibilities. The first is that the various model stages are located in different anatomical areas. In this case the inverse model which converts the view of a gesture to a corresponding command would most likely be located along the path leading from STS to F5 (possibly via 7b). The reciprocal path from F5 to superior temporal sulcus would provide the direct model, ENN. It is equally probable, however, that both ENN and MP are located in F5 and the interplay between stages occurs entirely within F5. If the latter interpretation is accepted, the role of STS areas would be that of giving a merely "pictorial", though highly elaborated, description of gestures – with the observation/execution system entirely located in the frontal lobe.

The integrated model of Figure 6.4 thus relates the "grasp an object" system to the "view a gesture" system. The expectation network is driven by F5 irrespective of whether the motor command is "object-driven" (via AIP) or "gesture-driven". It thus creates expectations for what a hand movement will look like when "object-driven" (an instrumental action directed towards a goal) or "gesture-driven" (a "social action" aimed at making a self-generated movement approximate an observed movement). The right hand path of Figure 6.4 exemplifies "learning by doing", refining a crude "innate grasp" – possibly by a process of reinforcement learning, in which the success/failure of the grasp acts as positive/negative reinforcement. The left hand path of Figure 6.4 exemplifies another mode of learning (the two may be sequential or contemporary) which creates expectations about gestures as well as exemplifying "social learning" based on imitation of gestures made by others.

"Declarative" and "procedural" abilities

Some recent clinical studies have shown a double dissociation between the "declarative" ability to communicate the size of an object, whether verbally or by pantomime, and the "procedural" ability to act upon objects. Since the anatomical location of the lesions (see below) responsible for the deficits appear to contradict the view we presented on communication evolution in primates, it is important to briefly discuss here those findings.

Goodale *et al.* (1991) studied a patient (DF) who had developed a profound visual form agnosia following a bilateral lesion of occipitotemporal cortex. The pathways from occipital lobe toward the parietal lobe appeared to be intact. When the patient was asked to indicate the width of a single block by means of her index finger and thumb, her finger separation bore no relationship to the dimensions of the object and showed considerable trial to trial variability. Yet, when she was asked simply to reach out and pick up the block, the peak aperture between her index finger and thumb changed systematically with the width of the object, as in normal controls. A similar dissociation was seen in her responses to the orientation of stimuli. In other words, DF could preshape her hand accurately, even though she appeared to have no conscious appreciation (either verbal or by pantomime) of the visual parameters that guided the preshape.

Jeannerod *et al.* (1994) reported the case of a woman (AT) who was the "opposite" of DF. AT had a lesion of the occipito-parietal region that interrupted the dorsal route of visual processing, but left the inferotemporal lobe and the occipitotemporal pathways intact. AT could use her hand to pantomime the size of a cylinder, but could not preshape appropriately when asked to grasp it. Instead of an adaptive preshape, she would open her hand to its fullest, and only began to close her hand when the cylinder hit the "web" between index finger and thumb. But there was a surprise! When the stimulus used for the grasp was not a cylinder (for which the "semantics" contains no information about expected size), but rather a familiar object – such as a reel of thread, or a lipstick – for which the "usual" size is part of the subject's knowledge, AT showed a relatively adaptive preshape. This suggests that the inferotemporal-parietal pathways provide the parietal areas with "default values" of action-related parameters, i.e., values that can serve in place of actual sensory data to, for example, represent the approximate size of a known object to help the parieto-frontal system.

In the model presented in the previous section (Figure 6.4), we posited the following paths:

(i) *The execution system:* view of object → AIP → F5 → grasp of object
(ii) *The observation matching system:* view of gesture → gesture description (STS) → gesture recognition (mirror neurons in F5 and possibly 7b)
(iii) *The expectation system:* F5 → ENN (F5?) → MP (mirror neurons in F5 and possibly 7b).

The data on AT lead to the introduction of an additional pathway (not shown in the figure):

(iv) *The object recognition system:* this is the "what" system based on visual input to the inferotemporal cortex. The AT data tell us that there is a path from IT to AIP (or F5?) which can provide information on the grasp parameters of a familiar type of object when objects of this class have a restricted range of values for the parameters.

The evolution of this pathway can be understood in motoric terms, independently of our theory on the gestural basis of language evolution. Our view is that path (i) extracts affordances based on the shape (rather than the "semantics") of an object, and that the object recognition system evolved in the first place to allow the choice of grasp to depend on more subtle knowledge of the object – so that, for example, having recognized an object as a piece of fruit, the recognition of whether or not it is ripe will bias the decision as to whether or not to act upon the affordance that it offers. The object recognition system is also involved in prefrontal systems which enter into the more subtle planning of action which may in turn provide the evolutionary basis (moving far beyond the focus of this chapter) for more abstract processes of thought which can affect language behavior as much as pragmatic behavior.

On this basis we may argue that path (ii) provides the basis for the evolution of naming actions, while path (iv) provides the basis for the evolution of naming objects. Their integration in determining courses of action then lays the basis for the syntactic integration of noun phrases and verb phrases in language, a point to which we all too briefly return in the section on "A Pre-Linguistic 'Grammar' of Action in the Monkey Brain". Of course, recognition of what an object "is" is a major step beyond the basic monkey story of how to grasp an object and requires extensive epistemological analysis of the "construction of reality" – whether by a community or within the head of an individual – as a network of interacting schemas (Arbib and Hesse, 1986). Neuroscience is very much at the beginning of charting how such knowledge may be mediated by, for example, rich links between inferotemporal and prefrontal cortex, associating an object with a wide variety of coordinated control programs (Arbib, 1981) for both immediate action and abstract thought.

Returning from these philosophical heights, we can use our analysis of the four pathways to reconcile our evolutionary story with the suggestion, based on the AT and DF data, that "declarative" ability appears to depend on the integrity of inferotemporal lobe and the visual areas ventrally located in the occipital lobe, while the "procedural" ability depends on the integrity of posterior parietal lobe and the visual areas located more dorsally. In contrast, for the thesis we are presenting here, we need to implicate F5 in the "communicative" use of hand movement, at least to the extent of providing an evolutionary basis for gesture as a precursor to language. The distinction between path (i) and paths (ii) and (iv) is fundamental for understanding the clinical data, but does require some expansion. According to this view, the lesion of visual input to the posterior part of the parietal lobe – path (i) – determined the "procedural" deficit of AT, with the integrity of path (iv) leaving her "declarative" capacity intact. In contrast, the integrity of posterior parietal lobe and more generally of path (i) allowed correct grasping movements in DF, but damage and deafferentation of inferotemporal lobe – path (iv) – determined her profound deficit in "declarative" capacities. More generally, path (ii) for the observation/matching system coupled with path (iv) for the object recognition system provides, in our hands, the evolutionary basis for the paths to Broca's area that serve pantomime and gesture for the signing of actions and objects, respectively.

An evolutionary view of communication and consciousness

The dichotomy between "declarative" and "procedural" proved crucial to the distinction between the two patients AT and DF. However, the notion of the "declarative" cannot be tackled without an attempt to model at least some aspects of the phenomenology of consciousness – for what distinguishes the two patients is that DF is conscious of the size of objects, whereas AT is not (although she can use the parietal perception of object size in shaping her hand to grasp an object).

A similar distinction has been dissected in observations of "blindsight". Neurologists long held that a monkey (or human) without a visual cortex was blind. However, noting that the role of the frog's tectum in visually directing whole body movements is analogous to the role of mammalian superior colliculus in directing eye movements, Humphrey (1970) showed that a monkey without visual cortex could use visual cues to grab at moving objects, and use changes in luminance for navigation. Similarly, humans without visual cortex can also "see" in this action-oriented sense but are not conscious of the visual stimuli for their actions (cf. Weiskrantz *et al.*, 1974; this is the phenomenon called "blindsight"). Thus, even schemas that we think of as normally under conscious control can in fact proceed without our being conscious of their activity.

The relation of visual cortex to superior colliculus exemplifies the evolutionary ideas of the British nineteenth-century neurologist Hughlings Jackson who viewed the brain in terms of levels of increasing evolutionary complexity (e.g., Jackson, 1878–79). An evolutionary more primitive system allows the evolution of higher-level systems; but then return pathways evolve which enable the lower-level system to evolve into a more effective form. Jackson argued that damage to a "higher" level of the brain disinhibited "older" brain regions from controls evolved later, to reveal evolutionarily more primitive behaviors. Evolution not only yields new schemas connected to the old, but yields reciprocal connections that modify those older schemas. We now apply these general ideas to present a view (due to Arbib, 1985; Arbib and Hesse, 1986) of the evolution of communication and consciousness which seems well suited to support the view of language communication offered in this chapter.

Primitive communication subserves primitive coordination of the members of a social group, but processes that coordinate a group need not involve consciousness. Indeed, the social insects demonstrate a subtlety of group coordination that is in no way a precursor to consciousness. Here, we speculate about a "mammalian scenario" in which group coordination may indeed lay the basis for the co-evolution of consciousness and language. As communication evolves, the "instructions" that can be given to other members of the group increase in subtlety. For coordination of the actions of a group to progress, the brain of each group member must be able not only to generate such signals, but also to integrate signals from other members of the group into its own ongoing motor planning. The key idea here seems to be a migration in time from:

(i) an execution/observation matching system enabling an individual to recognize the action (as distinct from the mere movement) that another individual is making, to
(ii) the individual becoming able to pantomime "this is the action I am about to take".

In the earliest stages of the evolution of this second ability, communication may have involved the accidental release of a motor plan from inhibition, thus allowing a brief prefix of the movement to be exhibited before the full action was released – but this "warning gesture" may have sufficed to alert others in time to bias their action, yielding benefits of adaptive value for groups that could both offer "signals of intention" and make use of them. This yields positive reinforcement to the individual accidentally releasing prefixes of actions, serving in turn as the basis for group selection, favoring the reproduction of those groups that can learn to emit and interpret such signals. This marks, at both the individual and species levels, the beginning of real communication as distinct from the release of signals.

However, Arbib and Hesse (1986) do not emphasize this external process of "group selection" in the population as a whole, but rather the changes within the individual brain made possible by the availability of a "précis" – a gesturable representation – of intended future movements (as distinct from current movements). We now examine the suggested consequences of such a précis as it enriches the "information environment" for the rest of the brain. Arbib and Hesse use the term *communication plexus* for the circuits involved in generating this representation. The Jacksonian element of their analysis is that the evolution of the communication plexus provides an environment for the further evolution of older systems. Since the "précis" is now available to other schemas, these can potentially adjust their activity in light of reports of what is going on elsewhere. A new process of evolution may thus begin whereby the précis comes to serve not only as a basis for communication between the members of a group, but also as a resource for planning and coordination within the brain of the individual. The "communication plexus" thus evolves a crucial role in schema coordination.

Arbib and Hesse's thesis is that it is the activity of this communication plexus that constitutes consciousness, i.e., that "consciousness" is defined by a neurally represented précis of potential behavior. Such a view does not explain the phenomenology of consciousness – i.e., the way consciousness "feels" to each of us – but it does accord well with this phenomenology. The fact that lower-level schema activity can often proceed successfully without the high-level coordination afforded by the communication plexus explains why consciousness may sometimes be active as a monitor rather than as a director of action. In other cases, the formation of the précis of schema activity plays the crucial role in determining the future course of schema activity, and thus of action – and this accords with those occasions in which we experience a conscious effort in weighing a number of courses of action before we commit ourselves to behave in a specific way. The reader may consult Arbib and Hesse (1986) for an articulation of the philosophical debate between those who, in line with the above argument, see the "self" as embodied within the neural circuitry and the body which contains it, and those dualists who view the self as in some sense separable from brain and body (e.g., Popper and Eccles, 1977).

Hand gestures and phonetic gestures

Let us now come back to the discussion of the similarities between Broca's area and F5. There is a general consensus that animal calls and human speech are different phenomena. Among the many aspects that differentiate them, such as the strict relation of animal calls (but not of speech) with emotional and instinctive behavior, there is also a marked difference in the anatomical structures responsible for the two behaviors. Animal calls are mediated primarily by the cingulate cortex together with diencephalic and brain stem structures (Jurgens, 1987; MacLean, 1993). Speech is mediated by a circuit whose main nodes are the classical Wernicke and Broca's areas of the dorsolateral cortical convexity (see Dejerine, 1914; Benson, 1988; Cappa and Vignolo, 1996).

The data reviewed above on the observation/matching system suggest that what determined the speech development in the lateral cortical circuit was that a part of this circuit, and Broca's area in particular, was endowed before speech appearance with the capacity of recognizing actions made by others. It is obvious that there is a great conceptual difference between recognition of gestures with communicative intent and gestures without it. In any case, the mechanisms that allow the recognition of hand actions must, in principle, be no different from those for recognition of facial-mouth movements having a communicative intent (e.g., monkey "lipsmacks") and those for recognition of "phonetic gestures". It is only the input–output coupling which is different, not the recognition process.

Two sets of data reinforce the validity of this conclusion. The first is based on neurophysiological findings concerning neurons coding face-mouth movements in F5. Preliminary experiments carried out in Parma (unpublished observations) showed that in F5 there are face-mouth neurons that become active when the monkey makes "lipsmacking" movements. Some of these neurons also fire when the monkey observes similar movements made by another individual. It appears therefore that the mirror mechanism is not limited to actions devoid of communication purposes such as grasping movements, but also mediates communications between individuals.

The second set of evidence comes from phonological studies of Liberman *et al.* (1967; Liberman and Mattingly, 1985; Liberman and Studdert-Kennedy, 1978). On the basis of empirical findings and general considerations of plausibility, they formulated what is usually referred to as the "motor theory" of speech perception. According to this theory, the "objects" of speech perception are not the sounds, but the phonetic gestures of the speaker. These gestures are represented in the brain as invariant motor commands. The phonetic gestures are "the primitives that the mechanisms of speech production translate into actual articulator movements, and they are also the primitives that the specialized mechanisms of speech perception recover from the signal" (Liberman and Mattingly, 1989). The common link between sender and receiver is not therefore sound, but motor pattern. The analogy with the function proposed for mirror neurons is striking. In both speech perception and gesture recognition the basic mechanism appears to be that of matching the neural activity resulting from observation of a gesture with that underlying its execution. Since the meaning of the latter is "known" the gesture is, to a first approximation, recognized.

The force of the phrase "to a first approximation" is to emphasize (as Arbib and Caplan, 1979 did in their early analysis of neural computations underlying language) that, since phonemes may be hard to distinguish in isolation, hearing a sound may well rest on cooperative computation between representations at multiple levels, including the lexical and the phrasal, before contextual constraints yield a coherent interpretation of an utterance. In this spirit, note, for example, that some Japanese speakers who acquire English late enough may be unable to hear the difference between "lid" and "rid" yet can pronounce them distinctly. In terms of Figure 6.4, we would say that, for such people, the network for "gesture recognition" has been stabilized for the Japanese phonemic repertoire before English is learned. Thus, although careful attention to mouth shape and tongue placement can be used to form an "l" and "r" distinguishable by English speakers, the gesture recognition system of the Japanese speaker is by then insufficiently plastic to acquire this distinction. On the other hand, this Japanese speaker is well able to understand English when context can settle whether "l" or "r" occurred in a particular utterance.

We agree, then, with A.M. Liberman on a "motor theory of perception" – that the basic mechanism appears to be that of matching the neural activity resulting from observation of a gesture with that underlying its execution. But where Philip Lieberman (1985) argues for speech as the basic modality in the evolution of human language, we stress its manual basis, seeing spoken language as derivative from skills for complex sequential behavior that emerged prior to the evolution of speech. As one example to support this view, we note that a speech-centered evolution of language mechanisms would render highly implausible the ability of deaf children spontaneously to use signing to communicate, and to acquire sign language as readily as normal children acquire spoken language. We develop this theme in the discussion of American Sign Language (ASL) in the next section.

The sequence we propose is the following: facial gestures first, then manual gestures, finally speech gestures. Facio-visual communication is used in a wide variety of social circumstances by non-human primates. It is produced both by males and females, regardless of their rank, and is accompanied by eye contact. Note that this specific relation between the sender and the receiver of the message may be absent during emission of vocal calls – the latter may be directed to the whole tribe rather than to a single individual. The use of manual gesture for communication marks an important evolutionary step because it allows the possibility of introducing a third, new element in the basically dyadic communication based on facial gestures. By using manual gestures the sender may indicate to the receiver the position of a third person or object, and may represent the speed and direction of a movement. These possibilities are very limited with visuo-facial communication, even if facial movements are accompanied by head movements.

Both facial and arm gesture can be used only when light conditions are suitable. Sound may overcome this drawback, but the advantage the basic vocalizations bring to communication are rather limited. They simply stress a facial message. The advantage of associating sound to gesture becomes far more important when manual gestures convey information on objects and events. The appearance of such flexibility was one of the most important evolutionary steps toward speech. The ability to use sound alone then followed, we suggest, at which stage speech takes off. Note that the Broca's area has the neural structure for all the above discussed gestures: face movements, oro-laringeal movements, hand-arm movement. Moreover, as we have stressed repeatedly, it is endowed with an observation/execution matching system.

What the hands reveal about language

The hypothesis that the language specialization of human Broca's area derives from an ancient mechanism related to the observation/execution of motor acts is made more plausible by the fact that language is not necessarily rooted in the vocal-auditory domain of speech but can be exhibited in the brachio-manual-visual domain of sign language. Moreover, the same circuitry that subserves speech may underlie signing as well. To this end, we briefly discuss the work of Poizner, Klima and Bellugi (1987) to establish the continuity of language with visuomotor skills. This is obscured when language is identified with speech.

In American Sign Language (ASL) syntax, space is crucial in signed descriptions. In signing a "sentence", the signer may indicate objects using "nouns" in the form of specific hand gestures encoding the object, with the signs for different objects made at different points in the peripersonal space of the signer. The positioning of the "nouns" may be arbitrary, or may offer a suggestive pantomime of the spatial relations among the objects being described. In any case, mere pointing to a location may then serve as a "pronoun" for an object previously signed there, obviating the need to repeat the signed description of that specific object. Note the direct building upon "natural" manual gesture. This is much harder in speech, and so might well have provided an evolutionary bridge from manual gesture to (more arbitrary) speech gesture.

Poizner *et al.* described three signers with left-hemisphere lesions. The impairments in visual-gestural language in these patients were similar to the impairments in auditory-spoken languages following left hemisphere lesion. Gail D., a Broca-like patient, exhibited extreme dysfluency and almost exclusive use of referential open-class nouns. She used almost ten times as many nouns as pronouns. Karen L. tended to make free use of pronominal indexes without specifying the associated nominals and used only half as many nouns as pronouns. Paul D. used more than five times as many nouns as pronouns. His overuse of nouns appeared to be a means to avoid using pronouns. By contrast to these three (very different) subjects, the language of right-lesioned signers was indistinguishable from controls, whose noun/pronoun ratio is about 2 : 1.

Poizner *et al.* also studied three signers with right-hemisphere lesions. On drawing tasks, the right-lesioned patients were markedly impaired, in contrast to left-lesioned patients who performed reasonably well. They were unable to indicate perspective in their drawings, even when copying from another drawing, and would omit portions of a drawing of a recognizable object that they would not omit in copying a similarly complex but meaningless collection of lines.

The data (whose sparseness must be emphasized) included a striking double dissociation: Gail D., who suffered massive damage to the left frontal lobe, was the most severely aphasic patient, yet her non-language visuo-spatial processing was the most intact of any of the six patients. By contrast, Sarah M., whose stroke yielded massive damage to the right hemisphere involving most of the territory of the right cerebral artery, showed massive left hemifield neglect in her visuo-spatial non-language functioning, yet her signing (including spatially expressed syntax) was unimpaired.

Lesion results also suggest that the dual uses of space in signing – for spatial mapping and spatialized syntax – may be dissociated. Syntactic relations are disrupted by left-hemisphere lesions, and spatial relations by right hemisphere damage. Right-lesioned Brenda I. described her room in sign but with great spatial distortion: the major pieces of furniture were correctly enumerated, but all spatial loci were placed indiscriminately in the right half of the spatial field. Left-lesioned Karen L. had trouble finding the appropriate nominal for an object, but close analysis of videotape revealed that she did sign (ambiguous) classifiers for the various objects and that she correctly indicated the spatial placement and orientation for each classifier. While left-lesioned Paul D.'s signing is full of grammatical paraphasias and tends to omit some details, it shows no evident spatial distortion – yet he showed impaired spatialized syntax. Brenda I. established syntactic loci throughout the signing space (including on the left) and maintained consistent co-reference to spatial loci.

Kimura (1993) argues that the left hemisphere is specialized, not for language *per se*, but for the complex motor programming functions that are essential for language production. Early studies of signing-disordered cases assumed that the defect was specifically linguistic. Sarno, Swisher and Sarno (1969) found the ability to imitate using a toothbrush, hammering, etc., was adequate, but such familiar movements may often be relatively spared when less familiar movements are affected. Kimura notes that unfamiliar movements, sensitive to manual apraxia, were found to be poorly copied by a patient with sign-language aphasia (Kimura, Battison and Lubert, 1976), and deaf signers denied any linguistic content in the movements presented. However, language may require its own "copy" of motor sequencing mechanisms, with the adjacency of these to "old" mechanisms making lesions that dissociate the two very rare.

Poizner *et al.* (1987) claim to find no deficit in copying non-linguistic movements in at least one case of signing aphasia (see the above discussion of Gail D.), but Kimura (1990) found this case to be manually apraxic and argues that the signing disorders seen after left-hemisphere pathology are manifestations of manual apraxia, just as most vocal aphasias are manifestations of disordered oral-vocal motor control. This still leaves open the issue of what language adds to the monkey's motor repertoire. Is it more than is added in, for example, the abstract ability to recognize sequence matching as a general property rather than to have to learn each sequence *ab initio*? We have stressed a link to social behavior: inferring the *intentions* of others as a basis for interacting with them.

Signing comprehension is also affected after left-hemisphere pathology, which Kimura, Davidson and McCormick (1982) interpret as evidence that the system for programming movements also participates in their perception, which fits well with our view of the role of expectation networks and mirror neurons.

Errors produced by patients with signing aphasia range from unrecognizable movements, through errors recognizable as a sign unrelated to the target, to errors within linguistic classes. The fact that errors can occur within a morphological category has been used by Poizner *et al.* (1987) to argue that the signing deficit must be linguistic in nature. It may be a more general property that errors in *any* performance have some "associative link" with the target. Kimura (1993) stresses that there is no evidence of a case where all errors stayed within the class of linguistic movements – but note, again, that if there were a "separate" language system, it would remain highly unlikely that pathology would be restricted to it.

Given such evidence, Kimura argues that linguistic and motor control functions evolved in an interactive manner, and that it would be extremely inefficient to duplicate the motor control mechanisms in a separate language system. We suggest that the issue is, rather, one of partial "separation". Recall our gloss on "Jacksonian" systems: old systems change as new systems "emerge". More recently, Hickok *et al.* (1996) examined the linguistic abilities of a large sample of sign-language users with unilateral brain lesions. Despite the fact that sign language is based on visuo-spatial rather than temporal information, the left-hemispheric dominance typical for speech emerged in left-lesioned signers. The ASL data thus suggest that the left cerebral hemisphere in humans has an innate predisposition for language, independent of language modality. Furthermore, in spite of the strong spatial component necessary for the production of sign language, the basic communicative function is, as for speech, localized in the left hemisphere and, basically, in the same areas where speech is localized in individuals without auditory deficits (Neville *et al.*, 1996). These data strongly support our contention that Broca's area has a somatotopic organization and that its fundamental property is the capacity to match execution and observation. In any case, we may agree with Kimura (1993) that

> Only overt behavior can interact with the environment, and thus it is the genetic substrate of *behavior* which is subjected to the laws of natural selection. Approaches to the study of language which ignore this, or take a linguistically solipsist view of communication are therefore unlikely to be productive.

A pre-linguistic "grammar" of action in the monkey brain

It is not our task in the present chapter to show how language evolved, but rather to provide a novel analysis of the "grasp system" of the monkey which makes extremely plausible the claim that this system provides the basis for the evolution of language. Thus, we will not carry the analysis of how· speech became the dominant medium for human language beyond the preliminary notes presented above. Instead, we devote this section to showing how a "pre-linguistic grammar" may be assigned to the control and observation of action; the idea is to make more plausible the notion that evolution could then yield a language system "atop" the grasp system of Figure 6.4, especially because this system already includes an "action recognition system".

We have chosen case grammar as a representation of sentence structure that adapts well to providing abstract expression of the "meanings" of neural activity in F5, and of the systems of which F5 is part. Case grammar organizes sentences around action frames with slots for different roles. For example, the sentence "John hit Mary with his hand" is viewed as the "surface structure" for a case structure *Hit(John, Mary, John's hand)* which is an instance of the case frame *Hit(Agent, Recipient, Instrument)* which makes explicit the roles of "John", "Mary", and "John's hand". Clearly, many different sentences can express the same underlying case structure. The key paper for case structure is "The case for case" by Fillmore (1996), but it is worth noting that many of the ideas about case have now been absorbed in the thematic structure of the lexicon which is an integral component of the Chomskian approach to syntax known as Government and Binding (GB) theory (Van Riemsdijk and Williams, 1986).

Case structure for "classical" F5 neurons

We view the activity of "classical" (non-mirror) F5 neurons as part of the code for an *imperative* case structure, for example,

Command: $Grasp_A(raisin)$

as an instance of $Grasp_A(Object)$, where $Grasp_A$ is a specific kind of grasp, the precision grasp, which is to be applied to the raisin. Here, grasp type generalizes across similar grasps of varied objects as postulated in opposition space theory (Iberall, Bingham and Arbib, 1986). Note that this case structure is an "action description", not a linguistic representation. We say it is *part* of the code because we argue that F5 activity encodes the action $Grasp_A(-)$, and this must be linked to activity elsewhere in the brain to bind the specific raisin to the role of Object.

The slots in a case frame come with restrictions on what can fill those slots, for example, any x in $Grasp_A(x)$ must be a small object. As actions become more refined, and as the transition to language occurs, the constraints on slot fillers may become more rigorous. From this it follows that, if the same principle holds for linguistic commands as for motor commands, Broca's area would code "verb phrases" and constraints on the noun phrases that can fill the slots, but not details of the noun phrases themselves. This knowledge (objects/noun phrases) could be completely outside F5/Broca's area, for example in the temporal cortex, and reach F5/Broca's area via the parietal or prefrontal lobe (recall our earlier discussion of how "path (iv)" may tie the object recognition system into the system for object manipulation, building upon the three paths shown in Figure 6.4).

Case structure for mirror neurons

Having viewed the activity of "classic" F5 neurons as coding a command (cf. an *imperative* sentence), we might say that the firing of "mirror" F5 neurons is part of the code for a *declarative* case structure, for example,

Declarative: $Grasp_A(Luigi, raisin)$

which is a special case of $Grasp_A(Agent, Object)$, where $Grasp_A$ is a specific kind of grasp applied to the raisin (the Object) by *Luigi* (the Agent). Again, this is an "action description", not a linguistic representation. If attention is focused on Luigi's hand rather than on Luigi himself, then the appropriate case structure would be $Grasp_A(hand, object)$ as a special case of $Grasp_A(Instrument, Object)$. Thus, the same act can be perceived in different ways: "Who" grasps vs. "What" grasps. An interesting aspect of the Parma data (unpublished observations) is that the mirror neurons did not fire when the monkey observed the experimenter grasp the raisin with pliers rather than his hand . . . until after a long period of observation. We thus see the ability to learn new constraints on a case slot – in this case the observed generalization of the *Instrument* role from hands alone to include pliers.

What binds the specific raisin to the role of object of an observed action, rather than (as in the "imperative" of the previous section) as the goal of an intended action? In observation, as distinct from execution, neural activity need not include many of the sublinguistic parameters to do with the specification of reach and grasp (as is also the case with linguistic description). The F5 mirror neuron activity might be thought of as coding a declarative "observation". But then what makes the activity "declarative" rather than a command to be executed? It is a representation without a necessary commitment to the action motorically coded by the neuron. Thus, the system for action control becomes a system that registers actions and can use this capacity to produce actions similar to those observed (imitation) or actions that are motorically unrelated to the observed ones (as in sign language).

In the case of $Grasp_A(Object)$, once the grasp is initiated, can one assert that the activity in F5 now becomes part of the declarative "$Grasp_A(Self, Object)$"? It is difficult to answer this question. The neuron discharge observed after the onset of hand shaping may have different functions. It may reinforce the initial command to open the hand, it may command the hand closure, it may represent a corollary discharge or be related to a proprioceptive input triggered by the active hand movement. When tested "passively" (passive joint movements) some "classical" F5 neurons show a remarkable proprioceptive discharge (Rizzolatti *et al.*, 1988; Hepp-Reymond *et al.*, 1994). Thus, at least for some neurons, one can posit that the discharge following the beginning of the movement is the declarative "$Grasp_A(Self, Object)$".

Conclusions

As stated in the Introduction, the idea of linking the evolution of language to manual gesture is an old one. However, new neurophysiological and PET data have allowed us to present a new view of the issue, much more rooted in the physiological reality. Our key novelty was the proof that there is a mechanism in the grasp system able to recognize actions. Without such a mechanism, the motor system would lack a fundamental property of language, i.e., that of being able to recognize messages as well as to send them. The recently discovered mirror neurons in monkey premotor cortex provide the primate motor system with an intrinsic capacity to compare the actions it generates with those generated by other individuals. It has therefore the potential to be both the sender and the receiver of messages.

Electrophysiological and PET experiments in humans showed that the human motor system becomes active during observation of gestures made by others and that Broca's area and the left temporal lobe are consistently activated during action observation (Fadiga *et al.*, 1995; Rizzolatti *et al.*, 1996b; Grafton *et al.*, 1996b). It appears, therefore, that the lateral brain system (temporo-frontal) that in humans mediates speech is also involved in gesture recognition, a function involving the homologous areas in the monkey. Our proposal is therefore that a fundamental, evolutionarily old mechanism for recognition of actions devoid of communicative intent is at the basis of the recognition of facial and manual gesture endowed with this intent. Generation and recognition of sounds connected with communicative gestures was, we hypothesize, the next step toward speech. It was here that speech started.

As far as grammar is concerned, we adopted a "case structure" grammar for analyzing hand actions. We have been careful to distinguish (i) "case structure" as studied in the monkey: a search for the neural representations of perceptually guided actions, from (ii) "case structure" as studied in the human: a search for the neural representations of linguistic structures. However, by relating "uttering a sentence" to "achieving a goal", we have "reduced the evolutionary distance" between action and utterance, thus increasing the plausibility of our overall hypothesis.

The problem of transforming an underlying case structure to a sentence (one of many possibilities) which expresses it may be seen as analogous to the non-linguistic problem of planning the right order of actions to achieve a complex goal. Suppose the monkey wants to grab food, but then – secondarily – realizes it must open a door to get the food. Then in planning the action, the order food-then-door must be reversed. This is like the syntactic problem of producing a well-formed sentence, but now viewed as going from "ideas in the head" to a sequence of word/actions in the right order to achieve some communicative/instrumental goal.

Finally, in our analysis of the "grammar" of actions we made explicit that the neural principle underlying organization of action is that of a combinatorial system. Each of the "classical" F5 neurons codes a discrete motor act (e.g., precision grip, whole hand prehension, wrist rotation). Action planning consists in selecting the appropriate neurons and combining them into appropriate patterns of temporal activation. The action structure does not belong, therefore, to a "blending" system, like, for example, color coding where the properties of the combination lie between the properties of its elements and the properties of single elements are lost in the average. On the contrary the basic structure of motor activity is formed by a lexicon of neurons and the acts they stand for. Not surprisingly (if one admits the common origin), the analogy with language is very strict. Unfortunately, very little can be said on the neurophysiological basis of the rules that combine the motor words. A possible guess is that this organization depends on medial cortical areas such as pre-SMA as well as the basal ganglia. Any conclusion on this point is, however, too premature.

References

Arbib, M.A. (1981) Perceptual structures and distributed motor control, *Handbook of Physiology, Section 2: The Nervous System*, Vol. II, Motor Control, Part 1 (V.B. Brooks,

Ed.), American Physiological Society, New York: Oxford University Press, pp. 1449–1480.

Arbib, M.A. (1985) *In Search of the Person: Philosophical Explorations in Cognitive Science*, Amherst: University of Massachusetts Press.

Arbib, M.A. and Caplan, D. (1979) Neurolinguistics must be computational. *Behavioral and Brain Sciences* 2: 449–483.

Arbib, M.A. and Hesse, M.B. (1986) *The Construction of Reality*, Cambridge: Cambridge University Press.

Armstrong, D.F., Stokoe, W.C., and Wilcox, S.E. (1995) *Gesture and the Nature of Language*, Cambridge: Cambridge University Press.

Bell, B.D. (1994) Pantomime recognition impairment in aphasia: an analysis of error types. *Brain and Language* 47: 269–278.

Benson, D.F. (1988) Classical syndromes of aphasia. In F. Boller and J. Grafman (Eds), *Handbook of Neuropsychology*, vol. 1, Amsterdam: Elsevier, pp. 267–280.

Bonda, E., Petrides, M., Frey, S., and Evans, A.C. (1994) Frontal cortex involvement in organized sequences of hand movements: evidence from a positron emission tomography study. *Society for Neuroscience Abstracts*, 152.6.

Brain, W.R. (1961) *Speech Disorders: Aphasia, Apraxia and Agnosia*, Washington, DC: Butterworth.

Bruce, C.J. (1988) Single neuron activity in the monkey's prefrontal cortex. In P. Rakic and W. Singer (Eds), *Neurobiology of Neocortex*, Chichester: Wiley, pp. 297–329.

Bruce, C.J., Goldberg, M.E., Bushnell, M.C., and Stanton, G.B. (1985) Primate frontal eye fields. II. Physiological and anatomical correlates of electrically evoked eye movements. *Journal of Neurophysiology* 54: 714–734.

Cappa, S.F. and Vignolo, L.A. (1996) Le basi neurologiche del linguaggio. In G.F. Denes and L. Pizzamiglio (Eds), *Manuale di neuropsicologia*, Bologna: Zanichelli, pp. 210–238.

Chollet, F., Di Piero, V., Wise, R., Brooks, D.J., Dolan, R.J., and Frackoviak, R.S.J. (1991) The functional anatomy of functional recovery after stroke in humans. *Annals of Neurology* 29: 63–71.

Decety, J., Perani, D., Jeannerod, M., Bettinardi, V., Tadary, B., Woods, R., Mazziotta, J.C., and Fazio, F. (1994) Mapping motor representations with positron emission tomography. *Nature* 371: 600–602.

Dejerine, J. (1914) *Sémeiologie des affections du système nerveux*, Paris: Masson.

Di Pellegrino, G., Fadiga, L., Fogassi, L., Gallese, V., and Rizzolatti, G. (1992) Understanding motor events: a neurophysiological study. *Experimental Brain Research* 91: 176–180.

Duffy, J.R. and Watkins, L.B. (1984) The effect of response choice relatedness on pantomime and verbal recognition ability in aphasic patients. *Brain and Language* 21: 291–306.

Fadiga, L., Fogassi, L., Pavesi, G., and Rizzolatti, G. (1995) Motor facilitation during action observation: a magnetic stimulation study. *Journal of Neurophysiology* 73: 2608–2611.

Fagg, A.H. and Arbib, M.A. (1996) Modeling parietal-premotor interactions in primate control of grasping, to appear.

Fillmore, C.J. (1966) The case for case. In E. Bach and R.T. Harms (Eds), *Universals in Linguistic Theory*, New York: Holt, Rinehart and Winston, pp. 1–88.

Gainotti, G. and Lemmo, M. (1976) Comprehension of symbolic gestures in aphasia. *Brain and Language* 3: 451–460.

Gallese, V., Fadiga, L., Fogassi, L., and Rizzolatti, G. (1996) Action recognition in the premotor cortex. *Brain* 119: 593–609.

Goodale, M.A., Milner, A.D., Jakobson, L.S., and Carey, D.P. (1991) A neurological dissociation between perceiving objects and grasping them. *Nature* 349: 154–156.

Grafton, S.T., Fagg, A.H., Woods, R.P., and Arbib, M.A. (1996a) Functional anatomy of pointing and grasping in humans. *Cerebral Cortex* 6: 226–237.

Grafton, S.T., Arbib, M.A., Fadiga, L., and Rizzolatti, G. (1996b) Localization of grasp representations in humans by PET: 2. Observation compared with imagination. *Experimental Brain Research* 112: 103–111.

Hepp-Reymond, M.-C., Husler, E.J., Maier, M.A., and Qi, H.-X. (1994) Force-related neuronal activity in two regions of the primate ventral premotor cortex. *Canadian Journal of Physiology and Pharmacology* 72: 571–579.

Hewes, G. (1973) Primate communication and the gestural origin of language. *Current Anthropology* 14: 5–24.

Hickok, G., Bellugi, U., and Klima, E. (1996) The neurobiology of signed language and its implications for the neural basis of language. *Nature* 381: 699–702.

Humphrey, N.K. (1970) What the frog's eye tells the monkey's brain. *Brain, Behavior and Evolution* 3: 324–337.

Iberall, T., Bingham, G., and Arbib, M.A. (1986) Opposition space as a structuring concept for the analysis of skilled hand movements. *Experimental Brain Research Series* 15: 158–173.

Jackson, J.H. (1878–79) On affections of speech from disease of the brain. *Brain* 1: 304–330; 2: 203–222, 323–356.

Jeannerod, M. (1994) The representing brain: neural correlates of motor intention and imagery. *Behavioral and Brain Sciences* 17: 187–245.

Jeannerod, M., Arbib, M.A., Rizzolatti, G., and Sakata, H. (1995) Grasping objects: the cortical mechanisms of visuomotor transformation. *Trends in Neurosciences* 18: 314–320.

Jeannerod, M., Decety, J., and Michel, F. (1994) Impairment of grasping movement following a bilateral posterior parietal lesion. *Neuropsychologia* 32: 369–380.

Jurgens, U. (1987) Primate communication: signalling, vocalization. In G. Adelman (Ed.), *Encyclopedia of Neuroscience*, Boston: Birkhauser.

Kimura, D. (1990) How special is language? Review of book by H. Poizner, E.S. Klima and U. Bellugi entitled *What the Hands Reveal about the Brain*. *Sign Language Studies* 66: 79–84.

Kimura, D. (1993) *Neuromotor Mechanisms in Human Communication*, New York, Oxford: Oxford University Press.

Kimura, D., Battison, R., and Lubert, B. (1976) Impairment of non-linguistic hand movements in a deaf aphasic. *Brain and Language* 3: 566–571.

Kimura, D., Davidson, W., and McCormick, C.W. (1982) No impairment in sign language after right-hemisphere stroke. *Brain and Language* 17: 359–362.

Leinonen, L. and Nyman, G. (1979) II. Functional properties of cells in anterolateral part of area 7 associative face area of awake monkeys. *Experimental Brain Research* 34: 321–333.

Lieberman, P. (1985) On the evolution of human syntactic ability. Its pre-adaptive bases – motor control and speech. *Journal of Human Evolution* 14: 657–668.

Liberman, A.M., Cooper, F.S., Shankweiler, D.P., and Studdert-Kennedy, M. (1967) Perception of the speech code. *Psychological Review* 74: 431–461.

Liberman, A.M. and Mattingly, I.G. (1985) The motor theory of speech perception revised. *Cognition* 21: 1–36.

Liberman, A.M. and Mattingly, I.G. (1989) A specialization for speech perception. *Science* 243: 489–494.

Liberman, A.M. and Studdert-Kennedy, M. (1978) Phonetic perception. In R. Held, H.W. Leibowitz, and H.L. Teuber (Eds), *Handbook of Sensory Physiology, Vol. VIII: Perception*, New York: Springer-Verlag.

Maclean, P.D. (1993) Introduction: perspectives on cingulate cortex in the limbic system. In B.A. Vogt and M. Gabriel (Eds), *Neurobiology of Cingulate Cortex and Limbic Thalamus: A Comprehensive Handbook*, Boston: Birkhauser.

MacNeilage, P.F. (in press) The frame/content theory of evolution of speech production. *Behavioral and Brain Sciences*.

Matelli, M., Camarda, R., Glickstein, M., and Rizzolatti, G. (1986) Afferent and efferent projections of the inferior area 6 in the macaque monkey. *Journal of Computational Neurology* 251: 281–298.

Matelli, M., Luppino, G., and Rizzolatti G. (1985) Patterns of cytochrome oxidase activity in the frontal agranular cortex of macaque monkey. *Behavioral and Brain Research* 18: 125–137.

Matelli, M., Luppino, G., Govoni, P., and Geyer, S. (1996) Anatomical and functional subdivisions of inferior area 6 in macaque monkey. *Society for Neuroscience Abstracts*.

Matsumura, M. and Kubota, K. (1979) Cortical projection of hand-arm motor area from postarcuate area in macaque monkey: a histological study of retrograde transport of horseradish peroxidase. *Neuroscience Letters* 11: 241–246.

Milner, A.D. and Goodale, M.A. (1995) *The Visual Brain in Action*, Oxford: Oxford University Press.

Muakkassa, K.F. and Strick, P.L. (1979) Frontal lobe inputs to primate motor cortex: evidence for four somatotopically organized "premotor" areas. *Brain Research* 177: 176–182.

Neville, H., Bavelier, D., Corina, D., Padmanabahn, S., Clark, V.P., Braun, A., Rauscheker, J., Jezzard, P., and Turner, R. (1996) Effects of experience on cerebral organization for language: fMRI studies of hearing and deaf subjects. *International Journal of Psychology* 31, Abstract no. 434.

Parsons, L.M., Fox, P.T., Hunter Downs, J., Glass, T., Hirsch, T.B., Martin, C.C., Jerabek, P.A., and Lancaster, J.L. (1995) Use of implicit motor imagery for visual shape discrimination as revealed by PET. *Nature* 375: 54–58.

Passingham, R. (1993) *The Frontal Lobes and Voluntary Action*, Oxford: Oxford University Press.

Penfield, W. and Roberts, L. (1959) *Speech and Brain Mechanisms*, Princeton: Princeton University Press.

Perrett, D.I., Harries, M.H., Bevan, R., Thomas, S., Benson, P.J., Mistlin, A.J., Chitty, A.K., Hietanen, J.K., and Ortega, J.E. (1989) Frameworks of analysis for the neural representation of animate objects and actions. *Journal of Experimental Biology* 146: 87–113.

Perrett, D.I., Mistlin, A.J., Harries, M.H., and Chitty, A.J. (1990) Understanding the visual appearance and consequence of hand actions. In M.A. Goodale (Ed.), *Vision and Action: The Control of Grasping*, Norwood, NJ: Ablex, pp. 163–180.

Petrides, M. and Pandya, D.N. (1994) Comparative architectonic analysis of the human and the macaque frontal cortex. In F. Boller and J. Grafman (Eds), *Handbook of Neuropsychology*, vol. IX. Amsterdam: Elsevier, pp. 17–58.

Poizner, H., Klima, E.S., and Bellugi, U. (1987) *What the Hands Reveal about the Brain*, Cambridge, Mass.: MIT Press/Bradford Books.

Popper, K. and Eccles, J. (1977) *The Self and its Brain*, Berlin: Springer-Verlag.

Rizzolatti, G. (1987) Functional organization of area 6. In *Motor Areas of Cerebral Cortex* (Ciba Foundation Symposium 132), Chichester: Wiley, pp. 171–186.

Rizzolatti, G., Camarda, R., Fogassi, L., Gentilucci, M., Luppino, G., and Matelli, M. (1988) Functional organization of inferior area 6 in the macaque monkey: II. Area F5 and the control of distal movements. *Experimental Brain Research* 71: 491–507.

Rizzolatti, G., Fadiga, L., Gallese, V., and Fogassi, L. (1996a) Premotor cortex and the recognition of motor actions. *Cognitive Brain Research* 3: 131–141.

Rizzolatti, G., Fadiga, L., Matelli, M., Bettinardi, V., Perani, D., and Fazio, F. (1996b) Localization of grasp representations in humans by positron emission tomography: 1. Observation versus execution. *Experimental Brain Research* 111: 246–252.

Rizzolatti, G., Gentilucci, M., Camarda, R., Gallese, V., Luppino, G., Matelli, M., and Fogassi, L. (1990) Neurons related to reaching-grasping arm movements in the rostral part of area 6 (area 6ab). *Experimental Brain Research* 82: 337–350.

Sakata, H., Taira, M., Mine, S., and Murata, A. (1992) Hand-movement related neurons of the posterior parietal cortex of the monkey: their role in visual guidance of hand movements. In R. Caminiti, P.B. Johnson, and Y. Burnod (Eds), *Control of Arm Movement in Space, Experimental Brain Research Suppl. 22*, Berlin: Springer-Verlag, pp. 185–198.

Sarno, J., Swisher, L., and Sarno, M. (1969) Aphasia in a congenitally deaf man. *Cortex* 5: 398–414.

Schlaug, G., Knorr, U., and Seitz, R.J. (1994) Inter-subject variability of cerebral activations in acquiring a motor skill: a study with positron emission tomography. *Experimental Brain Research* 98: 523–534.

Taira, M., Mine, S., Georgopoulos, A.P., Murata, A., and Sakata, H. (1990) Parietal cortex neurons of the monkey related to the visual guidance of hand movement. *Experimental Brain Research* 83: 29–36.

Van Riemsdijk, H. and Williams, E. (1986) *Introduction to the Theory of Grammar*, Cambridge, Mass.: MIT Press.

Weiskrantz, L., Warrington, E.K., Sanders, M.D., and Marshall, J. (1974) Visual capacity in the hemianopic field following a restricted occipital ablation. *Brain* 97: 709–728.

7   Is "mind" a scientific kind?

Andy Clark

1 Three models of mind and cognition

The title question (Is "mind" a scientific kind?) invites a consideration of just about every major problem in Philosophy of Science and several in Philosophy of Mind. Needless to say, I do not propose to attempt anything quite so grand. Instead, I will address the somewhat narrower question: how should we conceive the relation between scientific studies of cognition and the folk ontology that depicts minds as loci of beliefs, desires, concepts, propositional attitudes, etc.? In particular, I shall first consider and reject two extreme options, viz.:

(a) That the folk ontology must, on pain of eliminativism, be reconstructible using only the resources of some scientific study of cognitive processes.
(b) That the folk ontology is legitimated by gross behaviour patterns alone and is conceptually independent of whatever science can tell us about inner states and processes.

As a kind of rough shorthand, I shall describe position (a) as the thesis that the various items in the folk ontology, to be real, must turn out to name inner scientific kinds. And I shall describe (b) as the thesis that such items name purely observational kinds. The rejection of (a) will flow from a discussion of the point and purpose of folk psychological talk. The rejection of (b) will flow from a discussion of familiar counter-examples to the thesis that mind is just an observational kind, viz. another look at the contemporary Cartesian demons: Giant Look-up Tables and Quantum Fluke Beings. I shall end by developing an alternative thesis:

(c) That the folk ontology of minds and mental contents, although not required itself to pick out scientific kinds, is none the less required to be broadly *intelligible* given a correct scientific understanding of cognition.

The challenge, of course, is to make clear what this notion of intelligibility amounts to insofar as it is something weaker than the requirement that folk constructs must name scientific kinds. I take some steps in that direction by introducing requirements concerning the intelligibility of depicting a system as issuing recall-dependent judgements and the intelligibility of depicting it as a locus of conscious mental states and/or qualitative experience. I suggest that our intuitions about the contemporary demons (Giant Look-up Tables etc.) are best treated as rooted in such requirements.

In sum, I shall argue that the folk ontology of mind is in essence a practical tool which makes minimal (but real) demands on the types of inner workings compatible with its correct deployment. The product is thus a version of Dennett (1987), but one that tries also for a concrete picture of some minimal inner requirements on True Believers. Or, if you prefer, it is a version of Ryle (1949), but without the total rejection of science as impacting upon the conception of mind.

2 Against Super-Fodorian realism

The thesis that the folk ontology of mental states must, on pain of eliminativism, be neatly reconstructible in some more scientific milieu amounts to a doctrine which I label Super-Fodorian realism (Clark, 1993). The doctrine is *super-*Fodorian in that where Fodor sees the existence of a folk-content encoding inner code as an empirical fact (the a posteriori explanation of the systematicity of thoughts ascribed using the apparatus of folk psychology), the Super-Fodorian sees the existence of such a code as conceptually essential to the truth of belief/desire citing explanations. If science were to show us that *concepts* and *propositions* do not exist as scientifically identifiable inner items the folk mentalistic ontology would (according to the Super-Fodorian) be bankrupt. Why should this be so? Although there exist a variety of Super-Fodorian arguments in the contemporary literature, they all share a basic structure. I shall first exhibit that structure, then flesh it out with a single representative example. The basic structure involves an argument from *disunity*. It goes like this.

Argument from disunity

1   Folk psychology individuates mental states using an apparatus of attitudes (belief, desire, etc.) and propositions. And it individuates propositions as distinct structures of concepts.
2   Folk psychology is thus committed to a specific account of *sameness for mental states*, viz. that distinct mental states may involve different attitudes to the *same* propositional content, and that different propositional contents may involve the *same* concept.
3   But suppose a good scientific story about our inner cognitive workings fails to identify scientifically respectable inner states that recapitulate these judgements of sameness? Suppose the inner story posits unstable, elusive or fragmentary items where the folk story posits a recurrent entity (concept or proposition)?

4   In such cases the folk story must be abandoned as the order it depicts is
     revealed as illusory.

Versions of the argument from disunity can be found in Davies (1991), Stich
(1983) and Ramsey, Stich and Garon (1991). To report a single example,
Davies (1991) depicts the folk as committed to a vision in which an individual's mastery of a given concept (say, the concept of "bachelor") is invoked
to explain a host of behaviours (e.g. all their inferences from the information
that so and so is a bachelor to the conclusion that so and so is unmarried).
The folk thus invoke a single item (the concept "bachelor") in a variety of
explanations of someone's behaviour (verbal behaviour, in this case). But,
Davies insists, the mere fact that there is a discernible pattern in the individual's inferential behaviour cannot guarantee that it is mastery of a single
concept that explains the behaviour. What if our hero/heroine is a big look-
up table with a separate entry for the inference for each possible name in the
language? The folk story, in discerning an underlying unity in the observed
behaviours, is committed (Davies argues) to a certain kind of inner scientific
story, viz. one in which the concepts picked out by folk psychology exist as
discrete and literally recurring inner syntactic items. In short, there had better
exist something very like an inner language of thought if the folk explanations
are to be accepted as legitimate.
   The trouble with such Super-Fodorian arguments is that they trade on ambi-
guities in the notion of sameness. In Davies' case, the ambiguity is between
the claims

(a) that the same *concept-mastery* is implicated in several behaviours; and
(b) that the same concept (conceived as a kind of discrete inner data struc-
     ture) is present and active in several behaviours.

Thus suppose that learning to use the word "dog" in a way that meets public
criteria involves training several disparate and internally disunified cognitive
resources. What the training results in is thus a kind of tuning of many different
parts of an overall system. Upon successful completion of such training, we say
of someone that he has mastered the concept. If on one occasion he then uses
inner resource X to power an appropriate response and on another occasion
he uses a different inner resource, Y, it remains true to say that it is, in a sense,
the single *concept mastery* that explains each behaviour. Yet it is also true that
(in Davies' terminology) there need be no causal common factor active on
each occasion. Grasp of a concept, I therefore want to say, may be akin to
possession of a *global skill* (cf. Evans, 1982, pp. 101–102). Just as an individual
may be said to have a skill at golf (a skill that explains both successful putting
and successful driving) and yet deploy quite distinct cognitive sub-skills to
power various manifestations of this global skill, so she may possess global
conceptual skills whose internal cognitive underpinning is various and fragmentary.

Such an image (of folk psychology as naming global skills emergent out of potentially messy and disunified complexes of inner workings) allows folk-individuative practices to co-exist with several recent lines of scientific conjecture concerning cognition, viz.:

1   The evidence of internal disunity between brain systems responsible for verbal and non-verbal behaviours (used misguidedly by Stich (1983) as an argument in favour of eliminativism).
2   The evidence for an unexpectedly strange and rich body of possible dissociations of cognitive abilities coming from cognitive neuropsychology (Ellis and Young, 1988; Warrington and McCarthy, 1987; Shallice, 1988; Humphreys and Riddoch, 1987).
3   The distributed connectionist model of lexical knowledge in which local contextual information results in subtly different internal representations corresponding to the same folk-individuated content on different occasions (cf. Elman's (1991) comment that in his lexical categorization network there are no recurrent canonical representations of lexical items and that instead "it is literally the case that every occurrence of a lexical item has a separate internal representation").

In the inner economy, the folk items may well dissolve, reform or fragment. Things fall apart. But if our description of the folk vocabulary as specifying global skills evidenced in the daily behaviours of whole agents is correct, then such fragmentation, in and of itself, is interesting but harmless. The folk mentalistic ontology need not specify integral scientific kinds. It is an easy mistake, however, to think that the folk ontology, if it is not required to name scientific kinds, is altogether immune to the influence of scientific discoveries. Not so, as we shall now see.

3 Against mere ascriptivism

In attempting to insulate folk psychology from the misguided demands of the Super-Fodorian realist, it is tempting to fall back on a position in which all that matters, as far as the acceptability of the folk ontology and explanations goes, are the patterns in gross behaviour. The presence of these patterns is then seen as exhausting the commitments of the folk discourse. Where such patterns exist, according to this vision, the folk discourse is properly deployed. The most famous (albeit most slippery) proponent of such a pure ascriptivism is the Daniel Dennett of Dennett (1987, 1988). Dennett calls the practice of explaining something's behaviour by reference to beliefs/desires etc. "taking the intentional stance" towards that object. And he comments that "Any object – whatever its innards – that is reliably and voluminously predictable from the stance is in the fullest sense of the word a believer" (Dennett, 1988, p. 496).

    The trouble with such a forthright ascriptivism, famously, is that it threatens to let in bizarre cases in which we have strong intuitions that, voluminously predictable from the intentional stance or no, the object in question just ain't a True Believer (a haver of genuine beliefs and desires). A classic case is the Giant Look-up Table: a super-fast, super-large computer that stores a distinct output for each and every one of a vast number of inputs and uses this brute force approach to produce behaviour in which Dennett style patterns are rife. Or you may prefer my own example, the Quantum Fluke Being: a cosmic accident creature that gets all the behaviours right but does so by an increasingly unlikely (but never 100 per cent impossible) series of accidents. Its innards are disorganized mush, yet it exhibits nice patterns in gross behaviour. Or you may prefer Lycan's Zombies (Lycan, 1988, pp. 518–519), or Chris Peacocke's Martian Marionettes (Peacocke, 1983). The moral is the same: the folk's commitments don't stop at the surface of the skin.

So where do they stop? Davies had a neat story (section 1 above) in which the lack of re-usable syntactic entities corresponding to the semantic items of the folk story torpedoed look-up tables and their ilk. But we found it too demanding. Bennett (1991) offers, interestingly, an almost diametrically opposed thought, viz. that genuine intentionality requires not just a behaviour pattern susceptible to an intentional description but *also* that that pattern should *not* be the result of the operation of a single mechanism. Instead, Bennett argues, we have genuine intentionality only when the intentional description reveals a unity which is not visible at the mechanistic level. Bennett thus insists on what he calls a *unity position* which posits, as a necessary condition on genuine intentional descriptions, that the description depicts as conceptually unified some set of facts which *cannot* be so unified by reference to the underlying mechanistic story. Thermostats fail the test, as a single mechanistic explanation can replace the ones citing desires to achieve certain temperatures etc. By contrast, Bennett expects that there will be no single mechanism that mediates all the behaviours that we might describe in a higher animal using a generalization such as "it is doing x because it thinks x will bring food". Why? Because the range of behaviours that might fall under this rubric includes different kinds of bodily motion and responses to different inputs. Hence "We are soberly entitled to suppose that no one mechanism explains all this behaviour" (Bennett, 1991, p. 180).

Bennett thus *insists* that the True Believers' innards be fragmentary relative to the folk description. What Davies saw as downright inimical to the proper use of the folk talk, Bennett seems to depict as essential! My own view is that the whole approach of *counting mechanisms* is importantly misguided – not least because it depends on some very slippery notion of how to individuate mechanisms (when is it right to speak of one mechanistic route mediating an input/output pattern, and when of two, etc. I doubt if there are principled answers to such questions). The view developed in section 1 is rather that the inner story may be fragmentary OR non-fragmentary (relative to the folk ontology) without thereby compromising the integrity of the folk talk. In short, I count the Davies/Bennett lines as orthogonal to the question of the commitments of the folk discourse.

Dennett himself does not propose any form of mechanism counting as a response to the worries we raised. But he does feel driven to concede that "If one gets confirmation of a much too simple mechanical explanation – this really does disconfirm the fancy intentional level account" (Dennett, 1988, pp. 542–543). This is clearly the kind of intuition that Bennett sought to make precise by insisting on a multiplicity of mechanisms underlying each genuine intentional generalization. But it is hard to justify. Why should the possession of relatively simple innards unfit a being for the ranks of the True Believers? Simplicity *per se* is not a crime. And suppose it did turn out that a simple inner mechanism was mediating all of a certain sub-set of my behaviours. Why should that, in and of itself, work against an intentional/folk psychological description of those behaviours? The various moves in the debate, it seems to me, are curiously unmotivated: more an *ad hoc* attempt to regiment intuitions than to explain or justify them. Pure ascriptivism, just about everyone (including Dennett) agrees, won't quite do. But the shape of an alternative remains elusive.

4 The intelligibility constraint[1]

To get a better (workable) grip on the conceptual bonds linking the folk discourse and scientific studies of cognition, we need to give up a certain obsession. What has to go, I believe, is the obsession with reductive relations between types of description of complex systems. Both Davies' and Bennett's attempts to pin down the nature of the folk's inner commitments revolve around attempts to specify the necessary shape of reductive relations between individual items in the folk ontology and inner mechanisms. But a better tack, I suggest, may be to concentrate rather on the broad *properties* that the folk ascriptions assume and then to ask (of any given account of underlying mechanisms) whether the scientific story renders intelligible the possession of such properties. If it renders the possession of a property unintelligible, and if the property seems to be close to the heart of the folk framework, we may conclude that the truth of that scientific description is indeed incompatible with the acceptability of the folk framework. Otherwise (and regardless of the neat fit, or of a lack of it, between the folk and scientific ontologies) all is well.

To get a sense of the kind of approach I have in mind, consider the case in which someone claims to have made a mistake in his deployment of a concept. Thus imagine that one day I say to you "I must admit I made a mistake when I said that all fish-meat was soft: I now recall eating some shark-meat which was quite tough." On hearing this, you might characterize me, in folk-psychological mode, as believing that I made such and such a mistake and as being prompted to recognize that mistake by recalling a certain experience. But suppose you then discover that my inner cognitive economy takes the form of a big look-up table. One implication of this is that each of my various judgements and behaviours is issued in full informational isolation from the rest. That is to say, my response today to a question such as "Are you sure that what you said about all fish-meat being soft is correct?" is in fact issued without recourse to any causal process in which a memory of my previous judgement is retrieved and a comparison of that judgement against a body of stored information is made. To learn this, I assert, is to learn that the folk description of my behaviour (as being prompted, by recalling a previous experience, to judge that I previously judged incorrectly) is untenable. Note that it is not rendered untenable because of a failure to isolate neat internal analogues to the folk items. Rather, it is untenable because once we know how the inner processing system operates, we can see that some very general assumptions we had been making (viz. that the "agent" could recall previous judgements and compare such judgements against a body of stored knowledge) cannot be sustained.

Whether such a discovery would undermine the whole folk psychological enterprise would then depend on how essential these properties are to the picture of intentional agency. In the case imagined, they strike me as sufficiently central to warrant the elimination of the folk framework. Fortunately, nothing in the real scientific stories mentioned in section 2 threatens to have any such effect. All those stories depict us as complex information processing devices capable of recall, generalization and inference. Their only "crime" was to fail to recapitulate the detailed taxonomy of the folk discourse. But this, I contend, is no crime at all. As long as the global properties assumed by the folk discourse can intelligibly be supposed to be possessed by beings with a given inner constitution, folk psychology is innocent.

I will give one more example of the kind of global property I have in mind, though this one may prove contentious. I am willing to assert that the folk practice of ascribing grasp of a concept assumes some kind of potential consciousness of content on the part of the beings to whom it is correctly applied. For example, it strikes me as conceptually incoherent to depict a being as, on the one hand, knowing the meaning of the concept "dog", and on the other hand being incapable of enjoying any conscious episode in which the idea of a dog figures. Even if I cannot persuade you of that, you might at least agree that very often, folk psychology depicts agents as consciously entertaining specific thoughts. Suppose, then, that we one day achieve a satisfying scientific theory which depicts a certain (no doubt very high-level and abstract) computational organization as a necessary condition of conscious experience.[2] And suppose, in addition, that a certain recently encountered alien life-form, which we had hitherto regarded as grasping certain concepts and having a variety of conscious experiences, failed to possess the requisite inner organization. Then (unless we take this to cast doubt on the scientific theory – a live option) we should, I claim, at least conclude that parts of our folk description were wrong. And we might (depending on the extent to which we are willing to tie concept grasp to consciousness) even feel that most of our folksy descriptions of the being had been undermined. Once again, the moral is that the folk framework trades on large-scale properties (consciousness, recall, and others I have not discussed such as generalization and inference) whose presence gross behaviour is simply insufficient to guarantee. Only innards whose scientific description leaves intelligible the possession of such properties are to be countenanced as fit for True Believers.

5 The bearable vagueness of believing

In attempting to dodge between the counterbalanced infelicities of the Super-Fodorian and the Pure Ascriptivist, I am exposed to a variety of worries and criticisms. I therefore end with a brief defensive tour.

First worry: mental causation

In recent years, the issue of mental causation has come to dominate the discussion of the putative virtues and vices of the folk framework. Thus Fodor (1987) clearly sees it as a major virtue of any reductive/syntactic inner story that it allows us to make easy mechanistic sense of the idea of a specific belief (or whatever) being a cause. If we are willing to give up on the hope of such straightforward reduction without thereby giving up on the folk framework, what are we to say about mental causation?

One swift, clean move is to give up on the image of beliefs as mechanistic causes and instead to focus on the (purely) explanatory virtues of the folk framework. This is the kind of move that Dennett makes in speaking of the way folk content ascriptions allow us to predict who will or will not appreciate a certain joke and so on (Dennett, 1987). The folk talk here tells us what bodies of information the subject is familiar with. This is useful information regardless of whether neat reductive analogues to specific belief contents are to be found. Something that falls far short of a detailed description of the specific inner events that enter into the push and shove of creation can none the less tell us a lot about the likely patterns of behaviour of other agents. We may thus give up on the individual, folk-described, beliefs as discrete causes and yet still value and exploit the intentional descriptions of agents.

Alternatively (less neatly, I concede) we may question the assimilation of causation to simple mechanistic episodes of push and shove. I remain tempted by (though I shall not attempt to defend) the idea that our understanding of caustion is parasitic on our understanding of explanation and that all good explanation is, in at least some indirect sense, causal explanation. But whichever: either broaden the notion of causal to encompass global, emergent phenomena as causes, or insist that the folk talk is explanatory, though not causal explanatory. The point is, a discourse can be powerful and valuable regardless of whether its favoured entities have neat reductive analogues that participate in the push and shove of low-level creation. (Compare: "The car crashed because of its poor cornering." Cornering is a global property not reducible to any single mechanistic fact. Instead, a car corners well or badly due to the combined influence of several internal and external factors. Yet poor cornering, more's the pity, really can cause crashes.)

Mental causation, I conclude, is more a red herring than a fulcrum of debate, I hereby bracket it, and move on to:

Second worry: semi-believers, and demi-semi-believers

The characteristic items of the folk mentalistic ontology are, I suggested, in all likelihood names for highly fragmented bags of subpersonal cognitive competences. Thus to say of someone that he grasps a given concept, or that he believes a certain proposition, is to comment on an overall (gross behavioural) competence whose internal roots may be almost (but not quite) arbitrarily fragmented. One upshot of this, which some people find uncomfortable, is that the notion of sameness of belief becomes rather fluid. Two agents (or one agent at two times) may share enough sub-competences to count, for some purposes, as sharing the belief; yet differ with respect to enough subcompetences to count, for other purposes, as not sharing the same belief. Likewise, if grasp of a concept is subserved by a panoply of disparate subpersonal abilities, a being may count as more or less grasping a concept according to how many such abilities it possesses. Nor need there be any neat answer to the question: if we subtract these sub-abilities, will the agent still count as grasping the concept/having the belief or whatever?

I confess to being secretly pleased with this turn of events. The macro-level folk constructs will apply to a greater or lesser extent, and in ways largely determined by the contingencies of a specific deployment of the folk discourse. In problem cases (infants, animals, brain-damaged patients – see Stich, 1983) there will indeed be no answer to the question "does the organism fall under this folk description or not?" In respect of some sub-abilities, yes. In respect of others, no. For this purpose, yes. For that purpose, no. This strikes me as entirely intuitive. There really is no God-given answer in such cases. And (as a rule of thumb) where God fails, Philosophy and Cognitive Science had better not succeed!

Third worry: the fragmentation of the global properties

The scientific commitments of the folk image of mind are exhausted, I claim, by some set of rather global information-processing properties, for example having innards that support genuine recall and comparison, that allow qualitative experience, etc. But what if these global properties should themselves fragment: what if, for example, we found a being who met the scientific criteria for conscious experience yet who, surprisingly, failed to meet the criteria for genuine recall – a Giant Conscious Look-up Table if you will? In such cases, I am again happy to concede that there is no good answer to the question "Is that a True Believer?" In cases where a host of features co-occurrent in, and conceptually central to, our original exemplars of a certain type come apart, we may rightly say that nothing in our previous usage determines a hard and fast answer to the question. If we then proceed to refine and alter our original conception so as to marginalize some once-central properties and to centralize others, we are engaging in a useful process of stipulative conceptual development. I am quite certain that the concept of a True Believer will undergo such change. But when it does so we should not be misled into imagining that we are literally discovering the proper extension of the original concept.

The potential fragmentation of the kind of global properties I have highlighted is thus no cause for concern. In such cases some of our folk discourse allows us to pose questions that simply have no answers. If, for some new purpose, an answer is positively demanded, that may be a catalyst for conceptual change.

Final worry: what if we fail the tests?

If the folk discourse does indeed make some assumptions about inner stories, it must be logically possible that we ourselves, seen in the naked light of scientific advance, turn out to fail all the tests. For some theorists, the mere logical possibility that *we* could turn out not to be True Believers is a compelling reduction of the attempt to allow the folk discourse to make any contact with scientific stories. For some reason, I cannot get excited about this. I cannot seem to worry about failing a test that I am completely certain I will pass! I agree that were science to one day tell me, for example, that my present outputs in fact never draw on stored knowledge about my past behaviour and experiences, that would be full-scale disaster. But in such a case, turning out not to be a True Believer would, I suggest, be about the least of my worries!

6 Conclusion: a very robust parrot

What is the relation of mind (the folk mentalistic arena of concepts, beliefs, propositions and all the rest) and cognition (the scientific arena of vectors, state spaces, languages of thought or whatever)? We sketched and rejected two extreme views. The first (Super-Fodorian realism) depicted the folk discourse as embodying a commitment to a specific, language-like inner story. The second (pure ascriptivism) lifted every vestige of scientific commitment from the over-burdened shoulders of the folk. As an antidote to both extremes, I have tried to depict folk psychology as assuming some global, quite high-level properties which certain kinds of inner organization may demonstrably fail to underwrite. But these commitments fall far short of demanding that the specific explanatory posits of the folk discourse (concepts, propositions, attitudes) be vindicated by the discovery of corresponding inner scientific kinds. Indeed, the inner story may, consistent with underwriting the global properties, be quite fragmentary and fluid.

Paul Churchland once complained of Dennett's ascriptivism that it was akin to the insistence of Monty Python's famous pet shop owner that a certain terminally inert parrot was not dead but 'just resting'![3] Pure ascriptivism, Churchland argued, was just nailing the parrot to its perch. I have tried for an equally efficient but less drastic solution. The folk psychological parrot, I claim, is merely a very robust kind of animal needing only the minimum of cooperation from scientific advance to live and thrive.

Postscript added in 1997

I think it may be valuable to consider a somewhat different way of presenting the third or middle option (the one that demands only a minimal consonance between the facts about in-the-head processing and the shape and structure of the folk discourse). This way (as per the preceding text) recognizes an increasingly substantial mismatch between the constructs that seem well suited to describing the personal level facts and the emerging constructs of the sciences of the mind. But whereas the original argument seeks to reconcile these two discourses by simply treating the personal level ("folk") discourse as picking out behaviour patterns whose origination is then subject to a few (fairly weak) constraints of the form detailed in section 4, the new defence adds an additional observation concerning one reason we are so easily misled in this particular debate. The idea, to put it very bluntly, is that we fail to see that the folk talk is really targeted not on the profile of the bare biological brain but on the cognitive profile of the embodied, embedded agent.

Thus consider an agent equipped with biological brain, mobile body, public language and a few additional props such as pen and paper. Such an agent constitutes, I would like to say, an extended cognitive system. This system (unlike the bare biological brain) is very clearly a locus of real symbol-manipulating abilities. It can write symbols onto a static medium, and it can manipulate discrete symbol strings in that medium in ways that help to manage decision-making, planning and reasoning. Classical AI itself began as an attempt to get machines to perform the kinds of calculating task that biological agents normally perform using a variety of external aids (see e.g. Hutchins, 1995, Chapter 9). The original vision of classical AI may thus constitute an apt and revealing model not of what goes on in the head but of the abilities of biological brains embedded in the powerful scaffolding environment of body, word and text. To that extent, classical AI may have (somewhat perversely, given its historical roots) mistaken the cognitive profile of the agent-plus-the-environment for that of the naked brain. Many features of the classical vision then fall neatly into place. The neat separation of data and process, of symbol strings and CPU, may ultimately reflect the very real separation between the biological brain and a variety of external information stores persisting on paper, in filing cabinets, and in other media. (For further development of this angle, see Clark, 1989, p. 135; Hutchins, 1995, Chapter 9; Clark, 1997, Chapters 3 and 10; Clark and Chalmers, in press).

Returning to the issues foregrounded in the present volume, we may thus suggest that any full and satisfying reconciliation of the folk and scientific images must elude us as long as we persist in focusing all our scientific attention on the capacities and profile of the naked biological brain. For the folk talk is, after all, meant to illuminate the behaviours and capacities of whole agents, embedded in rich local environments. To assume that the patterns and problem-solving profiles of such highly scaffolded agents directly reflect the computational shape of individual brains is to neglect a major part of what makes human reason so truly special, viz. its capacity to parasitize, structure and exploit a seemingly endless supply of environmental props and aids so as to simplify and transform the problems confronting the biological brain. (See Dennett, 1995, and Clark, 1997, for much more on these themes.)

I thus stand by the basic argument of the original paper. The folk discourse is indeed only weakly and indirectly answerable to scientific accounts of in-the-head reason. But a full defence of this position should do more: it should explain and diagnose the apparent mismatches between the folk and the scientific images. In pursuit of this additional goal, we would do well to see the biological brain for what it truly is: an on-board controller of embodied, environment-exploiting action.

Notes

1   The use of the term "intelligibility" here may recall Cussins' use of a (semi-technical) notion of "Intelligible Connection" in the development of his Construction Constraint (see Cussins, 1990, pp. 374–378). But in fact the two notions are very different. Cussins' notion of an "Intelligible Connection" between levels applies just so long as the "marching in step" of the two kinds of description does not appear as a "miraculous coincidence". But from that perspective, there exists a perfectly "Intelligible Connection" (the capitals indicate Cussins' semi-technical term) between, for example, the innards of the Look-up Table being and the folk level of descriptions of its behaviour. It is no coincidence – but it is not an acceptable implementation because it is UNINTELLIGIBLE (my, non-technical sense) how the folk commitments to normativity (see text) can be met by such a being.
2   For an argument against such an outcome, see Patricia Churchland (1986). For an argument in favour, see Lahav (1993).
3   In a reply to Dennett, reprinted in Churchland (1989), p. 127.

References

Bennett, J. (1991). "Folk Psychological Explanations", in J. Greenwood (ed.) *The Future of Folk Psychology*, Cambridge: Cambridge University Press.

Churchland, P.M. (1989). *The Neurocomputational Perspective*. Cambridge, MA: MIT/Bradford Books.

Churchland, P.S. (1986). *Neurophilosophy: Toward a Unified Science of the Mind-Brain*. Cambridge, MA: MIT Press.

Clark, A. (1989). *Microcognition*. Cambridge, MA: MIT Press.

Clark, A. (1993). *Associative Engines: Connectionism, Concepts and Representational Change*. Cambridge, MA: MIT Press.

Clark, A. (1997). *Being There: Putting Brain, Body and World Together Again*. Cambridge, MA: MIT Press.

Clark, A. and D. Chalmers (in press). *The Extended Mind*.

Cussins, A. (1990). "The Connectionist Construction of Concepts", in M. Boden (ed.) *The Philosophy of Artificial Intelligence*, New York: Oxford University Press, pp. 368–440.

Davies, M. (1991). "Concepts, Connectionism and the Language of Thought", in W. Ramsey, S. Stich and D. Rumelhart (eds) *Philosophy and Connectionist Theory*, Hillsdale, NJ: Erlbaum, pp. 229–258.

Dennett, D. (1987). *The Intentional Stance*. Cambridge, MA: MIT Press.

Dennett, D. (1988). "Précis of the Intentional Stance (and Author's Response)", *Behavioral and Brain Sciences* 2: 495–546.

Dennett, D. (1995). *Darwin's Dangerous Idea*. New York: Simon and Schuster.

Ellis, A. and Young, A. (1988). *Human Cognitive Neuropsychology*. London: Erlbaum.

Elman, J. (1991). *Incremental Learning or the Importance of Starting Small*, Technical Report 9101, Center for Research in Language, University of California, San Diego.

Evans, G. (1982). *The Varieties of Reference*. Oxford: Oxford University Press.

Fodor, J. (1987). *Psychosemantics: The Problem of Meaning in the Philosophy of Mind*. Cambridge, MA: MIT Press.

Humphreys, G. and Riddoch, M. (1987). *To See But not to See: A Case Study of Visual Agnosia*. London: Lawrence Erlbaum.

Hutchins, E. (1995). *Cognition in the Wild*. Cambridge, MA: MIT Press.

Lahav, R. (1993). "What Neuropsychology Tells Us About Consciousness", *Philosophy of Science* 60: 67–85.

Lycan, W. (1988). "Commentary on D. Dennett, *The Intentional Stance*", *Behavioral and Brain Sciences* 2: 518–519.

Peacocke, C. (1983). *Sense and Content: Experience, Thought and Their Relations*. Oxford: Clarendon Press.

Ramsey, W. and Stich, S. (1991). "Connectionism and Three Levels of Nativism", in W. Ramsey, S. Stich and D. Rumelhart (eds) *Philosophy and Connectionist Theory*, Hillsdale, NJ: Erlbaum, pp. 287–310.

Ramsey, W., Stich, S. and Garon, J. (1991). "Connectionism, Eliminativism and the Future of Folk Psychology", in W. Ramsey, S. Stich and D. Rumelhart (eds) *Philosophy and Connectionist Theory*, Hillsdale, NJ: Erlbaum, pp. 199–228.

Ryle, G. (1949). *The Concept of Mind*. London: Hutchinson.

Shallice, T. (1988). *From Neuropsychology to Mental Structure*. Cambridge: Cambridge University Press.

Stich, S. (1983). *From Folk Psychology to Cognitive Science: The Case Against Belief*. Cambridge, MA: MIT/Bradford Books.

Warrington, C. and McCarthy, R. (1987). "Categories of Knowledge: Further Fractionations and an Attempted Integration", *Brain* 110: 1273–1296.

8 Evolution and self-evidence

William S. Robinson

Abstract

Robert Nozick (1993) has offered an evolutionary account of self-evident beliefs that comes into conflict with a "mild realist" (Dennett, 1991a) view of beliefs. This chapter summarizes both views, and explains the conflict. Emergence is examined. Mild realism is found to embrace "emergence" in an acceptable sense, and to eschew it in its problematic sense. Nozick's cases of self-evident beliefs are examined and difficulties in his account are explained. An alternative approach is developed that avoids the difficulties in Nozick's account and is compatible with mild realism. Implications of mild realism for concepts are drawn.

Robert Nozick (1993) has given an interesting evolutionary account of the development of self-evident beliefs. In broad strokes, his idea is that long-term constancy of environmental features permits evolution of structures that take advantage of those features, and beliefs that reflect those features are examples of such advantageous structures. For truly pervasive and constant features, quickness in arriving at a corresponding belief and stability of the belief in the face of superficial variety could confer increments in fitness. Self-evidence of belief would promote quickness and stability. Thus, self-evidence of belief could itself be selected for, and this may explain why we find certain matters to be self-evident.

In examining this account of self-evident beliefs, I shall begin by describing what Dennett (1991a) has called a "mild realist" view of the nature of beliefs in general. We shall find that this view is in conflict with a "strong realist" causal assumption about beliefs upon which Nozick's account of self-evidence rests. This conflict by itself might, of course, be taken as a reason to doubt mild realism. However, after clarifying the relation of mild realism and "emergence" in section II, we shall find, in section III, that there are reasons independent of mild realism to question Nozick's account. Discussion of these difficulties leads to the development, in section IV, of a positive understanding of an approach to evolutionary explanations that fits well with a mild realist stance. Section V develops some consequences for our understanding of concepts.

I

The view of belief summarized here has been developed in Robinson (1986; 1988; 1990; 1995). On this view, beliefs are properties of (whole) subjects – typically people, but also some other animals. This is to be contrasted with a common practice of identifying beliefs with brain states. The difficulties of this practice have been explained in detail in Robinson (1990); here, I will explain the point by reference to Dennett's (1991b) Multiple Drafts Model (MDM). At any one time, according to MDM, I have many representations, and even many complex representations that have a quasi-judgmental form. Not all of the quasi-judgmental representations are compatible and many of them are suppressed before making any contribution to behavior. For both reasons, not all of our quasi-judgmental representations can be regarded as our *beliefs*. But this conclusion implies that our having a certain belief does not consist just in our having a quasi-judgmental representation. On the MDM, a subject S's having a belief that *p* involves at least S's having a quasi-judgmental representation that survives competition with other such representations for access to behavioral control. This view, however, makes having a belief to be a global fact about the whole organization of S's system of quasi-judgmental representations and behavioral control mechanisms.

Let us add to this the fact that many beliefs – what we might call our nonperceptual beliefs – extend over considerable periods of time. This fact is crucial for the predictive utility of belief attributions, of which much is made by, for example, Fodor (1987). The more frequently we postulate a change of nonperceptual beliefs, the less attribution of such beliefs can serve as a guide to expectations of future behavior. Or, to put the point positively, predictive utility of belief attributions depends on nonperceptual beliefs' remaining stable over the time between prediction and action. Since attributions of nonperceptual beliefs are indeed useful, those beliefs do, in general, possess the required stability. Thus, in general, for nonperceptual beliefs, S's believing that *p* is a fact not only about S's global organization at one time, but about the organization of S's representing and behavioral control mechanisms over a considerable period of time.

Attributing a belief with a particular content requires us to use a sentence to specify that content. This fact does not imply that subjects to which beliefs are attributed have language. What it does imply is that their actions exhibit a pattern that resembles a pattern of behavior (in appropriate circumstances) that is indicated by the sentence that language users use in ascribing the belief. Thus, a cat can believe (roughly) that food is behind a cupboard door; it shows its belief by meowing by that cupboard or scratching at the door when it is hungry. We do have to be careful here, because any sentence we use will overdescribe the cat's belief in some way – the cat, after all, presumably lacks representations that correspond fully to our concepts of *food*, *cupboard*, *door*, etc. Nonetheless, the cat can exhibit a pattern of behavior that is similar to the pattern we would exhibit if we believed that food lies behind the cupboard door and were hungry – always allowing for the fact that the similarity must be adjusted to the behavioral repertoire of a cat.

When we attribute beliefs, we are attributing expected patterns of behavior – that is, patterns of behavior that are expected under some circumstances.[1] Thus, there must *be* patterns in our behavior. Some of these patterns will require language, e.g., one cannot believe that mind supervenes on the physical unless one is capable of coherently discussing the concepts involved in this claim. But neither belief attributions nor language itself could develop unless there were *some* patterns in our behavior that did not require language use. Thus, if we are to think of ourselves as subjects that are organized in such a way as to be able to have beliefs, we must first think of ourselves as subjects that are organized in such a way as to be able to have language-independent patterns of behavior.

A further step now suggests itself. Language-independent patterns of behavior can hardly depend on linguistic organization. Thus, if we agree with the foregoing, we must hold that there is a level of brain organization that is non-linguistic in character, but capable of sustaining patterns of behavior – patterns of behavior that may be attributed to subjects by the use of sentences, but that are explained by a pre-linguistic type of brain organization. When I say "non-" or "pre-linguistic" here, I do not mean nonrepresentational. There is abundant evidence that animals represent objects that are not present, and if a cat goes to the kitchen when it is hungry, or a dog to the door when it needs relief, the explanation of these patterns will undoubtedly involve representation of kitchens or doors (or some roughly corresponding feline or canine representations). What I do mean to emphasize is that the organization of whatever representations are necessary must be thought of on some principles *other* than those of linguistically organized concepts in sentence-like groupings. The latter correspond to the form of the *report* of what is believed, but cannot occur in the (causal) *explanation* of the pattern that is reported.

Some of our actions, of course, do depend on language. For example, in signing a contract, I agree to be bound by its words. Such high-level cases depend on a complex background. (a) As we have just seen, there must be patterns of behavior that arise from pre-linguistically organized representations. (b) Language must be learned. This requires connecting words to (at least) things, actions, properties, changes, and facts. On pain of regress, some of this connecting must be produced by processes that, while involving representations, are not yet linguistic. Parsimony suggests that we think of these processes as variations (by small changes or small additions) on the same pre-linguistic organizing mechanisms that are necessary for the pre-linguistic patterns of behavior in (a). (c) Only after these first two stages are present can we suppose that linguistic organization can enter into the *explanation* of (as opposed to the reporting of) patterns in our behavior. (d) Only after the language has become well developed do we have the basis for metalinguistic beliefs, or for the reporting of another's beliefs. These are closely related matters. In order to have a full concept of belief, one has to distinguish between the truth of p and the fact that S believes that p; and this means that one has to be able to understand and be able to work with what "p" says without asserting (for oneself) that p.[2]

We are now in a position to clarify the conflict, alluded to above, between mild realism and Nozick's account of self-evidence. We often say that people did things *because* they believed p and desired that q. I have no quarrel with such statements, and in so far as they lead to correct expectations about people's further behavior they are quite in order. I believe, however, that they are very superficial statements, and I have argued (Robinson, 1995) that we err if we mistake them as having any serious *causal* import. In short, beliefs are not causes of behavior, they are patterns of behavior. Causation is to be sought in the underlying brain organization, which is an organization of representations, but not of beliefs. But if beliefs are not causes of behavior, then they are not what natural selection is selecting for, nor could their self-evidence be selected for. We can, of course, say that the principles of brain organization that are selected for are those that lead to quickly acquired and stable patterns of behavior that are useful given longstanding and pervasive environmental facts. What remains is the question what this has to do with self-evidence of belief.

II

Before turning to this question about self-evidence, I want briefly to consider whether the account of belief just described makes beliefs "emergent". In one innocuous sense, the answer is affirmative. This sense is just that, on the foregoing account, beliefs are attributable only to whole persons. Whole persons are composites of body parts (notably including neurons and clusters of neurons) standing in a very complex set of relations. Beliefs are attributable only to composites thus organized and related to other things, and not to any of the parts of such composites.

Most accounts of "emergence", however, build into this concept considerably more than what we have just described.[3] Parts of trees are not generally trees, nor parts of walls walls; but trees and walls hardly qualify as emergents. What makes for emergence is *irreducibility*, that is, inability to be explained by the properties of whatever emergents are said to emerge *from*. To take a traditional case, if conscious experiences, for example, pains, are said to *emerge* from neural firings, that would imply that the properties and relations of neurons and their activations cannot explain why it is that, given those properties and relations, pains should occur.

What is irreducible need not, as a matter of logic, have any causal role. But those who have made claims for emergence have generally thought that they had evidence for their emergents and, moreover, evidence in the form of events that would not have occurred but for the proposed emergents. That is, they have generally attributed causal roles to emergents. This attribution of causal roles, combined with irreducibility, gives us a sense of "emergence" that we may call "robust emergence". What we now need to see is how robust emergence leads to a difficult problem.

Both things having emergent properties and things on which these have effects are composed of parts that lack the emergent properties. Consider the nonemergent properties that are supposed to occur as effects of an emergent property. If the emergent property of the cause both makes a causal contribution and is not reducible to a complex of nonemergent properties of the cause, then the nonemergent properties of the effect cannot follow from the laws of nature applied to the nonemergent properties of the cause. This situation guarantees that the nonemergent effects will appear to be violations of the laws of nature. To illustrate, suppose pains are regarded as (irreducible) emergents, and held to have effects upon neurons that eventually lead to pain behavior. Their irreducibility implies that we cannot explain why they occur, given their neural bases; their possession of causal properties implies that they are necessary to cause the neural events leading to pain behavior. These two points imply (see Robinson, 1982) that the neural predecessors of pains will not be sufficient to explain why the neural events that lead to pain behavior occur; these latter events will thus appear to violate the electro-chemical laws that ought to apply to the chemicals and membranes of which neurons are composed and the solutions that surround them.

Meehl and Sellars (1956) showed that this situation need not involve any contradiction. Contradiction can be seen to be avoided by imagining a partitioning of the explanatory space. Within the domain where the relations required for emergents do not obtain, one set of laws governs items at the basis level (in the case of our example, these would be chemicals, solution strengths, membrane constructions, and so on). Within the domain where the relations that give rise to emergents do obtain, a different set of laws governing the basis level elements holds sway. So long as the domains are distinct, there is no contradiction.

The division of the laws of chemistry into those holding for the domain of conscious brains and those holding in nonconscious (or nonliving) structures is a radical solution that few have been willing to accept. Alternative views that embrace robust emergence often merely obscure the difficulty, or propose solutions that are scarcely less problematic. It is thus fortunate that the account of belief given in section I does *not* imply that beliefs are emergent in the robust sense. In particular, it does not imply that beliefs cannot be explained by neural architecture and activations. There is, of course, no *practical* possibility of doing this: patterns of behavior are readily observable, their neural causes are not. But the account I have given does assume that our patterns of circumstance-dependent behavior do have causes that lie in our inputs and the construction of our neural systems, and it looks forward to learning more and more about the principles that enable the neural apparatus to maintain useful patterns of behavior over long periods of time while conforming to the ordinary laws of organic chemistry.

III

Let us now return to the matter of explaining the self-evidence of certain of our beliefs. We shall proceed by considering Nozick's examples. Let us begin with the longstanding (to say the least!) and pervasive fact that unsystematically acquired samples are apt to resemble the sampled population. A species whose internal organization allows this fact to influence its members' behavior will have, *ceteris paribus*, an advantage over its rivals that are not similarly endowed. Thus, if a species has survived for some considerable time, it is extremely likely that successful action of an individual member of that species in a saliently distinctive set of circumstances will raise the probability of the same action by that individual in similar circumstances.[4] Repeated success will further increase the probability of repeating the action in similar circumstances and, perhaps, broaden the set of circumstances that will elicit that action.

It may very well occur to us to describe the individuals just imagined as "acting inductively". We must, however, be careful. What we have actually described is a capacity for operant conditioning, and this is evidently insufficient for attributing to an organism (which might be a cat or a chimp) a belief in the principle of induction. To hold such a belief one must be able to represent sets of circumstances in general, and actions in general, and form a representation of the very general fact that actions that are successful in a set of circumstances will likely be successful if repeated in the same or similar circumstances. Now, I do not wish to argue that it is impossible that such a general representation could occur outside of a system that would be properly called "linguistic". Perhaps a pattern of neural activation could come to be caused by any case in which several properties and a successful action have gone together more than once or twice, and perhaps this could contribute some beneficial effect, even in a nonlinguistic organism. But something *like* a linguistic level of representation seems necessary. And even if we stretch our imaginations to allow nonlinguistic, general representations, we face the following problem. It looks as if the belief – the general representation – has nothing to do with behavior and so, cannot be selected for. What is evolutionarily important is that we *act* inductively: our believing the principle of induction seems, so far as fitness goes, an afterthought. Not only is its self-evidence not explained, its occurring as a belief at all is not explained by evolution. Let me spell this out.

We have seen that in order for there to be beliefs, there must be coherent, lasting patterns of behavior that are to be explained by some (as yet not well understood) pre-linguistic mechanisms. However language is learned, there must be some mechanisms (as yet even less well understood) that adjust language to what it is about. It is, presumably, the operation of these mechanisms that accounts for the concordance between our belief in the principle of induction and our behaving inductively (i.e., repeating what has worked in similar circumstances). And, since mechanisms that support the development of language *have* developed, and thus presumably have had some evolutionary advantage, we can surmise that the mechanisms that adjust language to what it is about have been selected for. But, as far as I can see, the fact that we believe the principle of induction is only a consequence of these mechanisms. If so, we have a (very preliminary) sketch of an explanation for our believing the principle of induction, but this kind of explanation holds out no hope of explaining the self-evidence of the principle of induction through selection for such a self-evident belief.

I am, of course, not denying that there must *somehow* be an explanation of self-evidence. I am arguing only that the appeal to natural selection operating on beliefs does not seem capable of providing it. Evolution gives us the mechanisms of language; what we need to see, but cannot yet see, is why these mechanisms yield such self-evidence as they do, for certain claims.

It may be that induction is a bad example. Considered abstractly, its self-evidence is perhaps not as strong as the self-evidence of some other cases. We can imagine what it would be like for it to be false in general, and we can imagine particular cases, like Thanksgiving turkeys, where its application would lead to disaster. Nozick has other examples: Euclidean geometry and principles of deductive logic (p. 110), and belief in other minds and the external world (p. 121). Perhaps we will have better success with some of these other cases.

Consider Euclidean geometry. We can certainly agree with Nozick that it might have been neurally costly and practically useless for earth-bound organisms to have learned to behave as if space were not exactly Euclidean. The following passage, however, goes far beyond this point of agreement.

> Given Euclidean geometry's close approximation to the truth, and given the attendant advantages of its seeming self-evidently true to us – advantages including quickness of inference, believing serviceable (approximate) truths, and avoiding other more divergent falsehoods – we can imagine Euclidean geometry's seeming self-evident as having been selected for; we can imagine selection for that geometry as our form of sensibility.
>
> (Nozick, 1993, p. 110)

The problem in this passage is that there is a conflation of perception and thought. The error involved in treating light as traveling in straight lines (even near massive bodies) will never make the difference between successful and unsuccessful fighting, fleeing, feeding or mating, and this does support the idea that evolution should not have made our perceptual apparatus represent anything other than an inert space describable by straight lines and Euclidean planes. But these considerations can be presumed to apply to the perceptual apparatus of animals who lack any beliefs, not to mention self-evident ones, about the truth of geometrical propositions.[5] Thus, they do not explain self-evidence of *belief* in any geometrical propositions. For an account of geometrical beliefs, I think we will need to add a theory that explains how our beliefs about geometry are constrained to match our pre-linguistically developed perceptual space. While we do not now have such a theory, I believe we have a significant clue, namely that such conformity is necessary if language is to be developed at all. Of course, in that case one can certainly say that mechanisms that produce the conformity are selected for: or better, that any language-like mechanisms that failed to produce the conformity would have been useless and selected against. But this concession still leaves us with a beginning of an explanation that is quite different from what Nozick seems to have in mind. Specifically, the sketch that I have suggested does not suppose that quickness of (conscious) inference or belief in approximate truths plays any causal role in the development of self-evidence of geometrical truths. (If one tries to rescue Nozick here by supposing that he means to refer to unconscious inferences, one threatens to trivialize the issue. For example, nonlinguistic animals will have to be counted as inferring conclusions from their geometrical beliefs.)

It may be objected that the line I am taking here is inconsistent with my description of beliefs as patterns of behavior. This objection can be answered by paying careful attention to the contents of the beliefs that we have reason to attribute to nonlinguistic animals, and by distinguishing these from other belief contents. While there are many complications, I think it is acceptable to think of some nonlinguistic animals as believing that there is prey over there (even, in some cases, where "over there" is out of sight). Circumventing an obstacle to get to the prey may reveal that an animal has a Euclidean perceptual space, and even that it can make a kind of spatial inference. For example, Tolman and Honzik (1930) showed that rats that have learned three routes to food, each longer than the previous one, will proceed immediately to the third route when they encounter a blockage of the first route that occurs after the place where the second route joins it, whereas they will try the second route if the blockage in the first route occurs before the place where the routes join. In this case, we may well attribute beliefs about whether the second route is open or closed. But neither having beliefs of this kind nor being able to generate them is the same thing as believing that space is "flat", or that diagonals of a rectangle are equal, or even that, in general, blockages in a point common to two routes are always blockages of both routes.

Similar considerations apply to simple arithmetical beliefs and principles of deductive logic. A nonlinguistic animal, or a human infant, may see two attractive objects go into a box, and one come out. Exploration of the box, or staring at it, may convince us that the animal or infant believes that there is still an attractive object in the box. It seems correct to say that this cognitive capacity depends on representing objects, representing something numerical about them, and even that it depends on subtractive processing. For all that, it seems evident that there is not sufficient basis in what has been said for attributing a belief that $2 - 1 = 1$. Likewise, if every A in an organism's experience has had a B behind it, and it tries to get behind a new A when we have reason to think it wants a B, we *may* say that it has modus ponens "built into it". This is quite different, however, from attributing to it either a belief that if A and if A then B, then B, or the self-evidence of such a belief.

Let us turn to a belief in other minds. This seems to me to raise two distinct issues: (a) belief in others' conscious experiences, and (b) belief in others' propositional attitudes, most notably, their beliefs and desires. Let us take these in turn.

The immediate difficulty about others' conscious experiences, from an evolutionary point of view, is that they are additional to the behavior upon which evolutionary considerations might be thought to depend. To explain this, let us begin by noting that quick recognition of others' incipient behavior can enhance fitness. People can better avoid attacks from others if they recognize when such attacks are likely. They are more likely to succeed in the hunt, or in battle, if they can anticipate what other members of their group are about to do. However, none of these things requires the belief that others have conscious experiences. Even if one adds a premise that conscious experiences are required in order to cause behavior, others cannot perceive those causes, and so cannot use them in predicting others' behavior. Thus, quite apart from the kinds of considerations we have already advanced in this chapter, we ought to be suspicious of an evolutionary account of belief in others' conscious experiences.

Belief in others' beliefs requires a different commentary. Beliefs, I have held, are (certain) patterns in behavior. If we can perceive such patterns, and use them to anticipate others' behavior, we may increase our own fitness, and possession of this ability across a group may enhance group fitness. Thus, there is some reason to suppose that ability to recognize beliefs in others could have been selected for. We should note, however, that allowing this does not commit us to any causal role for beliefs. I have already suggested that attributing beliefs depends on several other levels of cognition. Attributing causal roles directly to beliefs tends to mask the complexity of the achievement of belief attribution. Thus, it would be better to say that what is selected for are the abilities that, once in place, permit the recognition of complex patterns in the behavior of others.

I have pointed out that belief contents can be of various kinds and that having beliefs with some contents requires language while having beliefs with other contents does not. The case may be similar with attributions of beliefs to others. For example, some evidence suggests that (non-language using) chimpanzees can learn to follow the directions of an experimenter whom they have seen watching the placement of food (without themselves being able to see where the food was placed) and to ignore the directions of an experimenter whose view of the food placing they have seen to have been obstructed (Povinelli, Nelson, and Boysen, 1990).[6] It may be that a supportable summary of this evidence is that (non-language using) chimpanzees can learn to form beliefs about the knowledge of experimenters (and, therefore, about some belief of an experimenter). If so, language possession is not necessary to have a belief about a belief. Still, it may be that in order to have a belief about *some* beliefs, language possession is required. Consider, for example, beliefs that are about knowledge in general (as opposed to beliefs that are about some particular subject's knowledge of some particular fact). In this case, it would seem that the behavioral pattern that constitutes the (general) belief includes some linguistic performance (e.g., a disposition to say that what is known must be justifiable, or true, or believed). Because of this inclusion, the ability to have a belief that is about this (general) belief would also seem to require the ability to recognize linguistic patterns.

Let us return to the question of self-evidence of beliefs about other minds. Why am I so sure, to the point of not being able to take the denial seriously, that you have conscious experiences? The reason for the belief has often been represented as involving an inference from similarity of behavior in my own and others' cases. As is well known, difficulties have been found in this procedure. Elsewhere (Robinson, 1997a) I have argued for a different approach: we believe others have conscious experiences because we believe they are made very much like ourselves. From this point of view, similarity of behavior is only confirmatory evidence: the primary evidence is that we look similar, feel similar (i.e., another's body feels much the same to my touch as does my own body), eat the same things, bleed when cut, and so on. Our belief in others' conscious experiences is, on this account, a conclusion from the principle that like causes have like effects. The propensity to treat any individual other person (or mammal) we may encounter as sentient can be regarded as a consequence of a built in – i.e., selected for – propensity to treat things that are much alike in many respects as alike in some further respect.

The self-evidence of our belief in other people's having beliefs could be taken as merely the result of a very well-confirmed induction. That is, by the time the philosophical question is encountered, most people have years of observation of other people behind them, and so are in a good position to have noticed patterns in others' behavior and to have come to be able to form generally satisfiable expectations on the basis of partial observation of such patterns. The inductive character of belief in others' beliefs is further supported by the general point just outlined, that is, the point that we have an immense amount of evidence for the likeness of others to ourselves. Once we have mastered the concept of belief as applied to ourselves, we immediately have a further reason for attribution of beliefs to others, that is, they are extremely similar to us.

We have been sketching explanations for our beliefs about other minds. The conclusion I draw from our discussion is that the explanation for beliefs about beliefs does not require an evolutionary account that invokes a special mechanism for such beliefs, and the explanation for conscious experiences positively resists that kind of account. Of course, our belief in other minds and its self-evidence are consequences of *some* brain mechanisms, and these developed under selectional pressures, but this fact does not suggest either causal roles for beliefs or the kind of account of self-evidence that Nozick offers.

Let us turn, finally, to the self-evidence of our belief in an external world. What we should say here depends on just what we think this belief is. We might suppose that it is the belief that the world is mind-independent. It seems very unpromising to try an evolutionary account of such a belief, as it depends on possessing the concept of mind, and thus must have arisen quite late in human development. However, when Nozick discusses this belief, he gives a version that any worthy Berkelian could easily accommodate:

> [T]hose cousins of our ancestors who could not manage to learn that there was an independently existing "external world", one whose objects continued on trajectories or in place even when unobserved, did not fare as well as those who quickly recognized obdurate realities.
>
> (Nozick, 1993, p. 121)

There is something right about this, but what is right surely applies equally well to nonlinguistic animals. They too need to track prey, predators, or potential mates when they disappear behind rocks or into the tall grass. Shall we then say that they believe in an external world? I believe we *could* say that without too much risk of being misleading, but without further commentary it seems too general, or too sophisticated, to attribute to most nonlinguistic animals. If one doesn't think one's cat has *considered* the question whether there is an external world (external to what, exactly?) it is decidedly odd to think that it believes, or finds self-evident, an answer to it. (On the other hand, it seems quite in order to say that the cat that chases a mouse up to a hole, and then positions itself motionlessly facing the hole, believes there is (or may be?) a mouse in there.)

The conclusions that this discussion of cases leads me to are these. We need to distinguish between the embodiment of certain detection skills and habits of expectation, on the one hand, and belief in general propositions that sum up many cases of such habits of expectation, on the other. Natural selection may have a pretty direct connection to the skills and the habits, but it has no such direct connection to general beliefs. General beliefs seem to depend on language. Of course, the mechanisms of language had to be developed over evolutionary time, and can be presumed to have been selected for. It is a further problem to account for the meshing of our general beliefs and our habits of expectation, but it seems likely that this account will be a special case under the general need for language to mesh with nonlinguistic reality in order to prove useful. The picture I have sketched does not intend to place development of the beliefs we have considered wholly outside the realm of matters to which evolution is relevant, nor does it do so. But it does make the relation of evolution to belief in fundamental principles considerably less direct than Nozick's descriptions suggest. It does not require beliefs to have the kind of causal role that selectionist mechanism demands. It promotes an interest in genuine explanations by pointing us toward (a) mechanisms that we share with animals in dealing with the world, and (b) mechanisms that adjust all language to realities. Attention to the levels at which such mechanisms operate will, I believe, produce, in the end, an account that is much more explanatorily satisfying than the kind of account that Nozick suggests.

IV

The approach taken here favors explanation by a plurality of mechanisms that are individually not very rich in their consequences but can be deployed in many contexts, in contrast with explanations that invoke relatively specific propensities toward highly complex behavior. One reason for this preference concerns explanatory depth or elegance: whenever we *can* give an explanation in terms of a plurality of less rich but more widely deployable mechanisms, the more powerful but more specific propensity becomes explanatorily redundant. That is, it becomes explainable by reference to mechanisms that we need to account for other things, and thus must in any case retain in our whole theory. A further consideration is that satisfaction with a richer, more specific explanation may cause us to be less assiduous than we should be in seeking out more fundamental explanations.

A case that can be used to illustrate these points is provided by Nozick's treatment of desire for accumulation of wealth. I should say at the outset that he offers this treatment only as a *possible* account. I too think it is a possible account, so strictly speaking we are in agreement about this case. Nonetheless, it serves well as an illustration of the difference of approaches to which I want to call attention.

Briefly, the possibility that Nozick explores is that we may have a strong desire for accumulation of wealth because of the following three facts: (a) except in industrialized societies in the last 150 years, the wealthy have tended to leave more offspring than their less wealthy contemporaries (presumably because of better care, access to food and, often, more wives); (b) people with a strong desire for wealth tend to be wealthier than those who lack it; and (c) a genetic disposition toward a strong desire for wealth is heritable. On these assumptions, strong desire for wealth could have been selected for.

As I have said, such an account seems possible. Nozick himself suggests an alternative, namely, "a social explanation in terms of the institutions that shape people's psychological concerns and motivations and the way particular motivations aid the functioning and propagation of those institutions" (p. 126). However, the approach I have taken in this chapter suggests that a third option should be explored and found unworkable before accepting either of Nozick's proposals. This kind of alternative seeks to derive the strong interest in wealth from more basic interests in acquiring necessities of life, and the benefits of planning and foresight. It seems that we will in any case need to hold that these desires and abilities were selected for, and it seems likely that they might explain the desire for wealth, because foresight would connect acquisition now with ability to secure necessities of life in the future. If this explanation is successful, we would not need to suppose that an additional desire for wealth must be postulated as a heritable disposition.

It is possible to lose track of the issue here by supposing that the desire for wealth can be decomposed into an ensemble of abilities such as the ones just indicated. It may then seem a merely verbal point whether we say that a disposition is what is selected for, or that an ensemble of abilities is selected for. We can reinstate a sense of distinction here by observing that there is a clear difference between the following two scenarios: (1) each member of an ensemble of desires and abilities is independently selected for, so that the persistence of the ensemble follows from the evolutionary pressures to maintain each of its components, and (2) the persistence of the components of the ensemble is explainable only through the fact that they confer advantage only when they occur together.[7] This second situation is indeed possible, and would support a claim that the ensemble (or its corresponding disposition) is what is being selected for. The point I want to make here, however, is that we are entitled to (2) only when we have tried to supply an account along the lines of (1) and have found such an account to be unavailable.

It is worth emphasizing that in arguing for a preference for accounts like those in (1) I am not supposing that they must always be available. Nor should it be thought that I am supposing that the mechanisms in accounts like (1) are "general purpose" mechanisms. Suitability for solving problems of whatever sort is not the same thing as suitability for solving a certain specific problem that recurs in many different contexts. A hypothetical illustration may be helpful, and can be gleaned from Cosmides and Tooby (1994, p. 331). They suggest a possible preference for participation in coalitions. If we think of such a preference as depending on a single mechanism, or an ensemble of mechanisms that individually have no other useful function, we must imagine a relatively large felicitous mutation. If we keep (1) in mind, we will be more likely to look for components that might exist outside a political context. For example, perhaps one thing necessary for acceptability of coalitions is a degree of trust that, under certain conditions, somewhat exceeds what is warranted by one's actual evidence. A mechanism that produces such trust is perhaps useful in hunting parties, food storage systems, and many other cooperative activities. Such a mechanism would be specialized, and not a general problem solver, but could be a component of the evolutionary solution to many problems. Development of such a limited mechanism would seem to require less presumption of a large, felicitous mutation than development of a preference for participation in coalitions. This would make explanation by such a limited mechanism preferable, provided that it can be found.

There are two remarks that should be made before concluding this section. The first is a recognition that the approach I have just been recommending poses a problem for which I have no solution. If we have a number of specialized mechanisms for relatively small tasks, and these contribute to the accomplishment of many larger tasks, we must suppose that these mechanisms will be accessed on appropriate occasions and that, over the course of evolutionary time or individual lifetimes, their outputs can become connected to new behavioral outputs. Here, there is an element of generality; that is, theories of how appropriate accessing and development is brought about will not be explanatory unless they apply to many mechanisms and tasks. Unfortunately, no such theory is available. However, this problem of appropriate connection of mechanisms is one that arises for a wide class of views. For example, even if our models contain mechanisms that have rich consequences but work only on special problems, we must face the fact that many situations will present several special problems. Thus, we will have to have something in our theory to handle integration of the outputs of several mechanisms, or selective temporary suppression of some of them. It is to be hoped that clear understanding of this problem of appropriate connection, and recognition of its pervasiveness, will stimulate efforts to solve it.

The second remark concerns the resolution of the conflict described in section I, i.e., the conflict between mild realism and Nozick's account of self-evidence. Mild realism emphasizes the global nature of the patterns that constitute belief and, by implication, deprives beliefs of a causal role that is often attributed to them. The explanation of the organization of behavior that constitutes believing is to be sought, according to mild realism, not in the effects of beliefs, but in relatively local facts about brain events and principles of their interconnection.[8] In the last two sections of this chapter there have been several occasions on which we have discussed beliefs without attributing causal roles to them. We have also found some difficulties in Nozick's account. Finally, we have seen reasons in support of a view that once again directs our explanatory search in the direction of relatively simple mechanisms. Taken together, these latter developments seem to me to support a resolution of the conflict described in section I that favors mild realism.

V

I have presented mild realism as a view primarily about beliefs. Extension of the view to cover desires should be straightforward, and I leave that task to readers. Extension of the view to concepts (which subjects of beliefs and desires must surely possess) is perhaps not quite so straightforward, and I shall briefly outline how concepts fit into a mild realist outlook.

We remarked in section I that beliefs are attributed by using sentences. It was implicit in that discussion that concepts correspond to words. In fully developed, paradigmatic cases, believers will possess the concepts corresponding to the words in which their beliefs are attributed. Possession of concepts, like possession of beliefs, is possession of an overall internal organization that results in patterns of behavior. Full-blown possessers of the concept *cat*, for example, can reason about cats, describe cats, reject several kinds of impostors (e.g., robots that look like cats), and so on.

There can be partial or defective internal organizations that lead to degraded forms of behavior patterns that go with beliefs. In such cases, unqualified attributions of belief would be misleading, but attributions of belief together with suitable riders would still be useful guides for expectations of future behavior. We have discussed one fairly extreme case of this kind, namely, attributions of beliefs to animals. We must expect an analogous situation with concepts. For example, if we attribute to a cat the belief that there is a mouse behind the hole, we implicitly attribute to the cat the concept of a mouse. This means that we attribute an internal organization that supports a set of abilities regarding mice that extends to cases other than the single ability to wait for the mouse to reemerge.

In this chapter, I have made use of the notion of *representation*. The requirements for possession of representations are far less stringent than the requirements for possession of concepts. An event can be established as a representation if it is required for producing just a single reliable relation between some sensory input and a behavioral output. But a subject possesses a concept only if it has a complex repertoire of behaviors that are held together by its overall internal organization. Because of this difference, representations can be invoked in explanations in a way that concepts cannot. Representations *can* occur in absence of a global internal organization, and so a theory that explained how representations can come to be related in various ways could, in principle, explain how global internal organization arises and is maintained. Concepts cannot be appealed to in this way, for their possession already implies that global organization is in place. (See Robinson, 1997b, for further discussion.)

It is compatible with the foregoing way of looking at concepts that there should be cluster concepts, concepts with prototype structure, and concepts with necessary and sufficient conditions. The view I have been developing says that concept possession involves global internal organization, but it does not say *which kinds* of organization there may be, nor does it exclude any. Neither does it exclude the kind of change in organization that would seem required to yield the changes in the structure of verb classes described by Pinker and Prince (see this volume).

A final point exhibits the consonance of the foregoing view with that of Clark (see this volume). Mild realism indeed agrees that the patterns of behavior that constitute believing and possessing concepts are not mere accidents; they result from some kind of complex internal organization. Mild realism is, however, not committed to any particular kind of internal organization. It makes only the negative point that cognition cannot be *explained* by (mis)treating beliefs or concepts as *elements* of internal organization. Believing and possessing concepts are external, behavioral patterns to be explained, not internal brain-state explainers.

Notes

1 A whole literature on the difficulties of intentionality arises from the simple observation that some of the circumstances are desires and other beliefs. I have discussed these matters in Robinson (1988, 1986, and 1990).

2 I offer these distinctions only as necessary, not as exhaustive of our levels of organization.

3 See Kim (1993) for conceptual analysis of and historical references on emergence. The account given in the text follows this source, albeit in a very summary fashion.

4 This remark hides a deep problem about what counts as relevant similarity. I must forego discussion of this problem here.

5 It is interesting to speculate on possible differences of perceptual space for echo-locating bats, or for certain birds of prey (on this last see Akins, 1993).
6 Three of the four chimpanzees used in this experiment had been previously exposed to various experiments related to learning and cognition, but not to experiments involving linguistic abilities. The fourth subject had been a subject in studies involving linguistic abilities. Interestingly, this subject, possibly due to relatively advanced age, was the *least* competent of the four subjects in the task described in the text. Thus, even in the light of the possible linguistic involvement of this fourth subject, the view expressed here, that this experiment may show an ability available to *non-language using* animals, is well justified.
7 Such components might still be empirically separable by double dissociation under experimental conditions.
8 Perhaps I should say that this implication holds on my own view of mild realism, and not on Dennet's – although I think there are difficulties in his position. See Robinson (1995) for discussion.

References

Akins, K.A. (1993) "A Bat without Qualities?", in M. Davies and G.W. Humphreys (eds) *Consciousness*, Oxford: Blackwell.

Cosmides, L. and Tooby, J. (1994) "Better than Rational: Evolutionary Psychology and the Invisible Hand", *American Economic Association Papers and Proceedings*, 327–332.

Dennett, D. (1991a) "Real Patterns", *The Journal of Philosophy*, 88: 27–51.

Dennett, D. (1991b) *Consciousness Explained*, Boston: Little, Brown and Co.

Fodor, J. (1987) *Psychosemantics*, Cambridge, MA: MIT Press.

Kim, J. (1993) *Supervenience and Mind*, Cambridge: Cambridge University Press.

Meehl, P. and Sellars, W. (1956) "The Concept of Emergence", in H. Feigl and M. Scriven (eds) *Minnesota Studies in the Philosophy of Science, vol. I*, Minneapolis: University of Minnesota Press.

Nozick, R. (1993) *The Nature of Rationality*, Princeton: Princeton University Press.

Povinelli, D.J., Nelson, K.E., and Boysen, S.T. (1990) "Inferences about Guessing and Knowing by Chimpanzees (*Pan Troglodytes*)", *Journal of Comparative Psychology*, 104: 203–210.

Robinson, W. (1982) "Causation, Sensations, and Knowledge", *Mind*, 91: 524–540.

Robinson, W. (1986) "Ascription, Intentionality and Understanding", *The Monist*, 69: 584–597.

Robinson, W. (1988) *Brains and People*, Philadelphia: Temple University Press.

Robinson, W. (1990) "States and Beliefs", *Mind*, 99: 33–51.

Robinson, W. (1995) "Mild Realism, Causation, and Folk Psychology", *Philosophical Psychology*, 8: 167–187.

Robinson, W. (1997a) "Some Nonhuman Animals Can Have Pain in a Morally Relevant Sense", *Biology and Philosophy*, 12: 51–71.

Robinson, W. (1997b) "Representation and Cognitive Explanation", in A. Riegler and M. Peschl (eds) *Does Representation Need Reality?*, Austrian Society for Cognitive Science Technical Report 97–01, pp. 70–75.

Tolman, E.C. and Honzik, C.H. (1930) "Introduction and Removal of Reward and Maze Performance in Rats", *University of California Publications in Psychology*, 4: 257–75.

9 The development of scientific concepts and their embodiment in the representational activities of cognitive systems

Neural representation spaces, theory spaces, and paradigmatic shifts

Markus F. Peschl

Abstract

The goal of this chapter is to show how scientific concepts and processes are embedded in representational activities of cognitive systems. The most obvious fact is that science is conducted by cognitive systems whose neural systems enable them to represent and successfully interact with the world. In the course of this chapter it will turn out that concepts from computational neuroscience and artificial life provide interesting insights into the problem of knowledge representation and, as a consequence, into the understanding of science and of what is referred to as the context of discovery. It will be shown how the dynamics of theories and scientific concepts can be described by the dynamics going on in the neural representation space (activation and weight space). Furthermore, concepts from genetic algorithms and their combination with artificial neural networks could give a cognitively founded explanation for paradigmatic shifts.

1 Introduction

It seems to be an accepted fact that *science* is the result of *cognitive activities*. The production of theories, conducting experiments, "having new ideas", developing and "inventing" new perspectives on a well-known phenomenon, verifying a hypothesis, deducing implications, applying certain methods, neglecting certain results, etc. are not some abstract and detached "scientific processes"; they are deeply cognitive capacities which are closely tied to the activities of cognitive systems, their representational capabilities, their interactions with the environment, their interactions with each other, and their ability to produce artifacts, to generate and use language, and to manipulate the environmental dynamics. Recent publications in philosophy of science (e.g., Brakel 1994; Churchland

1989, 1991, 1995; Giere 1992, 1994) represent a first step toward taking seriously this connection between cognitive and scientific processes.

Nevertheless, many approaches in philosophy of science (e.g., Logical Positivism, Popper's philosophy of science, etc.) did not include (or even explicitly exclude) cognitive processes and the activities of a cognitive system in their theories and investigations. Their focus is on the "context of justification", i.e., these approaches are using methods and tools from logic in order to deduce theories, they are trying to verify or falsify already existing theories, etc. In any case, the really interesting part in the scientific process – "discovering", constructing, or developing a new theory – is more or less neglected. The reasons for this are manifold: the process of discovery is said to be a more or less irrational process and, thus, cannot be included in a theory about scientific knowledge; the psychological, neuroscientific, or cognitive processes involved in the context of developing new theories are said to be too complex and, thus, cannot be understood. In other words, the "context of discovery" is still somewhat shrouded in mystery for most traditional philosophers of science. They prefer to stay in their logical analyses, in their abstract and detached description of scientific processes (i.e., scientific theories are abstract and objective descriptions of the environmental dynamics or complex systems of logical sentences), despite the fact that the *cognitive* process of discovering or constructing new knowledge and theories is the really interesting and fascinating activity in science. However, as mentioned above, there is an increasing interest in these not so formal processes of science. Psychological as well as social studies of science are only a first step. The foundation of all these processes are cognitive activities of cognitive systems. The focus of interest has to shift from formal, social, or psychological investigations and descriptions of science to the "roots" of the scientific process: the investigation of cognitive systems, their ability to represent the world and to interact with it, and to construct new knowledge and theories. From this basis social, cultural, and scientific structures, and the dynamics of theories will appear in another light.

The situation of traditional philosophy of science can be compared to the development in cognitive science and artificial intelligence: for a long time there was the hope that intelligent behavior could be understood, generated, and simulated by applying logic, formal systems, symbol manipulation, and propositional approaches (e.g., Newell and Simon 1976; Newell 1980; Fodor 1975, 1983; Winston 1992; and many others). The concepts of a formal representation of the environment and logical operations on these representations were in the foreground. The problem of learning and acquiring new knowledge was approached in the context of this formal, (deductive) pseudo-inductive, and logical framework ("machine learning") – the results were rather disappointing and did not at all match the observations of human intelligent behavior or learning behavior. Recent developments in the fields of cognitive science (Posner 1989; Green 1996) and artificial life (e.g., Langton 1989, 1994, 1995, and many others) have revealed, however, that so-called lower cognitive processes, such as primary and sensorimotor processing, neural processing on any level of complexity, neural learning mechanisms, sensory systems, etc. are at least as important for generating, understanding, and simulating so-called higher cognitive activities.

With the advent of *neural computation* (e.g., Arbib 1995; Anderson 1988; Anderson *et al.* 1991; Churchland and Sejnowski 1989, 1992; Churchland *et al.* 1990; Hertz *et al.* 1991; Rumelhart *et al.* 1986; Schwartz 1990; Sejnowski *et al.* 1988; Varela *et al.* 1991; and many others), artificial life, dynamic systems (Gelder and Port 1995), etc. an epistemological as well as methodological – almost paradigmatic – shift has occurred in the cognitive science community. A new understanding of *knowledge representation* and *cognition* is the result of this process, which is still developing. The emphasis is on a more dynamic and not so rigid and formal view of cognition, of knowledge, and processing. It is based on the assumption that cognitive activities have their foundation in the neural and biological substratum and dynamics (and not in logical formulas). In this chapter philosophy of science (and its traditional understanding of scientific processes) will be confronted with these new perspectives, methods, and theories about cognition, knowledge representation, and cognitive processes. In contrast to artificial intelligence, which has been influenced by and which is based on principles stemming from philosophy of science and logic, I am trying to show that recent developments in cognitive science, neural computation, and artificial life have a crucial impact on epistemological concepts, such as knowledge representation. As a consequence, they will change our understanding of the process of science, of (scientific) theories, and of developing and constructing new theories.

The goal of this chapter is to sketch these rather new concepts of (neural) representation and to make explicit their implications for philosophy of science and epistemology. (Scientific) theories turn out to be only one form of representation embedded in the more general and flexible neural representation system of a cognitive system. Consequently, the development of scientific theories follows a similar dynamics to neural representations. This view has important implications for an alternative understanding of developing and constructing new theories. Construction processes in conceptual representation spaces (being neurally realized as activation and weight space) turn out to be more important than formal systems, complex deductions, or accurate mappings of the environment.

2 Cognitive science and (philosophy of) science

One of the aims of this chapter is to show that there exists a *close relationship* between philosophy of science and recent developments in cognitive science (see section 1). There is the obvious connection that science is done by cognitive systems; hence, cognitive science could perhaps contribute its models and theories to the investigation of the process of science. On a more fundamental level one can find at least two links that connect these two fields: an *epistemological* and a *methodological* link.

2.1 Epistemological link

It seems that both cognitive systems and science have a rather similar goal: the *representation of the world*. Both are interested in an adequate representation, description, explanation, prediction, and manipulation of the environmental dynamics.

Any cognitive system is a living system. In order to survive, it is necessary to maintain a state of homeostasis (Maturana and Varela 1980). From an abstract and system theoretic perspective, the process of life can be characterized as a sequence of transient equilibria – energy from the environment is necessary to maintain these equilibria. In order to achieve this goal the cognitive system has to have some *knowledge* about its environment so that it can look for sources of energy and avoid inadequate or dangerous environmental states or situations. In other words, it is *necessary to represent the environment* in some way, in order to survive in this environment. Phylogenetic and ontogenetic processes have brought about a wide range of more or less complex representation systems. The *nervous system* has turned out to be an extremely successful, flexible, and complex representational substratum which can be found in most complex organisms.

As shown in Peschl (1994a) (see also Peschl 1993, 1994b), a (recurrent) neural representation system can be understood as a *transformation system* which transforms the sensory input with respect to the current internal state into behavioral output.[1] The current input selects a(n internal representational) state out of the space of possible successor states. This space is predetermined by the current internal state and the neural architecture. The important point to note is that it is *not* the goal of the neural representation system to map the environment as accurately as possible (to representational states), but to *generate functionally fitting behavior* (see also Glasersfeld 1995; Roth 1994). Hence, representation in neural systems is a *strategy to survive* by externalizing behavior, rather than by depicting the environment.

The "goal" of evolutionary as well as ontogenetic processes (i.e., learning, development, etc.) is to generate and provide these representational structures (in the form of a specific neural architecture), which are capable of generating adequate behavior (being necessary for the organism's survival). In other words, the representational system aims at *manipulating* the organism's internal and external environmental dynamics in order to achieve desired states.[2]

From a constructivist perspective (e.g., Foerster 1973; Glasersfeld 1984, 1995; Steier 1991; Varela *et al.* 1991; Watzlawick 1984; and many others) scientific theories have similar goals: they are not understood as "objective descriptions" of the environment (which is impossible anyway from an epistemological and constructivist perspective), but as strategies for successfully coping with the environment. In other words, the aspect of manipulating and predicting the environmental dynamics is the central feature of scientific theories.[3] Think, for instance, of modern particle physics: an incredible effort is pushed into the development of huge particle accelerators in order to manipulate the environmental dynamics in such a way that a predicted effect can be "seen". Another example is modern genetics: the goal is to manipulate the genetic material in a desired way in order to produce a certain protein structure or organism. Of course, some kind of knowledge has to be developed about the genetic structure, its biochemistry, etc. However, it is only so far of interest as it provides *tools* or strategies for successfully manipulating the genetic material or predicting its effects. At best, the descriptive or explanatory aspect of scientific theories is captured in "if–then" rules in the following sense: if the environment is in a certain condition (either through its own dynamics or by penetration in an experiment), then the effect *x* is very likely.

Like in cognitive systems, the goal of scientific theories is to (a) find out, (b) describe, (c) predict, and (d) make use of *functional relationships* and *regularities* which are found in or constructed from the environment. What is referred to as "objective scientific description or explanation" is only a by-product which has its status as "true knowledge" only because of its success in predicting and manipulating the environment in a superior manner. From an epistemological and constructivist perspective the difference between so-called scientific theories and so-called common sense knowledge seems to get blurred; there seem to remain only quantitative differences concerning generality, accuracy in predicting the environmental dynamics, consistency, elegance, etc. Both are structures that can be used to generate behavior functionally fitting into the environment. As history of science as well as our own experience shows, there is no way to tell that there do not exist other knowledge, representational, or theoretic structures that are capable of generating the same or even "more fitting" behavior.

Hence, the epistemological link between scientific theories and neurally represented knowledge is closer than most philosophers of science (want to) assume. From the perspective that scientific theories are also a product of cognitive and neural representational processes it is no wonder that this artificial gap between scientific and common sense concepts and knowledge begins to collapse the more we understand cognitive systems and their (neurally based) representational capabilities.

2.2 Methodological link

The second link between cognitive science and (philosophy of) science is based on the epistemological assumptions from section 2.1 and concerns methodological questions. As neural processes are the foundation of any representational process, approaches in which neural systems, evolutionary processes, living systems, etc. are *simulated* are an important link for understanding epistemological issues. What makes these approaches interesting is the fact that they offer methods for explaining and understanding the dynamics of neural or evolutionary systems. Their theories and methods do not only provide rich details in the generated data, but also provide a *conceptual* framework and models for cognitive processes on various levels of complexity. As will be shown, these methods have also crucial implications for the epistemological realm: they give us new insights in the representational dynamics and the representational relationship to the environment. And this is the point where it becomes of interest for our original problem of trying to understand the process of science from a cognitive perspective. (Explanatory and simulation) methods from the fields of neural computation/connectionism, genetic algorithms (e.g., Belew 1990; Goldberg 1989; Holland 1975; Mitchell and Forrest 1994; and many others), artificial life, etc. offer a *conceptual* level of explanation (e.g., representational state spaces) which is of interest for both the scientific and the cognitive domain.

In the course of this chapter it will turn out that these concepts lead to an alternative understanding of scientific theories and how they are embedded and generated by the neural representation system. The claim is that the method of simulating cognitive systems provides conceptual tools that are not only relevant for the understanding of cognitive systems and epistemological questions, but also for philosophy of science.

It has hopefully become clear by now that cognitive science and the study of cognitive systems (as computational systems) in general can offer new perspectives and insights into understanding the process of science. Science is brought back to its "roots", i.e., science is not some abstract and detached process, but it is conducted by cognitive systems and it is based on the *representational capabilities* and *dynamics* of one or a group of cognitive systems. The goal of this chapter is to sketch the foundations and implications of such a "radically cognitive account of science" in the light of recent developments in cognitive science (e.g., neural computation, genetic algorithms, artificial life, etc.).

3 Scientific theories, representation, neural systems, and representational spaces

3.1 Structural similarities between scientific and cognitive processes

Comparing the process of science with the activities of cognitive systems one can see that both are trying to achieve rather similar goals:

(i) First of all, both are interested in *regularities* in the environment, i.e., science and cognitive systems are looking for environmental *patterns* that occur on a regular basis in the spatial and/or temporal domain. Before any knowledge or a theory is constructed, a cognitive system (perhaps in the context of a scientific investigation) discovers that certain phenomena in the environment happen according to some repeatable patterns or rules. These "primary regularities" are extracted by neurally realized feature detectors on various levels of abstraction. In the scientific domain these feature detectors can be compared to a theory-laden view of the world extracting those features of an observed phenomenon that seem to be relevant for the theory.

(ii) In a second step the highly inductive neural machinery isolates correlations and states in the environment that seem to be relevant for the observed

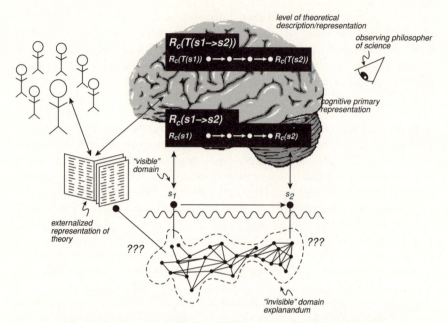

Figure 9.1 The relationship between the "hidden domain", the observable domain, and its representations in the brain (i.e., common sense or primary representation and representation of the theory (representing the environmental phenomenon))

regularities. Scientific as well as cognitive processes are based on the following assumptions: (a) there is some "hidden reality" that is not directly accessible by our sensory systems (see also Kosso 1992), and (b) furthermore, (hidden) mechanisms in this "hidden reality" are responsible for the regularities that can be observed in the accessible macro-domain. In other words, these regularities are emergent phenomena of processes occurring in the "hidden domain". Looking a bit closer, one can say that these emergent phenomena are emerging in the moment of *transduction*, i.e., the micro-processes of both the environment and the particular sensor interact and the result is a neural signal leading to a certain primary representation (= "observation") in the brain. Figure 9.1 sketches the relationship between these domains. Science aims at constructing abstract representations or mechanisms which fit into the observed phenomena by revealing one possible relationship between the hidden and observable domains. The criterion for a "successful theory" is a mechanism that predicts or manipulates the phenomenon in an expected manner.

Note that at least *two steps of constructions* are involved in this process:

(a) *Constructing the correlations*: we have to keep in mind that the regularities that are extracted by the cognitive system are *system relative*; i.e., they are a result of an active process of construction which has its substratum in the neural architecture. These regularities do not explicitly "lie around" out there in the environment. Of course, the environmental dynamics follows some kind of regular pattern, but the regularities, which are extracted by the cognitive system, are primarily regularities *with respect to* the representational system. In other words, the structure of the representation system constructs regularities according to its own regularities which fit into the constraints of the environmental dynamics. This process applies to both the cognitive as well as the scientific domain.[4]

(b) *Constructing a theory about the "hidden reality"*: as a result of the inaccessibility of the "hidden reality" the cognitive system has to *construct* a (common sense or scientific) *theory* about the mechanisms that govern this hidden domain and that lead to the observed phenomena and regularities. In other words, this representation has to account for the regularities by providing (theoretical or abstract) mechanisms that are capable of explaining, predicting, and/or generating the environmental phenomenon. This knowledge (e.g., models, abstract mechanisms, etc.) has to fit into the dynamics of the environment like a key fits into a lock (cf. the concept of *functional fitness*, Glasersfeld 1984, 1995).

The most simple form of such a representation is the model of a black box; of course, it is not a very powerful model, as it describes only the input–output relations of an observed system or phenomenon. However, in most cases such a model is the starting point for constructing more complex mechanisms, rules, dynamics, internal relationships, etc. which account for the observed behavior. The strategy of "opening up the observed system" by means of more or less sophisticated experiments is not only applied in the domain of science, but also in everyday life. The results of this strategy are twofold. First of all, the investigating cognitive system gets some hints as to how the externally observed behavior is generated by finding out more about the relationships and interactions between the internal subsystems of the system. Secondly, the observer realizes that with each internal subsystem a new black box is associated which has to be opened and explained. It depends on the cognitive system's question, the problem, the scientific sophistication, etc., at which level this (almost infinite) reductionist process stops.

In any case, there has to be *constructed* some model, knowledge, or theory (in the most general sense) in order to fill the black box, which is encountered whenever we are interacting with the environment. Keep in mind that the resulting theories are the outcome of an *active process of construction* rather than of a passive mapping. The only criterion, which has to be fulfilled by everyday as well as scientific theories, is that they are *consistent* with the environmental structures; i.e., that they fit into the environment. One of the implications is, of course, that there is more than one theory that meets this criterion. As long as this knowledge or theory can be *used* in a beneficial way for the survival (in the most general sense) of the organism or a group of organisms, it is a *functionally fitting* or adequate theory about an aspect of the environment.

(iii) The ultimate goal of all these (construction) processes is to *make use of these representations, knowledge, or theories*; in other words, to apply the more or less complex and abstract everyday or scientific models and theories in order to *predict* and/or to *manipulate* the environmental dynamics. This does not only apply to common sense knowledge, but also to scientific theories/knowledge that claim to "objectively describe" the environment. In each of these theories there is a "behavioral aspect". Most of them do not so much focus on describing the environmental dynamics, but on questions like "what happens, if . . . ", i.e., they are interested either in predicting the environmental dynamics under a given condition or in actively manipulating the dynamics of the environment by applying knowledge about its internal states, relationships, and state transitions.[5]

Note that (in both the cognitive and the scientific domain) knowledge or theories are never developed just *per se* or just for mapping or depicting the environment. All efforts of learning, adaptation, evolution, or developing common sense knowledge or representations as well as scientific theories *finally aim at externalizing* some kind of *behavior* that is beneficial for the organism.[6] The important thing I want to point out in this chapter is that the traditional notion of representation or theory suggests somehow mapping an aspect of the environment to some representational substratum – from an epistemological, neuroscientific, as well as philosophy of science perspective this understanding seems to be misleading, however. It can be shown that neither knowledge being represented in neural structures, nor knowledge being represented in scientific theories, primarily represent or map the world, but rather have to be seen as *strategies for successfully coping* and coupling with the world (Peschl 1994a, 1994b). That is, there is neuroscientific as well as epistemological evidence that it is not possible to have a direct access to the environment. Due to non-linear transduction processes and the recurrent neural architecture a stable referential relationship between the environment and its representation has to be given up as well. Thus, it is by no means clear what is meant by "mapping" or "describing" or "representing" (in the classical referential sense) the world. We lack an objective criterion for how "near" or accurate the mapping or theoretical description is to the real world, as any cognitive system is *always* and *only* confronted with neurally constructed representations of the world – they are the only verification criterion! At best, "negative statements" can be made about the environment, i.e., in the case when a theory or representation hurts an environmental boundary condition and, thus, does not functionally fit.

It seems to be only due to our already neurally constructed view and experience of the world that, in order to behave adequately, a pictorial (Kosslyn and Pomerantz 1977; Kosslyn 1990, 1994), linguistic (Fodor 1975, 1981), or referential representation of the environment is thought to be necessary.

As can be seen in Figure 9.2, cognitive and scientific processes do not only have similar goals, but also follow *structurally similar dynamics*. From an abstract and epistemological perspective both are organized as dynamic feedback systems

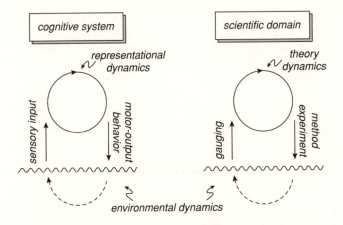

Figure 9.2 Structural similarities between the feedback processes in science and cognitive systems

interacting with the environment. Two feedback/recurrent loops and dynamics have to be differentiated: (i) the *internal feedback* represents the internal dynamics of knowledge or theories (i.e., the dynamics emerging from constructing, changing, etc. neural structures or theories); (ii) the second feedback dynamics concerns the *external interactions* with the environment: as a result of the internal representational dynamics the cognitive system externalizes behavior and causes changes in the environment which are detected by the sensory system which, in turn, perturbates the representational dynamics. Similarly, a scientific theory "externalizes behavior" by conducting an experiment. In this process the theory or knowledge is tested in the environment. On the input side the results of this experiment are measured and cause a confirmation or the need for change in the representational structure (= theory).

Of course, there is a close relationship and interaction between the internal and external feedback loops. The internal dynamics is responsible for *generating hypotheses* by continuously *adapting, constructing,* and *changing* the representational structures (i.e., neural architecture and, thus, the knowledge, theories, etc. being represented in the neural substratum). Furthermore, the internal dynamics is responsible for externalizing this knowledge in the form of behavior, experiments, applying methods, controlling motor devices, etc. On the other hand the internal dynamics is driven in part by the signals, inputs, stimuli, etc. entering the cognitive system or theoretical domain from the environment via the sensory system or via gauges (and their interpretation). As is shown in Peschl (1994a), the environmental input does *not* determine the internal dynamics, but only has *modulatory influence* on it.

In order to test and/or verify the fitness of internally constructed knowledge or theory, behavior is externalized according to the "instructions" from the representational structure. The organism's behavioral/motor output is the result of the internal representational dynamics/knowledge and *modulates* the environmental dynamics. In the scientific realm the behavioral output can be compared to the process of conducting an experiment, of applying a method, and/or of penetrating the environmental dynamics with some machinery. In any case the environmental dynamics is influenced in some way. These changes in the environmental states lead to a change on the organism's sensory surface or in the gauges. In this moment the new environmental state is transformed into a (neural, numerical, etc.) representation of itself ("transduction"). In the representational realm the results of these externalizations can be checked and verified, whether a desired state has been reached or not. The success or failure of this verification process indicates how well the knowledge or theory fits into the environmental dynamics. In other words, if it failed to modulate the environment in a desired way, it is necessary to make changes in the representational structure or theory. Sections 4 and 5 will explain these processes in more detail for the cognitive as well as scientific realm.

In any case the success or failure of the behavioral externalization ("empirical experiment") determines the level of functional fitness of the representational structure or theory of the particular aspect of the environment. After the representation or theory has been changed, the cycle described above and in Figure 9.2 starts again: behavior is externalized according to the new knowledge/theory, the environment is modulated, etc. Although Figure 9.2 suggests that the processes occurring in the scientific and the cognitive realm are two different and detached systems, one has to keep in mind that scientific activities, such as constructing new theories, conducting experiments, receiving input from the environment, etc. are all *embedded* in the feedback dynamics depicted on the left side of the figure. Perhaps that is why these processes are so similar.

3.2 Functional fitness and representation in neurally based cognitive systems

3.2.1 Deductive vs. inductive processes

The two cycles depicted in Figure 9.2 can be divided into two alternating subprocesses: the *deductive* part of externalizing behavior and the more *inductive* part of constructing, adapting, and changing the representational structures (e.g., theories, knowledge, etc.). From an abstract and epistemological perspective no new knowledge is developed in the deductive process of externalizing behavior. The only thing that happens is that already (implicitly) existing knowledge structures are applied for generating behavior. In terms of scientific processes this means that implications, predictions, methodological instructions, etc. are deduced from a theory. In other words, certain states of the space of (theoretic) possibilities, which is implicitly predetermined by the theory describing it, are made explicit by deduction.[7] In terms of cognitive/neural systems this means that the internal representational dynamics, which is determined by the neural architecture, the current internal state, and the current input, selects a state out of its predetermined and prestructured space of possible (representational) states. As has been mentioned, the externalized behavior is a subset of the space of possible representational states (i.e., many different internal representational states can lead to a single behavioral action; see Peschl 1994a, 1994b for further details).

In any case, behavior – be it in the form of an experiment or in behavioral actions of a cognitive system – always has to be interpreted as a result of a deduction in the internal representational dynamics. One could say that it is an externalization of a fraction of the organism's or theory's knowledge or representational structure (in a certain environmental context). Contrary to the deductive character of behavioral externalizations, new knowledge is constructed or existing knowledge is adapted or changed by inductive processes in cognitive systems and scientific activities. From an epistemological perspective this seems to be the more interesting process in science as well as in cognitive systems. In philosophy of science this aspect is referred to as "context of discovery"; in the context of investigating cognitive systems these processes of constructing new knowledge or changing representational structures are referred to as learning, adaptation, or evolutionary dynamics. As will be shown in the following sections, it seems that rather new theories and methods from cognitive science, which are investigating these inductive processes, could shed some light on the still mysterious process of developing new (scientific) theories.

3.2.2 Neural representation and transformation

For that reason a brief overview of representational mechanisms and processes in neural systems is given in the following paragraphs. As has been mentioned, any neural system can be understood as a non-linear (recurrent) transformation system which transforms an input into an output. Theoretically this transformation could be described by a recurrent function (and/or set of differential equations). Approaches in connectionism or neural computation describe this transformation by a computational neural structure or architecture which tries to model natural neural systems on a very abstract level. Thus, the behavioral and representational dynamics of a neural system can be simulated by a computer on an abstract level. From an epistemological perspective this is a very interesting process, as it becomes feasible to study representational processes and principles of neural systems in great detail and on various levels of complexity.[8]

3.2.3 Representational spaces and substrata

Computational neuroscience provides a theoretical and explanatory framework that is of interest not only for the study of neural dynamics, but also for a better understanding of representational issues in neural systems. The core idea of this framework is based on the concept of a *state space* (which originally was used in cybernetics and system theory: e.g., Ashby 1964; Wiener 1948; Heiden 1992; Port and Gelder 1995; and many others). In other words, the dynamics of (spreading) activations, the dynamics and changes in the synaptic weights, or the evolutionary dynamics can be explained and simulated by making use of states and state transitions in state spaces. I cannot go into details here – the focus of the following paragraphs will be only the epistemological implications for the problem of representation in neural systems.

The concept of representation changes radically with the introduction of neural activation spaces (see also Churchland 1989, 1995; Churchland and Sejnowski 1992; Peschl 1992a, 1992b; and many others). It seems that we have to give up the notion of linguistically transparent representations (Clark 1989) and replace it with the concept of *distributed representation* (Hinton *et al*. 1986; Rumelhart *et al* 1986; Gelder 1992; Elman 1991); furthermore, there is evidence (Peschl 1994a) that the concept of a *referential representation* (i.e., a representational state stands for a certain phenomenon in a stable way) has to be abandoned as well. Especially the second issue brings about the necessity for an alternative concept of representation. As will be shown in sections 4ff, this new perspective has crucial implications even for the understanding of scientific processes.

Generally speaking, three (four) representational substrata (state spaces) can be found in neural systems. Of course, there is strong interaction between these representational dynamics going on:

(i) *Activation space*: let's assume that a neural system consists of *n* neurons/units. Each neuron can assume a certain activation value. A state space describing the state or pattern of activations can be constructed by appointing the activation values of each neuron in one dimension. Hence, an *n*-dimensional activation space is created, where a certain state of activations (= a pattern of activations in the neural system at a certain time *t*) can be described as a single point.

From an epistemological perspective, such a state in activation space can be interpreted as the current *representational state*. However, this state does not represent an environmental phenomenon in the traditional sense: first of all many different neural activations contribute to the pattern of activations. So, it is impossible to find a single representational substratum (such as a symbol). Secondly, as most neural systems have a *recurrent architecture*, the internal representational state is determined not only by the current environmental input (which is supposed to be represented in the traditional view), but also by the previous internal state. The current input can only select from a set/space of possible successor states. However, this set of successor states is predetermined by the neural architecture and by the current internal state. So, there is no way of guaranteeing a stable referential relationship between repraesentandum and repraesentans.

As an implication of these facts, what is represented in the neural activation space can be characterized as follows: the current state or pattern of activations is *not* a stable depiction or mapping of the (transduced) environmental state. Rather, it represents a state that relates the current external input and the previous internal state to each other with the goal of generating functionally fitting behavior.

(i-a) *Trajectories in activation space* are (temporal) sequences of patterns of activations that have representational character (Horgan and Tienson 1996). In many cases a recurrent neural system "falls" into stable states, such as fixed point attractors, cyclic attractors, or chaotic attractors (Hertz *et al.* 1991). These stabilities sometimes can play the role of representations. However, the same problems with a stable referential relationship apply as in point (i).

(ii) *Weight space*: the synaptic architecture of the weights are responsible for the dynamics of activations. In other words, they control the flow and spreading of activations in the neural system. Thus, they play a rather important role in representational issues: they are responsible for generating patterns of activations (see (i)) and, thus, behavior. Abstractly speaking, the synaptic weights determine the space of possible state transitions (and, thus, behavioral externalizations) in the activation space. The current input and the current internal state only instantiate/select one of these predetermined states and state transitions.[9] Hence, the whole representational as well as behavioral dynamics is *embodied* in the synaptic weights. This implies that what an external observer refers to as "knowledge" of an organism is represented in the synaptic weights and architecture.

Of course, these weights are changing over time as well. This is referred to as ontogenetic adaptation or "learning". Section 4 will discuss these processes and their relevance for the development of scientific theories in detail. What is important at this point is that the weights and their dynamics can be represented in an m-dimensional weight space.[10] That is, a certain configuration of weights is a single point in weight space. The dynamics of learning can be represented as a *sequence of points* forming a *trajectory* through weight space. It is important to keep in mind that a certain point in weight space determines the whole structure and the dynamics of the activation space. Hence, whenever the point moves in weight space (= "learning") the dynamics changes in the activation space. This is exactly what we observe: we see that the behavior of the organism changes and say that it must have "learned" something. From this observation we imply that its knowledge, representation or theory about the environment must have changed.

Of course, there is a close interaction between the dynamics in the weight space and activation space: the success or failure of the externalized behavior (being the result of the current configuration in weight space) determines whether and how it is necessary to learn/adapt. The resulting changes in the weight space lead to changes in the behavioral dynamics which – hopefully – functionally fit into the environment.

(iii) *Genetic space*: the genetic code is the basic representational entity for any cognitive system. It determines the basic features of the body structure as well as of the representational structure. It has to be clear that the expression of the genetic code does not lead directly to these structures – a very complex process of *development* is involved (Edelman 1988; Berger and Singer 1992; Chiba *et al.* 1988; Jessel 1991; Lawrence 1992; Cangelosi *et al.* 1994). That is, there does not take place a 1 : 1 mapping from the genetic code to the mature organism. Rather, the body and representational structure develops in a complex process of interactions between the genetic code, the environment, and the body structures, which already have been produced and expressed. This implies that the genetic material has to be understood – similarly to the neural representational substratum – as representing a strategy for *generating* "behavior" in the form of an organism (which itself has to generate adequate behavior) in a process of development and interaction with the environment.

Again, via the criterion of success and failure (= reproduction) an interaction and feedback between the neural and the genetic representational substratum and dynamics is established. The goal is not to map the environment, but to develop representational/genetic structures that are capable of generating functionally fitting organisms. The fields of artificial life (e.g., Langton 1989, 1995; Steels 1996; Meyer and Wilson 1991; and many others), genetic algorithms (e.g., Mitchell and Forrest 1994; Belew 1990; Holland 1975; and many others), and of studying the interaction between evolutionary processes and neural dynamics (e.g., Belew 1990; Belew *et al.* 1992; Cangelosi *et al.* 1994; Harp *et al.* 1989; Hinton 1987; Miller *et al.* 1989; Nolfi *et al.* 1990; Nolfi and Parisi 1991; and many others) give new insights in this complex interplay between phylogenetic and ontogenetic dynamics. In the following sections these (computational) concepts will be applied to achieve an alternative view of scientific processes, and how they are embedded in cognitive activities.

3.2.4 Functional fitness and neural representation

In the context of neural as well as genetic representation the concept of *functional fitness* plays an important role. From section 3.2.3 above we learned that there is empirical evidence that the concept of referential representations (such as propositions) has to be abandoned. The aspect of *generating behavior* (or functioning organisms) seems to be the main task of representational structures, rather than depicting or mapping the environment. Constructivist approaches (e.g., Glasersfeld 1984, 1995; Maturana and Varela 1980; and many others) refer to this concept as adequate or *viable behavior*.

In other words, the externalized behavior has to functionally fit into the structures of the (internal and external) environment. As we have seen above, the behavior is the result of the internal neural dynamics being itself determined by the synaptic weight configuration, the internal state, and the input. From this perspective it can be seen that the knowledge being embodied in the synaptic architecture can be interpreted as a kind of theory or *strategy* for generating functionally fitting behavior in the context of the organism's task to survive. The goal is to manipulate the organism's internal and external environment in such a way that it is beneficial for the cognitive system's survival and reproduction. The behavior has to fit into the external and internal environmental constraints.

The goal of any representational dynamics can*not* be to create an accurate "picture" of the environment. Rather, constructive and adaptive processes, such as neural plasticity or evolutionary dynamics, have to change the neural architecture in such a way that it is capable of generating viable behavior. Hence, it is not surprising that we do not have real success in trying to find referential representations in any of the representational substrata discussed in section 3.2.3.[11] A categorical error seems to be involved in these investigations: how can we expect to find referential representational structures (such as symbols) in the substratum that is responsible for generating exactly these structures? In other words, the representational mechanisms and substrata being responsible for generating stable referential representations (e.g., neural activities) are confused with their results (e.g., propositions, mental images, etc.).

One of the consequences of such a view is that knowledge – and this applies to scientific theories as well – (i) is always hypothetical, (ii) is in a continuous flow, and (iii) characterizes the environment only to the extent of what it is *not*.[12] Furthermore, (iv) knowledge is always system-relative and (v) there can exist two or more (competing) theories or strategies that equally well fit into the same environmental constraints.

4 Acquiring new concepts, learning, the context of discovery, and moving around in theory space

4.1 Learning and dynamics in the neural representation space

What an external observer refers to as "learning" or acquiring new knowledge can be explained, as we have seen above, as adaptation and construction processes occurring in the neural substratum. The changes in the synaptic weights lead to a change in the dynamics of spreading activations which, in turn, lead to a change in the organism's behavioral dynamics which is interpreted as a change in knowledge or as the construction of a new theory or representation by an observer.

From empirical evidence as well as simulation experiments it is known that "learning" can be interpreted as a more or less directed *search process* in the weight space on a conceptual level. Abstractly speaking, a point is moving around in weight space. This process is physically realized as changes in the synaptic weights. There exists a wide variety of "learning algorithms and mechanisms" which are based in one way or the other on Hebb's (1949) concepts of learning. Long-term potentiation (LTP), long-term depression (LTD) (Brown *et al.* 1990; Churchland and Sejnowski 1992; Gazzaniga 1995; Dudai 1989; Singer 1990), or connectionist learning algorithms (e.g., Hertz *et al* 1991; Rumelhart 1989; and many others) are only instantiations of Hebb's principles. From an epistemological perspective, the basic principle can be summarized as follows: those physically realized relationships (i.e., synaptic configurations) that lead to successful behaviors are reinforced, whereas synaptic configurations that are responsible for generating inadequate behavior are changed or suppressed.

Changing the synaptic weights is an *inductive process* in which "new" knowledge or theories are generated on a hypothetical basis. These strategies for generating behavior are used and applied under the assumption "as if they were true or fitting". Only in the (deductive) process of externalizing them it becomes evident whether the theories or knowledge being represented in the current synaptic configuration are viable or not (see the feedback loop in Figure 9.2). The success or failure of the externalization leads to an internally or externally determined error[13] which has to be minimized in the following learning steps. From this perspective learning turns out to be a search process in which an error has to be minimized.

A minimal error means a(n epistemologically) stable relationship with the environment in the context of the organism's task to survive. This stability is physically realized as a stable homeostasis. In this cycle of alternately inductive and deductive processes a physical structure is developing which is capable of generating functionally fitting behavior. From an observer's perspective, one could say that this structure "represents" knowledge about the environment and has developed in a process of construction and adaptation. However, one should not make the error of assuming that there is some kind of convergence toward a "true" or "ultimate" knowledge about the environment. As has been discussed, this knowledge or theory is always *system-relative*, i.e., the success or failure does not depend only on how well the externalized behavior fits into the environment, but also on the internal organization of the whole organism which determines what is successful and what is a failure. In other words, the structure of the organism implicitly defines the premises under which knowledge can be successful or not. Thus, different organisms (even of a single species) will have more or less different criteria for successful, functionally fitting, viable, or adequate knowledge, theories, or behavior. In the scientific realm this is known as the phenomenon that – under different background assumptions and methods – different theories will be adequate or "true".

Of course, this does *not* imply – as is often done by many critics of the constructivist approach – that the resulting constructs or theories are completely arbitrary. Rather, they have to be understood as the result of a process that aims at constructing (transformation) mechanisms that are capable of coping with the *constraints* of the internal and external environment. The ontogenetic constructs are constrained by (a) the external environment, (b) the organization of the internal environment, and (c) by the genetically determined space of possible constructs (i.e., the basic architecture of a specific nervous system allows, despite the possibility of learning, only a certain space of possible constructs – and this space is implicitly defined by the genetic code). The dynamics of the genetic structure is constrained by the success or failure of the organism (= its reproduction rate), by the environmental resources, by the organism's body and representation architecture, as well as by the inherent mechanisms of genetic expression.

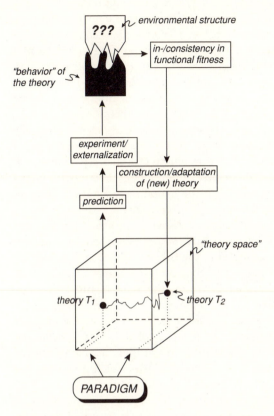

Figure 9.3 The dynamics in *theory space* and its interaction with the environment

4.2 Dynamics in theory space

What can we learn from the concepts discussed above for the process of science and, more specifically, for the process of acquiring new theoretic concepts? First of all, we have to keep in mind that the process of constructing new theories is a deeply cognitive process. In other words, it is rooted in the processes and the representational dynamics described above and in section 3.2. From this perspective it is not surprising that similar concepts can be applied to this still mysterious process of "discovery" in science. Discovery is not so much characterized as discovering new features or regularities in the environment; rather, it is the discovery and construction of new relationships and strategies for coping successfully and effectively with the environment – these processes are only occurring inside the neural representation system.

Scientific theories are represented in the same way as any other knowledge in the neural substratum. Therefore, they can be interpreted as certain states in a state space. To represent a certain theory T_i means to be in a certain state in synaptic weight space. To assume a certain weight configuration implies a set of behavioral strategies that can be externalized in/to the environment (in certain internal and external contexts). Figure 9.3 shows the situation for scientific theories on a more abstract level. The (implicitly assumed) scientific paradigm (in the sense of Kuhn (1970)) gives rise to a space of possible theories. Each point in this theory space instantiates a certain theory T_i. This space is embedded in the larger synaptic weight space. Thus, moving around in the synaptic weight space has an effect on the state of the theory space.

The process of constructing new theories or changing/adapting already existing theories is based on the same neural processes as any learning process (see above) – it can be characterized as a search process in a representational state space. In Figure 9.3 this cyclic process of developing theories is depicted in detail: the theory space is embedded in the neural representation space. A certain point in this (high dimensional) space represents a certain theory T_i. Similarly as in the common sense domain, this neural configuration leads to (i) a prediction which, in turn, can be (ii) *externalized* in the form of an *experiment*. The experiment can be compared to the behavior of a cognitive system. That is, some kind of direct or indirect motor action modulates, or perturbates the environmental dynamics. In other words, the theory represents knowledge or a strategy about how to penetrate the environment in such a way that a desired or predicted state is achieved. The theory also determines the methods that are applied to the environment. In the case of cognitive systems the "method" is the motor systems; in the scientific realm these motor systems are extended by more or less complex tools and/or machines which perturbate the environment according to the theory's rules and instructions.

As can be seen in Figure 9.3, the resulting "theory's behavior", which is externalized in an experiment, fits more or less into the structure of the environment. The level of functional fitness is determined by the *success* of penetrating the environment in a certain (desired) way. If the environmental dynamics does not "respond" in the desired or predicted way, this indicates that this particular (configuration of the) theory has failed (or is falsified), and that it is necessary to change, adapt or completely reconstruct it. The goal is to *reduce the inconsistencies* between the theoretical descriptions, predictions, and the actual environmental dynamics. Looking at this process the other way around, theories as well as any other (successful) representational structure can be described as results of a process that aims at establishing consistency between environmental and body constraints. The knowledge or theory is the mediating substratum which is responsible for generating functionally fitting behavior in the process of interaction between the organism and the environment. This consistency is achieved by a continuous process of adaptation and construction of functionally fitting strategies and behaviors. These construction and adaptation processes are realized by the neural dynamics shown in section 4.1. It can be described as an optimization process searching for an adequate transformation mechanism which is realized as a weight configuration in the synaptic weight space. In other words, a point moves around in theory space – each point instantiates a particular theory and moving points in theory space represent the transition from one theory to another.

The goal of these processes is to *extract relevant regularities* from the environmental dynamics. The representation of these system relative regularities are the foundation for any externalization of behavior or experiments. They are used for making predictions – and, in most cases, predictions enhance the chances for survival or, at least, simplify life, if they prove to be successful in the "real world". From this perspective, neural construction and adaptation processes are the heart of any scientific *inductive* process in which a new theory is created or an already existing theory is adapted or changed. Furthermore, it turns out that, as can be seen in Figure 9.3, the "creation" or construction of new theories or knowledge does not bring forth "really new" knowledge. Rather, the context of discovery can be described as a *search* process in an already predetermined space of possible theories. This space is predetermined by the paradigm (Kuhn 1970) that has been chosen by the cognitive system. The goal of this search process is to *optimize* the fit and the level of consistency within the boundaries of this paradigm.[14] Most research in modern natural sciences turns out to be optimizing sets of parameters, methods, experimental set-ups, etc. leading to a better fit and consistency between predicted and actual phenomena.[15]

This may sound a bit disappointing and provocative in the context of the epistemological and social status that scientific knowledge or theories normally claim to have. As an implication of the "cognitive view" as well as of a historic view of scientific processes, the notion of ultimate, objective, or true knowledge has to be seriously questioned. As has been mentioned already, I suggest replacing it with the concepts of system relativity, functional fitness, and viability. Scientific knowledge, nevertheless, remains at the peak of what we can know about our environment. However, it will always remain hypothetical, system relative, in steady flow, and does not describe or map the environment, but rather provides strategies for successfully coping, modulating, and manipulating the environmental dynamics.

In the picture about embedding scientific processes in neural dynamics, which has been presented above, a couple of questions remain unanswered: what happens if the search in theory space is not successful or unsatisfactory? What happens if the cognitive system's goals and desires change? Who defines the (semantics of the) dimensions of the theory space? Which role does the paradigm play, and what happens if the scientist (alias cognitive system) changes the paradigm or "invents" or constructs a new paradigm? These questions will be addressed in the following section.

5 Paradigmatic shifts and theory spaces

In the previous section we have seen that a paradigm (Kuhn 1970) gives rise to a space of possible theories (= "theory space") which is searched in the process of "normal science". In this context we are facing the problem of what happens

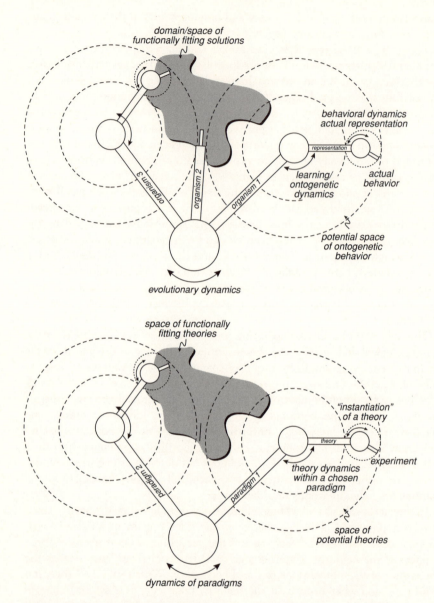

Figure 9.4 Comparing the evolutionary and ontogenetic dynamics of cognitive
systems and scientific processes in the "robot-arm analogy"

to the theory space when a paradigmatic shift occurs and, furthermore, which
(cognitive) mechanisms can be found to explain paradigmatic shifts. As is well
known from the history of science, in most cases a paradigmatic shift leads to
completely new concepts, perspectives, and categories of how to view and understand a certain environmental phenomenon. In constructivist terminology this

means that a completely new key is constructed in order to fit into the lock/environment.[16] How do these new categories, terminologies, and theories emerge? In order to approach this problem from a cognitive perspective, let's have a look at the interactions between evolutionary processes and ontogenetic dynamics in the neural representational substratum in a first step.

The upper part of Figure 9.4 shows the "robot-arm analogy" (Belew 1990) for cognitive systems. It is an analogy that demonstrates the interaction between phylogenetic/evolutionary and ontogenetic dynamics. This robot arm has three degrees of freedom:

(i) In the *evolutionary dynamics* a particular genetic code is instantiated and expressed. In the process of interaction with the environment an organism develops. This organism has a (neural) representation system at its disposal.

(ii) The second degree of freedom consists in the representational dynamics discussed in section 4.1 (i.e., learning, neural plasticity, search in weight space, etc.). The current state of the representation/weight space gives rise to a structure in activation space.

(iii) The dynamics of spreading activations instantiates states in the activation space and leads to the externalization of behavior. The success or failure of this behavior (= level of functional fitness of the behavior and of the representational structure) causes changes in the representational dynamics.

Over more generations the success or failure of the basic architecture of the representation system, the resulting behavior, as well as the genetically encoded basic body structures, developmental instructions, and learning/adaptation mechanisms cause a genetic drift ("evolution"). More abstractly speaking, the genetic code changes over time and gives rise to a newly structured representational space (= synaptic weight space, potential space of possible representational configurations of an organism) and, thus, to a new set of behavioral strategies. In the course of ontogenesis this space is searched, as has been described in section 4.1. A particular state in the weight space gives rise to a space of potential representations and behavioral strategies (= activation space).[17] The goal of the phylo- and ontogenetic dynamics is to turn the robot's arm in such a way that its tips find the region of functionally fitting solutions, behaviors, or knowledge.

What can these interactions between evolutionary and ontogenetic representational dynamics teach us for our problem of paradigmatic shifts? The lower part of Figure 9.4 shows how the dynamics of paradigms and theories fits into this picture. In section 4.2 it has been shown that "normal science" (in the sense of Kuhn (1970)) can be characterized as a search and optimization process in theory space. It is embedded in the adaptation, learning, and construction processes of the whole neural representation system. The goal is to find consistency between the environment and the theories that are generated (i.e., moving points in theory space) within the context and boundaries of the chosen paradigm. In this terminology a *paradigmatic shift* can be described as the construction of a whole *new theory space*. It consists of different dimensions, new and different semantics in the dimensions, and different representational and behavioral dynamics. This newly constructed theory space, of course, is embedded in the neural substratum and represents a whole new space of potential representational constructs, relationships, and behavioral patterns. In order to test this potential space of new theories, this new theory space has to be explored, as described in section 4.2.

Looking at examples from history of science, one can see that the introduction of new paradigms often brought about some kind of surprise about the new way of looking at and structuring well-known phenomena. It is the "irrational" and unexpected character that makes paradigmatic shifts so interesting – whereas in normal science most results are rather predictable and the theories responsible for them have to undergo only minor adaptations.[18] Contrary to already established paradigms, newly constructed and unexplored paradigms are based on completely new concepts, basic assumptions, terminologies, and methods in most cases. This "irrational" character suggests that the (cognitive) processes involved in generating paradigmatic shifts might have *evolutionary character*: a new paradigm is brought forth in a trial-and-error manner. It is even more hypothetical than the generation of a new theory in the context of an already established theory space/paradigm. This is due to the fact that at the moment of the introduction of a new paradigm a completely hypothetical framework and space of potential theories is being suggested and generated. Hence, there is relatively high risk involved in this process. It can be compared to the process of expressing a gene that has undergone some kind of mutation. It is completely unclear whether the resulting organism and its potential representational structures and behaviors will be capable of surviving. Similarly, at the moment of the conception of a new paradigm, a totally new potential theory space is created which has to be explored by the process of "normal science" – it is not at all clear whether this space of potential theories will be successful or not.

The mechanisms involved in paradigmatic shifts can be compared to *evolutionary operators* which are applied to cognitive/representational structures. The introduction of completely new and unexpected categories, making use of metaphors, combining aspects from different theories, etc. has a lot in common with random mutations, cross over operators, etc. By applying these operators, a completely new theory space is established – as can be seen in Figure 9.4 (bottom) the goal is to rotate the robot arm into the region of functionally fitting theories. From this perspective it is also clear that two or more different theories can account for the same phenomenon, that is, the same area of functionally fitting solutions can be reached with different robot-arm configurations (= different conceptual systems). In other words, a phenomenon is approached from two or more different sides or angles. As the goal is not to create an image or 1 : 1 mapping of the environment, but to construct consistencies in the form of functionally fitting behavior, it is no contradiction that two or more theories can account for the same phenomenon by making use of different representational categories. In any case, the interaction between evolutionary mechanisms and ontogenetic representational dynamics could shed some light on the mysterious phenomenon of paradigmatic shifts in science. Evolutionary operators act as "paradigm generators"; each of these paradigms establishes a space of potential theories which has to be searched according to the rules outlined in sections 4.2 and 4.1.

Critics of such an evolutionary perspective of growth and development of scientific knowledge (e.g., Thagard 1988) are right in stating that a purely blind search for new scientific concepts is not an adequate model. That is why the focus of this chapter is not only on phylogenetic processes, but also on ontogenetic learning/adaptation (see section 4). The important point is the *interaction* between the rather directed ontogenetic and neurally based learning, adaptation, and construction processes and the "blind" phylogenetic processes. Evolutionary variation "blindly" brings forth a completely hypothetical space of knowledge/strategies (paradigm) which is explored in a directed manner in the course of ontogenetic development. In this process of exploration the new paradigm will prove its in-/adequacy very soon.

Contrary to Thagard's view (1988) that "the biological roots of the human information processing system are not directly relevant to the task of developing a model for the growth of scientific knowledge" (p. 105), the presented concepts suggest that so-called scientific processes are not at all abstract processes occurring in a detached system called science. Rather, they are embedded in and results of the activities and dynamics of one or a group of neural systems and, thus, follow a similar dynamics.

6 Implications and conclusions

The approach suggested in this chapter does not aim to replace traditional theories and concepts in philosophy of science. Rather, the goal is to give (the explanation and theory about) science a new foundation – scientific processes are embedded in cognitive processes. Starting from this very basic assumption, it might be possible to view scientific processes and traditional approaches in philosophy of science from a new (cognitive) perspective which might lead to a reformulation of these theories. I am aware that there is still a very long way to go until satisfactory theories about the cognitive foundation of science will be available. Hence, the goal of this chapter is *not* to suggest such a detailed theory, but rather to show how basic principles and concepts that have emerged in the last decade in the fields of cognitive science, computational neuroscience, and artificial life can be used as *tools* for enabling the construction of such a theory.

Both cognitive systems and science have the representation of the world as their most important task. As has been shown, neither neural nor scientific representation aims at depicting or mapping the world. Of course, the obvious goal of science is to describe and explain environmental phenomena – however, as has been discussed in the context of the constructivist concepts, the epistemological status of theories (and any kind of knowledge, in general) is constructive rather than descriptive. Hence, theories, even if they have "descriptive character", are the result of complex processes of construction, which, in principle, cannot produce more than functionally fitting representations of the world. The goal is to *construct strategies* that are capable of adequately predicting and coping with the environmental dynamics. Even if it seems that our cognitive or nervous system provides us with "pictures of the environment", it can be shown that these pictures are the result of *active processes of construction* embodied in the architecture of the neural representation system. The goal of these construction processes is not to reconstruct the environmental structure as accurately as possible, but to provide the organism with relevant information and representations for generating adequate behavior, making reasonable decisions, etc. The representations or theories only have to fit into the environment. This constructive character of representations becomes even more obvious in the case of scientific theories. In most cases they do not speak about entities which can be perceived by our sensory systems – theoretic entities are constructs about hidden mechanisms[19] which fit (as explanations or predictions) into the perceivable environmental dynamics.

In this sense knowledge and/or theories become *tools* that are used for predicting, controlling, and manipulating the environment. In the common sense domain we use representational entities, such as concepts, symbols, language, etc., as means for manipulating and influencing the environmental dynamics and/or the (representational) dynamics of other cognitive systems. Although theoretic or scientific entities, such as concepts in physics (particles, waves, force fields, etc.), biology, or psychology (dynamics of propositions, "mind", etc.), have never been explicitly "seen" or felt, they turn out to be extremely powerful and useful tools in the domains of predicting, manipulating, and explaining environmental phenomena.

As has been shown, concepts from computational neuroscience and artificial life provide a conceptual framework enabling the embedding of scientific into cognitive processes. The dynamics of theories is realized in the dynamics occurring in the synaptic weight space and the genetic space. From this perspective the "context of discovery" and the construction of new scientific concepts can be operationalized in the sense that cognitive and neural mechanisms act as explanatory vehicles which account for the still mysterious process of discovering and constructing new scientific knowledge.

As an implication, scientific knowledge becomes some kind of "truth tool", which is not necessarily structurally equivalent or homomorphic with the environment. From studying neural systems we can learn that representation has to be understood as a *strategy for coping with the environment* in the context of the organism's task to survive. This is achieved by a mutual process of adaptation and construction leading to changes in the representational structure which enable the generation of (hopefully) adequate behavior. The resulting representational structure does not have anything to do with an "objective" description of the environment. The same can be applied in the scientific domain: why do we expect tools or strategies for manipulating the environment to map or represent the environment in an iso-/homomorphic and "objective" way? Do we expect a hammer or a tooth to be structurally equivalent to a nail or to the entities the tooth chews? Both represent knowledge in the sense that they are results of constructive processes that are based on evolutionary and cognitive dynamics. In both cases the goal is to cope successfully with some environmental phenomenon or problem. Similarly, scientific theories are not so much descriptions of an environmental phenomenon, but answers to questions of how to deal with this phenomenon in the form of functionally fitting solutions.

Notes

1 To be more precise, a new internal state is generated. The behavioral output is a subset of this internal state; that is, a subset of all neurons that constitute the internal state is connected to motor systems and, thus, controls the organism's behavioral dynamics.

2 These environmental states are "desired" in the sense that they are necessary for the organism's survival. Of course, the manipulation of environmental states includes also the organism's internal environment, such as blood pressure, body temperature, etc.

3 In its most extreme form the idea of successfully manipulating the environment – without being really interested in understanding what is happening – can be found in the development of modern *technologies*. The goal is not so much an adequate description of the environment, but a *functioning system*.

4 In the scientific domain this can be seen even more clearly: a variety of *different theories* exists for a single phenomenon. Most of these theories describe the environmental regularities quite well with respect to their assumptions and underlying theoretical framework.

5 This behavioral or manipulative aspect can be found in its minimal form whenever an *experiment* is conducted. One aspect of the environment is actively pushed into a certain state in order to produce a certain phenomenon – it does not matter whether this is the process of letting fall an apple, of accelerating electrons, or of putting a subject into a psychological lab and an experimental setting.

6 And this applies to any organism and to almost any form of knowledge.

7 This process has been investigated in great detail by *traditional* philosophy of science.

8 In many cases this would not be possible in empirical experiments (for practical, methodological, and/or ethical reasons).

9 This process of instantiating a certain state or state transition can be compared to the process of *deducing* certain predictions, behaviors, or experiments from theories; see also section 3.2.1 and the right side of Figure 9.2.

10 Under the assumption that the neural networks consist of m synaptic weighs.

11 See also the discussions about the representational capabilities of artificial and natural neural systems.

12 It characterizes the environment only *negatively*, i.e., it is the result of the "collisions" with the environment in the process of interacting and adapting with/to it.

13 In many cases this *error* is defined by the state of the organism's dis-/equilibrium or homeostasis.

14 This process could be compared to Kuhn's concept of puzzle solving (Kuhn 1970).

15 Think, for instance, of *serial experiments* in biology, physics, in the process of developing almost any theory.

16　Whereas in the search process (of normal science) described in section 4.2 only minor changes are made to the key.
17　The spaces of potential behaviors or representations are marked by dotted circles/regions in Figure 9.4.
18　That is, their main claims and the basic assumptions and categories on which they are based remain unquestioned and *untouched*.
19　That is, these mechanisms are not perceivable by human sensory systems. They are hidden in the sense that they seem to be responsible for the directly observable phenomena, but can be accessed only via sophisticated instruments which detect and transform these hidden dynamics into the perceivable domain according to the theories on which they are based.

References

Anderson, J.A., A. Pellionisz, and E. Rosenfeld (Eds.) (1991). *Neurocomputing 2. Directions of research*. Cambridge, MA: MIT Press.

Anderson, J.A. and E. Rosenfeld (Eds.) (1988). *Neurocomputing. Foundations of research*. Cambridge, MA: MIT Press.

Arbib, M.A. (Ed.) (1995). *The handbook of brain theory and neural networks*. Cambridge, MA: MIT Press.

Ashby, R.W. (1964). *An introduction to cybernetics*. London: Methuen.

Belew, R.K. (1990). Evolution, learning, and culture: computational metaphors for adaptive algorithms. *Complex Systems 4*, 11–49.

Belew, R.K., J. McInerney, and N.N. Schraudolph (1992). Evolving networks: using the genetic algorithm with connectionist learning. In C.G. Langton, C. Taylor, J.D. Farmer, and S. Rasmussen (Eds.), *Artificial life II*. Redwood City, CA: Addison-Wesley, pp. 511–547.

Berger, P. and M. Singer (1992). *Dealing with genes: the language of heredity*. Mill Valley, CA: University Science Books.

Brakel, J.v. (1994). Cognitive scientism of science. *Psycoloquy (electronic journal)* 5(20). Filename: scientific-cognition.3.vanbrakel.

Brown, T.H., A.H. Ganong, E.W. Kariss, and C.L. Keenan (1990). Hebbian synapses: biophysical mechanisms and algorithms. *Annual Review of Neuroscience 13*, 475–511.

Cangelosi, A., D. Parisi, and S. Nolfi (1994). Cell division and migration in a genotype for neural networks. *Network: computation in neural systems 5(4)*, 497–516.

Chiba, A., D. Shepherd, and R.K. Murphey (1988). Synaptic rearrangement during postembryotic development in the cricket. *Science 240*, 901–905.

Churchland, P.M. (Ed.) (1989). *A neurocomputational perspective – the nature of mind and the structure of science*. Cambridge, MA: MIT Press.

Churchland, P.M. (1991). A deeper unity: some Feyerabendian themes in neurocomputational form. In G. Munevar (Ed.), *Beyond reason: essays on the philosophy of Paul Feyerabend*, Dordrecht, Boston: Kluwer Academic Publishers, pp. 1–23. (Reprinted in R.N. Giere (ed.) (1992). *Cognitive models of science*, Minnesota Studies in the Philosophy of Science XV. Minneapolis: University of Minnesota Press.)

Churchland, P.M. (1995). *The engine of reason, the seat of the soul. A philosophical journey into the brain*. Cambridge, MA: MIT Press.

Churchland, P.S., C. Koch, and T.J. Sejnowski (1990). What is computational neuroscience? In E.L. Schwartz (Ed.), *Computational neuroscience*. Cambridge, MA: MIT Press.

Churchland, P.S. and T.J. Sejnowski (1989). Neural representation and neural computation. In A.M. Galaburda (Ed.), *From reading to neurons*. Cambridge, MA: MIT Press, pp. 217–250.

Churchland, P.S. and T.J. Sejnowski (1992). *The computational brain*. Cambridge, MA: MIT Press.

Clark, A. (1989). *Microcognition: philosophy, cognitive science, and parallel distributed processing*. Cambridge, MA: MIT Press.

Dudai, Y. (1989). *The neurobiology of memory: concept, findings, trends*. New York: Oxford University Press.

Edelman, G.M. (1988). *Topobiology: an introduction to molecular embryology*. New York: Basic Books.

Elman, J.L. (1991). Distributed representation, simple recurrent networks, and grammatical structure. *Machine Learning* 7(2/3), 195–225.

Fodor, J.A. (1975). *The language of thought*. New York: Crowell.

Fodor, J.A. (1981). *Representations: philosophical essays on the foundations of cognitive science*. Cambridge, MA: MIT Press.

Fodor, J.A. (1983). *The modularity of mind*. Cambridge, MA: MIT Press.

Foerster, H.v. (1973). On constructing a reality. In W.F. E. Preiser (Ed.), *Environmental design research*, Volume 2. Stroudsburg, PA: Hutchinson and Ross. (Reprinted in P. Watzlawick (Ed.) (1984). *The invented reality*. New York: Norton, pp. 41–61.)

Gazzaniga, M.S. (Ed.) (1995). *The cognitive neurosciences*. Cambridge, MA: MIT Press.

Gelder, T.v. (1992). Defining "distributed representation". *Connection Science* 4(3/4), 175–191.

Gelder, T.v. and R. Port (1995). It's about time: an overview of the dynamical approach to cognition. In R. Port and T.v. Gelder (Eds.), *Mind as motion*. Cambridge, MA: MIT Press.

Giere, R.N. (Ed.) (1992). *Cognitive models of science*, Minnesota Studies in the Philosophy of Science XV. Minneapolis: University of Minnesota Press.

Giere, R.N. (1994). The cognitive structure of scientific theories. *Philosophy of Science* 61, 276–296.

Glasersfeld, E.v. (1984). An introduction to radical constructivism. In P. Watzlawick (Ed.), *The invented reality*. New York: Norton, pp. 17–40.

Glasersfeld, E.v. (1995). *Radical constructivism: a way of knowing and learning*. London: Falmer Press.

Goldberg, D.E. (1989). *Genetic algorithms in search, optimization, and machine learning*. Reading, MA: Addison-Wesley.

Green, D.W. et al. (1996). *Cognitive science. An introduction*. Cambridge, MA: B. Blackwell.

Harp, S., T. Samad, and A. Guha (1989). Towards the genetic synthesis of neural networks. In J.D. Schaffer (Ed.), *Proceedings of the Third International Conference on Genetic Algorithms*. San Mateo, CA: M. Kaufmann Pub.

Hebb, D.O. (1949). *The organization of behavior; a neuropsychological theory*. New York: Wiley.

Heiden, U.a.d. (1992). Selbstorganisation in dynamischen Systemen. In W. Krohn and G. Küppers (Eds.), *Emergenz: die Entstehung von Ordnung, Organisation und Bedeutung*. Frankfurt/M.: Suhrkamp, pp. 57–88.

Hertz, J., A. Krogh, and R.G. Palmer (1991). *Introduction to the theory of neural computation*, Santa Fe Institute Studies in the Sciences of Complexity, Volume 1, Lecture notes. Redwood City, CA: Addison-Wesley.

Hinton, G.E. (1987). *Connectionist learning procedures*. Technical Report CMU-CS-87–115, Carnegie-Mellon University, Pittsburgh, PA.

Hinton, G.E., J.L. McClelland, and D.E. Rumelhart (1986). Distributed representations. In D.E. Rumelhart and J.L. McClelland (Eds.), *Parallel distributed processing: explorations in the microstructure of cognition. Foundations*, Volume I. Cambridge, MA: MIT Press, pp. 77–109.

Hinton, G.E. and S.J. Nowlan (1987). How learning can guide evolution. *Complex Systems 1*, 495–502.

Hinton, G.E. and T.J. Sejnowski (1986). Learning and relearning in Boltzman machines. In D.E. Rumelhart and J.L. McClelland (Eds.), *Parallel distributed processing: explorations in the microstructure of cognition. Foundations*, Volume I. Cambridge, MA: MIT Press, pp. 282–316.

Holland, J.H. (1975). *Adaptation in natural and artificial systems: an introductory analysis with applications to biology, control, and artificial intelligence*. Ann Arbor: University of Michigan Press.

Horgan, T. and J. Tienson (1996). *Connectionism and the philosophy of psychology*. Cambridge, MA: MIT Press.

Jessel, T.M. (1991). Neuronal survival and synapse formation. In E.R. Kandel, J.H. Schwartz, and T.M. Jessel (Eds.), *Principles of neural science* (3rd ed.). New York: Elsevier, pp. 929–944.

Kosslyn, S.M. (1990). Mental imagery. In D.N. Osherson and H. Lasnik (Eds.), *An invitation to cognitive science*, Volume 2. Cambridge, MA: MIT Press, pp. 73–97.

Kosslyn, S.M. (1994). *Image and brain. The resolution of the imagery debate*. Cambridge, MA: MIT Press.

Kosslyn, S.M. and J.R. Pomerantz (1977). Imagery, propositions, and the form of internal representations. *Cognitive Psychology 9*, 52–76.

Kosso, P. (1992). *Reading the book of nature*. Cambridge: Cambridge University Press.

Kuhn, T.S. (1970). *The structure of scientific revolutions* (2nd ed.). Chicago: University of Chicago Press.

Langton, C.G. (Ed.) (1989). *Artificial life*. Redwood City, CA: Addison-Wesley.

Langton, C.G. (Ed.) (1994). *Artificial life III*. Redwood City, CA: Addison-Wesley.

Langton, C.G. (Ed.) (1995). *Artificial life. An introduction*. Cambridge, MA: MIT Press.

Lawrence, P.A. (1992). *The making of a fly. The genetics of animal design*. London, Boston: B. Blackwell.

Maturana, H.R. and F.J. Varela (Eds.) (1980). *Autopoiesis and cognition: the realization of the living*, Boston Studies in the Philosophy of Science, Volume 42. Dordrecht, Boston: D. Reidel Pub. Co.

Meyer, J.A. and S.W. Wilson (Eds.) (1991). *From animals to animats: proceedings of the First International Conference on Simulation of Adaptive Behavior (SAB '90)*. Cambridge, MA: MIT Press.

Miller, G., P. Todd, and S. Hedge (1989). Designing neural networks using genetic algorithms. In J.D. Schaffer (Ed.), *Proceedings of the Third International Conference on Genetic Algorithms*. San Mateo, CA: M. Kaufmann Pub.

Mitchell, M. and S. Forrest (1994). Genetic algorithms and artificial life. *Artficial Life 1*(3), 267–291.

Newell, A. (1980). Physical symbol systems. *Cognitive Science 4*, 135–183.

Newell, A., P.S. Rosenbloom, and J.E. Laird (1989). Symbolic architectures for cognition. In M.I. Posner (Ed.), *Foundations of cognitive science*. Cambridge, MA: MIT Press, pp. 93–131.

Newell, A. and H.A. Simon (1976). Computer science as empirical inquiry: symbols and search. *Communications of the Association for Computing Machinery (ACM)* 19(3), 113–126. (Reprinted in M. Boden (ed.) (1990). *The philosophy of artificial intelligence.* Oxford: Oxford University Press.)

Nolfi, S., J.L. Elman, and D. Parisi (1990). *Learning and evolution in neural networks.* Technical Report CRL-9019, CRL, University of California, San Diego.

Nolfi, S. and D. Parisi (1991). *Growing neural networks.* Technical Report PCIA-91-18, Inst. of Psychology, C.N.R., Rome.

Peschl, M.F. (1992a). Construction, representation, and embodiment of knowledge, meaning, and symbols in neural structures. Towards an alternative understanding of knowledge representation and philosophy of science. *Connection Science* 4(3/4), 327–338.

Peschl, M.F. (1992b). Embodiment of knowledge in natural and artificial neural structures. Suggestions for a cognitive foundation of philosophy of science from a computational neuroepistemology perspective. *Methodologica 11*, 7–34.

Peschl, M.F. (1993). Knowledge representation in cognitive systems and science. In search of a new foundation for philosophy of science from a neurocomputational and evolutionary perspective of cognition. *Journal of Social and Evolutionary Systems 16*, 181–213.

Peschl, M.F. (1994a). Autonomy vs. environmental dependency in neural knowledge representation. In R. Brooks and P. Maes (Eds.), *Artificial life IV.* Cambridge, MA: MIT Press, pp. 417–423.

Peschl, M.F. (1994b). *Repräsentation und Konstruktion. Kognitions- und neuroinformtische Konzepte als Grundlage einer naturalisierten Epistemologie und Wissenschaftstheorie.* Braunschweig/Wiesbaden: Vieweg.

Port, R. and T.v. Gelder (Eds.) (1995). *Mind as motion: explorations in the dynamics of cognition.* Cambridge, MA: MIT Press.

Posner, M.I. (Ed.) (1989). *Foundations of cognitive science.* Cambridge, MA: MIT Press.

Roth, G. (1994). *Das Gehirn und seine Wirklichkeit. Kognitive Neurobiologie und ihre philosophischen Konsequenzen.* Frankfurt/M.: Suhrkamp.

Rumelhart, D.E. (1989). The architecture of mind: a connectionist approach. In M.I. Posner (Ed.), *Foundations of cognitive science.* Cambridge, MA: MIT Press, pp. 133–159.

Rumelhart, D.E., G.E. Hinton, and R.J. Williams (1986). Learning internal representations by error propagation. In D.E. Rumelhart and J.L. McClelland (Eds.), *Parallel distributed processing: explorations in the microstructure of cognition. Foundations*, Volume I. Cambridge, MA: MIT Press, pp. 318–361.

Rumelhart, D.E. and J.L. McClelland (Eds.) (1986). *Parallel distributed processing: explorations in the microstructure of cognition. Foundations*, Volume I. Cambridge, MA: MIT Press.

Rumelhart, D.E., P. Smolensky, J.L. McClelland, and G.E. Hinton (1986). Schemata and sequential thought processes in PDP models. In J.L. McClelland and D.E. Rumelhart (Eds.), *Parallel distributed processing: explorations in the microstructure of cognition. Psychological and biological models*, Volume II. Cambridge, MA: MIT Press, pp. 7–57.

Schwartz, E.L. (Ed.) (1990). *Computational neuroscience.* Cambridge, MA: MIT Press.

Sejnowski, T.J., C. Koch, and P.S. Churchland (1988). Computational neuroscience. *Science 241*(4871), 1299–1306.

Singer, W. (1990). Search for coherence: a basic principle of cortical self-organization. *Concepts in Neuroscience 1*, 1–26.

Steels, L. (1996). The origins of intelligence. In *Proceedings of the Carlo Erba Foundation Meeting on Artificial Life*. Milan: Foundazione Carlo Erba.

Steier, F. (Ed.) (1991). *Research and reflexivity*. London, Newbury Park, CA: Sage Publishers.

Thagard, P. (1988). *Computational philosophy of science*. Cambridge, MA: MIT Press.

Varela, F.J., E. Thompson, and E. Rosch (1991). *The embodied mind: cognitive science and human experience*. Cambridge, MA: MIT Press.

Watzlawick, P. (Ed.) (1984). *The invented reality*. New York: Norton.

Wiener, N. (1948). *Cybernetics; or, control and communication in the animal and the machine*. New York: Wiley.

Winston, P.H. (1992). *Artificial intelligence* (3rd ed.). Reading, MA: Addison-Wesley.

10 The concept of disease
Structure and change*

Paul Thagard

Abstract

By contrasting Hippocratic and nineteenth century theories of disease, this chapter describes important conceptual changes that have taken place in the history of medicine. Disease concepts are presented as causal networks that represent the relations among the symptoms, causes, and treatment of a disease. The transition to the germ theory of disease produced dramatic conceptual changes as the result of a radically new view of disease causation. An analogy between disease and fermentation was important for two of the main developers of the germ theory of disease, Pasteur and Lister. Attention to the development of germ concepts shows the need for a referential account of conceptual change to complement a representational account.

Laypeople are familiar with dozens of diseases such as influenza, chicken pox, and cancer. Medical personnel acquire concepts for thousands of additional diseases, from Alzheimer's to yellow fever. What is the nature of these concepts? Examination of historical and contemporary writings on disease suggests that disease concepts can best be viewed as causal networks that represent relations among the symptoms, causes, and treatment of a disease. Conceptual change concerning disease is primarily driven by changes in causal theories about diseases. To defend these claims, I will review some important developments in the history of medicine and describe the major changes that have taken place in the concept of disease.

I begin with the ancient Greek view of disease displayed in the writings attributed to Hippocrates, whose concepts are closely connected to the humoral theory of the causes of disease. This view dominated European medical thought until the development of the germ theory of disease, which was first hinted at in the sixteenth century but not developed and generally accepted until the nineteenth. Fracastoro, an Italian physician, wrote the first important work on contagion in 1546, but the modern germ theory of disease developed with the research of Pasteur, Lister, Koch, and others in the 1860s and 1870s. Transition from the humoral to the germ theory of disease required a major conceptual revolution, involving many kinds of conceptual change including a fundamental shift in how diseases are classified. Less radical conceptual changes occurred in the twentieth

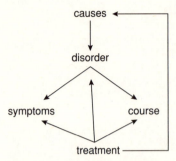

Figure 10.1 The causal structure of disease concepts

century with the discovery of genetic, nutritional, and immunological causes of disease.

Concepts

On the traditional, purely linguistic view, a concept is given by a definition that specifies necessary and sufficient conditions for its application. On this view, we should be able to provide definitions such as X is a disease if and only if __, and X is tuberculosis if and only if __. Like other concepts, however, the concept of disease has not succumbed to this kind of linguistic analysis (Reznek, 1987). Cognitive science has offered a different view of the nature of concepts, understanding them as mental representations; but the nature of conceptual representations has remained controversial. Theorists have variously proposed that concepts are prototypes, sets of exemplars, or distributed representations in neural networks (for reviews see Smith and Medin, 1981; Smith, 1989; Thagard, 1992, ch. 2; Thagard, 1996, ch. 4.).

Recently, a growing number of psychologists have emphasized the role of causal connections in understanding the nature of concepts (Carey, 1985; Keil, 1989; Medin, 1989; Murphy and Medin, 1985). The concept of a drunk, for example, is not just a set of prototypical features or typical examples, but also involves causal relations that can be used to apply the concept in an explanatory fashion: if someone falls into a swimming pool fully clothed, we can say that it happened because he or she is a drunk.

Disease concepts are particularly interesting from this theoretical perspective, because they display a rich causal structure schematized in Figure 10.1. Symptoms are the observable manifestations of a disease, which can develop over time in particular ways that constitute the expected course of the disease. The symptoms arise from the cause or causes (etiology) of the disease. Treatment of the disease should affect the symptoms and course of the disease, often by affecting the causal factors that produce the symptoms. For example, tuberculosis has a set of typical symptoms such as coughing and the growth of tubercles (nodules) in the lungs and elsewhere, along with a course

Table 10.1 Degrees of conceptual change

1	Adding a new instance of a concept, for example a patient who has tuberculosis.
2	Adding a new weak rule, for example that tuberculosis is common in prisons.
3	Adding a new strong rule that plays a frequent role in problem solving and explanation, for example that people with tuberculosis have *Mycobacterium tuberculosis*.
4	Adding a new part-relation, for example that diseased lungs contain tubercles.
5	Adding a new kind-relation, for example differentiating between pulmonary and miliary tuberculosis.
6	Adding a new concept, for example *tuberculosis* (which replaced the previous terms *phthisis* and *consumption*) or *AIDS*.
7	Collapsing part of a kind-hierarchy, abandoning a previous distinction, for example, realizing that phthisis and scrofula are the same disease, tuberculosis.
8	Reorganizing hierarchies by *branch jumping*, that is shifting a concept from one branch of a hierarchical tree to another, for example reclassifying tuberculosis as an infectious disease.
9	*Tree switching*, that is, changing the organizing principle of a hierarchical tree, for example classifying diseases in terms of causal agents rather than symptoms.

Source: adapted from Thagard, 1992, p. 35

that before the twentieth century often included wasting and death. The disorder most commonly affects the lungs, but tuberculosis can also infect many other parts of the body. In 1882, Robert Koch discovered that the cause of tuberculosis is a bacterium, now called *Mycobacterium tuberculosis*, and in 1932, Gerhard Domagk discovered that this microbe can be killed by the drug Prontosil. The drug streptomycin was discovered in 1944 and proved effective in treating the disease. Hence today tuberculosis has a well-understood cause and a kind of treatment that is effective except for the emergence of bacterial strains resistant to antibiotics.

Understanding a disease concept as a causal structure like that shown in Figure 10.1 is consistent with aspects of prototype and exemplar theories of concepts. Patients may have symptoms that approximately match a set of symptoms that typically occur in people with a particular disease. Medical personnel may have in mind particular examples of patients with a particular disease. But a disease concept is not fully captured by a set of typical symptoms or exemplars, because the causal relations are an important part of the conceptual structure, as historical examples will show.[1]

Conceptual change

Thagard (1992) identified nine degrees of conceptual change summarized in Table 10.1. Conceptual change is not simply a matter of belief revision, since concepts are not simply collections of beliefs. Rather, they are mental structures that are richly organized by means of relations such as *kind* and *part*. All the major scientific revolutions in the natural sciences – Copernicus, Newton, Lavoisier, Darwin, Einstein, quantum theory, and plate tectonics – involved major changes in conceptual organization involving kind and/or part relations (Thagard, 1992). Such changes are far more important, both psychologically and epistemologically, than mundane changes such as adding new instances or even adding new concepts. The most radical kind of conceptual change is tree switching, which changes not only the branches of a hierarchy of concepts but also the whole basis on which classifications are made. Such changes are rare, but occurred in the Darwinian revolution when the theory of evolution by natural selection brought with it a new principle of classification. Before Darwin, species were largely classified in terms of similarity, but the theory of evolution added a more fundamental mode of classification in terms of descent. Darwin's trees of kinds of organisms were based on history of descent, not just on similarity. Today, the relatedness of different species can be identified by the degree of similarity of their DNA, providing a genetic, historical basis for classification that sometimes overrules more superficial similarities.

All of these kinds of conceptual change occurred in the development of the concept of disease, particularly during the transition to the germ theory. Accounts of conceptual change by other researchers in the history, philosophy, and psychology of science are reviewed at the end of this chapter. With various kinds of conceptual change in mind, particularly branch jumping and tree switching, let us now look at some key developments in the history of the concept of disease.

Historical developments

Hippocrates and the humoral theory

Hippocrates was born on the Greek island of Cos around 460 B.C. We know little concerning what he himself wrote, but between 430 and 330 B.C. a body of medical writing was produced by him and his disciples. The Hippocratic approach to medicine, as interpreted by Galen and others, dominated European medical thought well into the nineteenth century.[2]

Hippocrates developed a naturalistic approach to medicine that contrasted sharply with the religious views that preceded him. Figure 10.2 shows the causal network that the Hippocratics rejected, for example in their discussion of the "sacred disease", epilepsy. On the traditional view, epilepsy was caused by divine visitation, and hence could only be cured by using an appeal to the gods or other magic. Little was said of the existence of a physical disorder responsible for the observable symptoms. The Hippocratics argued that epilepsy is no more sacred than any other disease, and contended that it is caused by an excess of phlegm, one of the four humors (fluids) that constitute the human body.

The following quotes from Hippocratic treatises concisely summarize the humoral theory:

> The human body contains blood, phlegm, yellow bile, and black bile. These are the things that make up its constitution and cause its pains and health.

Figure 10.2 Causal structure of religious disease concepts

> Health is primarily a state in which these constituent substances are in the correct proportion to each other, both in strength and quantity, and are well mixed.
>
> (Lloyd, 1978, p. 262)

> All human diseases arise from bile and phlegm; the bile and phlegm produce diseases when, inside the body, one of them becomes too moist, too dry, too hot, or too cold; they become this way from foods and drinks, from exertions and wounds, from smell, sound, sight, and venery, and from heat and cold.
>
> (Hippocrates, 1988, p. 7)

To modern ears, the humoral theory sounds odd, but contextually it possessed a great deal of conceptual and explanatory coherence. Many of Hippocrates' contemporaries believed that there are four fundamental elements: earth, air, fire, and water. These possess various combinations of the four qualities of moist, dry, hot, and cold; for example, fire is hot and dry. The four humors also possess these qualities in different degrees, so that bile tends to be hot and phlegm tends to be cold.

Diseases arise because of humoral imbalances. For example, too much bile can produce various fevers, and too much phlegm can cause epilepsy or angina. Imbalances arise from natural causes such as heredity (phlegmatic parents have phlegmatic children), regimen (diet and other behavior), and climate (temperature, wind, and moisture conditions). Different kinds of imbalance produce different diseases with symptoms and development that were acutely observed by the Hippocratics. They described in detail not only the symptoms of patients with a particular disease, but also the ways that the patients tended to develop toward recovery or death. The course of a disease was affected by the development of a particular humor, producing crises that signaled basic changes in patient outcome. Fevers were classified as tertian, quartan, and so on based on the number of days before a crisis occurred.

Treatment of a disease can address either the causes of the humoral imbalance by changing diet and environment, or the humoral balance itself. To rid the body of excess bile or phlegm, methods were used to induce vomiting or

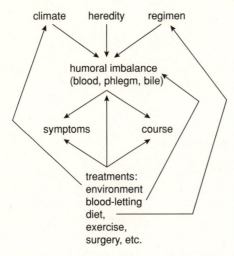

Figure 10.3 Causal structure of Hippocratic disease concepts

evacuation of the bowels, and veins were opened to let blood. The use of emetics, purgatives, and phlebotomy remained standard medical practice well into the nineteenth century. These techniques make sense within the Hippocratic framework because they are means of changing fluid balances. Figure 10.3 displays the structure of the causal network underlying the Hippocratic concept of disease.

The Hippocratics primarily classified diseases by symptoms, particularly in terms of the parts of the body affected by the diseases. The treatise *Affections* classified diseases as shown in Table 10.2. The four seasons played an important role in Hippocratic discussions of diseases, because different seasons brought with them different amounts of the four qualities of heat, cold, moist, and dry, and therefore affected humoral balance.

Fracastoro and the contagion theory

Although some Hippocratics recognized that consumption (tuberculosis) is contagious, contagion played little role in medical explanations of disease until the work of Fracastoro, who was born in Verona about 1478. In 1525 he published a long poem about the newly recognized disease syphilis, and in 1546 he published his major treatise on contagion.

Fracastoro did not deny the existence of bodily humors such as phlegm, but he contended that there is a large class of diseases caused by contagion rather than humoral imbalance. Persons can contract infections even if their humors are normally balanced. He defined a contagion as a "corruption which develops in the substance of a combination, passes from one thing to another, and is originally caused by infection of the imperceptible particles" (Fracastorius, 1930,

Table 10.2 Hippocratic classification of diseases

Diseases of the head
Diseases of the cavity
   Acute diseases
   Other winter fevers
   Summer fevers and pains
   Tertian and Quartan fevers
   White phlegm
   Large spleen
   Ileus [severe colic]
   Dropsy
   Intestinal diseases
   Strangury [painful urination]
   Articular diseases
   Jaundice
Skin conditions

Source: Hippocrates, 1988, pp. 2–3

p. 5). He called the particles the *seminaria* (seeds or seedlets) of contagion. (I translate Fracastoro's "seminaria" as "seeds" rather than the customary but anachronistic "germs".) Fracastoro was unable to say much about the nature of these conjectured particles; bacteria were not observed by van Leeuwenhoek until 1683, and their role in infection was not appreciated until the 1860s. Fracastoro nevertheless discussed the causes and treatment of various contagious diseases.

He described how contagion can occur by direct contact, by indirect contact via clothes and other substances, and by long-distance transmission. In addition, he stated that diseases can arise within an individual spontaneously. His book has chapters for the arrangement of contagious diseases shown in Table 10.3.

The differences between diseases are explained by their having different "active principles", i.e. different seeds. Fracastoro distinguished between

Table 10.3 Fracastoro's classification of contagious diseases

---

Contagious fevers
The poxes and measles
Pestilent fevers
Pestiferous fevers
Contagious phthisis
Rabies
Syphilis
Elephantiasis
Leprosy
Scabies

Source: Fracastorius, 1930

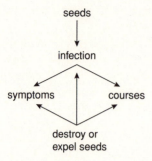

Figure 10.4 Causal structure of Fracastoro's disease concepts

different kinds of fevers in part on the basis of their being caused by different kinds of contagion. Rather than abandoning the humoral theory, he blended it with his contagion theory, suggesting that seeds for different diseases have different analogies (affinities) for different humors. For example, the principles of syphilis have an affinity with thick phlegm, whereas those of elephantiasis have an affinity with black bile.

Just as Fracastoro's contagion theory of disease postulates different causes than the humoral theory, it also recommends different treatments. Cure comes not from restoring a bodily imbalance, but from destroying or expelling the seeds of contagion. Remedies that destroy the seeds of contagion include extreme heat and cold, while evacuation of the seeds can be brought about by bowel movements, urination, sweating, blood-letting, and other methods. Methods of treatment thus overlap with those advocated by the Hippocratics, although Fracastoro urged that blood-letting not be used for contagious diseases that arise from without as opposed to those spontaneously generated from within. Figure 10.4 shows the causal structure of Fracastoro's conception of disease. The *seminaria* produce an infection that can be treated by destroying or expelling them.

According to Nutton (1990), Fracastoro's theory of contagion was respectfully received by his contemporaries, although they tended to assimilate his views to the Galenist metaphor of "seeds of disease" which did not, unlike Fracastoro's view, assume that such seeds are infectious agents transmitted from one person to another. Since no one had observed the *seminaria* postulated by Fracastoro, his hypothesis had no obvious advantage over Hippocratic assumptions that noxious airs rather than germs are a main source of epidemic diseases. After 1650, Fracastoro had little influence, although interest in his work revived in the nineteenth century when the modern germ theory emerged.

Pasteur, Lister, Koch and the germ theory

Louis Pasteur was a French chemist who in the 1850s turned his attention to the process of fermentation, including the production of lactic acid in sour milk and the production of alcohol in wine and beer. Many scientists at the time believed that fermentation and putrefaction were the result of spontaneous generation. Liebig, for example, contended in 1839 that fermentation in beer is not caused by yeast, but by the internal development of the beer. Pasteur was able to show that the yeast increased in weight, nitrogen, and carbon content during fermentation, and inferred that yeast is a living organism that is the cause of fermentation in beer and wine. He proceeded in the early 1860s to identify other organisms – bacteria – that produce lactic acid fermentation. To challenge directly the theory of spontaneous generation, he conducted ingenious experiments to show that fermentation does not take place in the absence of contamination by air. Pasteur's work greatly improved the manufacture of vinegar and wine, and he was invited in 1865 to investigate an epidemic of silkworm disease in the south of France, and he also took time to study cholera which had spread to France from Egypt. Naturally, Pasteur applied to silkworms some of the same microscopic techniques that had proven so fertile in his studies of fermentation.

Pasteur (and independently the British surgeon Joseph Lister) made the most important mental leap in the history of medicine, pursuing an analogy between fermentation and disease. They realized that just as fermentation is caused by yeast and bacteria, so diseases may also be caused by microorganisms. In 1878, Pasteur wrote concerning his work on fermentation:

> What meditations are induced by those results! It is impossible not to observe that, the further we penetrate into the experimental study of germs, the more we perceive sudden lights and clear ideas on the knowledge of the causes of contagious diseases! Is it not worthy of attention that, in that Arbois vineyard (and it would be true of the million *hectares* of vineyards of all the countries in the world), there should not have been, at the time I made the aforesaid experiments, one single particle of earth which would not have been capable of provoking fermentation by a grape yeast, and that, on the other hand, the earth of the glass houses I have mentioned should have been powerless to fulfill that office? And why? Because, at the given moment, I covered that earth with some glass. The death, if I may so express it, of a bunch of grapes, thrown at that time on any vineyard, would infallibly have occurred through the *saccharomyces* parasites of which I speak; that kind of death would have been impossible, on the contrary, on the little space enclosed by my glass houses. Those few cubic yards of air, those few square yards of soil, were there, in the midst of a universal possible contagion, and they were safe from it. Is it not permissible to believe, by analogy, that a day will come when easily applied preventive measures will arrest those scourges which suddenly desolate and terrify populations; such as the fearful disease (yellow fever) which has recently invaded Senegal and the valley of the Mississippi, or that other (bubonic plague), yet more terrible perhaps, which has ravaged the banks of the Volga?
>
> (for the original see Pasteur, 1922, vol. II, p. 547)

From silkworms, Pasteur moved on to diseases such as anthrax and rabies, applying his proverb to "seek the microbe". Some microbes such as the virus that causes rabies are too small to be identified by the microscopes available to Pasteur. The concept of germ underwent substantial changes as microbiology progressed, as I will describe in a later section.

According to Geison (1995, p. 36), "the old and widely accepted analogy between fermentation and disease made any theory of the former immediately relevant to the latter". But Pasteur's breakthrough was more than simple analogical transfer from the domain of fermentation to the domain of disease, for he had to revise the existing analogy. In an 1857 memoir, Pasteur disputed the influential view of Liebig that putrefaction is the cause of both fermentation and contagious diseases (Brock, 1988, p. 28). From Liebig's perspective, fermentation and contagion are analogous because they are both caused by putrefaction (rotting). After the establishment of the germ theory of fermentation, Pasteur concluded that disease can be viewed as analogous in that it too is caused by germs. A new analogical mapping supplanted Liebig's. Pasteur seems to have had the revised analogy in mind even before he began work on silkworms in 1865: in his work on problems with wine fermentation in 1864 he wrote of "les maladies des vins", i.e. diseases of wines. See Holyoak and Thagard (1995, ch. 8) for a discussion of scientific analogies.

Pasteur developed the technique of heating milk and wine to prevent development of bacteria, but what is now called pasteurization is no help with diseases of humans (compare Fracastoro's ideas about heat!). Pasteur had no direct way of killing microorganisms, but he discovered how to prevent rabies using vaccination, an ancient technique of exposing people or animals to an attenuated strain of an infectious agent that had been successfully applied by Jenner to smallpox in the late eighteenth century.

The British surgeon Joseph Lister was quick to appreciate the significance of Pasteur's ideas about fermentation, writing in 1867:

> Turning now to the question how the atmosphere produces decomposition of organic substances, we find that a flood of light has been thrown upon this most important subject by the philosophic researches of M. Pasteur, who has demonstrated by thoroughly convincing evidence that it is not to its oxygen or to any of its gaseous constituents that the air owes this property, but to the minute particles suspended in it, which are the germs of various low forms of life, long since revealed by the microscope, and regarded as merely accidental concomitants to putrescence, but now shown by Pasteur to be its essential cause, resolving the complex organic compounds into substances of simpler chemical constitution, just as the yeast plant converts sugar into alcohol and carbonic acid. . . . Applying these principles to the treatment of compound fracture, bearing in mind that it is from the vitality of the atmospheric particles that all mischief arises, it appears that all that is requisite is to dress the wound with some material capable of killing those septic germs, provided that any

Table 10.4 The discoverers of the main bacterial pathogens

Year	Disease	Organism	Discoverer
1877	Anthrax	Bacillus anthracis	Koch, R.
1878	Suppuration	Staphylococcus	Koch, R.
1879	Gonorrhea	Neisseria gonorrhoeae	Neisser, A.L.S.
1880	Typhoid fever	Salmonella typhi	Eberth, C.J.
1881	Suppuration	Streptococcus	Ogston, A.
1882	Tuberculosis	Mycobacterium tuberculosis	Koch, R.
1883	Cholera	Vibrio cholerae	Koch, R.
1883	Diphtheria	Corynebacterium diphtheriae	Klebs, T.A.E. Loeffler, F.
1884	Tetanus	Clostridium tetani	Nicholaier, A.
1885	Diarrhea	Escherichia coli	Escherich, T.
1886	Pneumonia	Streptococcus pneumoniae	Fraenkel, A.
1887	Meningitis	Neisseria meningitidis	Weischelbaum, A.
1888	Food poisoning	Salmonella enteritidis	Gaertner, A.A.H.
1892	Gas gangrene	Clostridium perfringens	Welch, W.H.
1894	Plague	Yersinia pestis	Kitasato, S. Yersin, A.J.E.
1896	Botulism	Clostridium botulinum	van Ermengem, E.M.P.
1898	Dysentery	Shigella dysenteriae	Shiga, K.
1900	Paratyphoid	Salmonella paratyphi	Schottmuller, H.
1903	Syphilis	Treponema pallidum	Schaudinn, F.R. and Hoffmann, E.
1906	Whooping cough	Bordetella pertussis	Bordet, J. and Gengou, O.

Source: Brock, 1988, p. 290

substance can be found reliable for this purpose, yet not too potent as a caustic.

(reprinted in Brock, 1988, p. 84)

As a surgeon, Lister had seen many of his patients die from infection, but he realized that Pasteur's finding that germs cause fermentation suggested not only an explanation for why wounds become infected, but also a possible means of preventing infection. Knowing that carbolic acid had been used in Carlisle on sewage to prevent odor and diseases in cattle that fed upon the pastures irrigated from the refuse material, Lister (analogically) began to use carbolic acid to sterilize wounds, dramatically dropping the infection rate.

In the 1870s and 1880s, the German doctor Robert Koch demonstrated that anthrax and tuberculosis are caused by bacteria. Koch realized that there are many different kinds of bacteria, and specific kinds are responsible for specific diseases. By the 1890s, researchers had recognized that microbes much smaller than bacteria are responsible for rabies and many other diseases, and the modern concept of a virus originated. Antibiotic cures for bacterial infections were not developed until the 1930s. But in the latter half of the nineteenth century, sometimes called the golden age of bacteriology, researchers identified

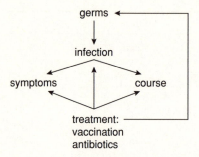

Figure 10.5 Causal structure of the germ theory of disease

the microbial causes of many diseases listed in Table 10.4. Even in recent years, new bacterial infections such as Lyme disease and legionnaire's disease have been identified, and evidence is mounting that peptic ulcers have a bacterial origin (see Thagard, forthcoming-a, forthcoming-b).

The germ theory viewed diseases in terms of a causal network similar to that of Fracastoro, but with much more detail about the nature of germs and possible treatments. Figure 10.5 displays very schematically the causal relations known to hold for many diseases by the end of the nineteenth century. The Hippocratics were largely confined to a taxonomy of diseases in terms of symptoms, and Fracastoro's theory allowed only a limited causal classification based on kinds of contagion; but the germ theory of disease made possible a detailed and clinically powerful taxonomy of diseases in terms of their microbial causes. Today, infectious diseases are typically classified as bacterial (e.g. syphilis, tuberculosis), viral (e.g. AIDS, herpes), protozoal (e.g. malaria), and so on. Knowing what bacteria are responsible for a particular disease indicates what antibiotic treatment to apply. Viruses have proven to be much more resistant to chemical attack.

Although classification in terms of superficial symptoms such as fever is no longer important, the taxonomy of infectious diseases in terms of microbial agents goes hand in hand with classification in terms of organ system affected. Textbooks are commonly structured in terms of organ systems, so that, for example, respiratory diseases are discussed together. The Hippocratics combined an emphasis on humoral imbalances with only a sketchy knowledge of anatomy; the doctrine that diseases have seats in particular bodily organs was developed by Morgagni in the eighteenth century

Current disease concepts

Although many diseases are infectious, research in the twentieth century has revealed other kinds of cause of disease: genetic, nutritional, immunological, metabolic, and cytological. The Hippocratics saw some traits such as being

Table 10.5 Organization of *Cecil Textbook of Medicine*

Cardiovascular diseases
Respiratory diseases
Renal diseases
Gastrointestinal diseases
Diseases of the liver, gall bladder, and bile ducts
Hematologic diseases
Oncology
Metabolic diseases
Nutritional diseases
Endocrine and reproductive diseases
Diseases of the bone and bone mineral metabolism
Diseases of the immune system
Musculoskeletal and connective tissue diseases
Infectious diseases
HIV and associate disorders
Diseases caused by protozoa and metazoa
Neurology
Eye diseases
Skin diseases

Source: Wyngaarden, Smith, and Bennett, 1992

phlegmatic as hereditary, but the first demonstration of the genetic basis of a disease was Archibald Garrod's work on alkaptonuria in 1901 (Devor, 1993). Many other kinds of genetic disorders have been identified, and in recent years genetic engineering has offered the possibility of new kinds of treatment for such disorders. Hippocrates placed great emphasis on diet as a factor on disease, and the value of citrus fruits in preventing scurvy was established in 1747, but identification of vitamin C as a nutritional requisite of health occurred only in 1932. Diseases caused by nutritional deficiencies can easily be treated by providing the missing vitamins or other nutrient. Knowledge of the immune system advanced rapidly in the 1950s, making possible the understanding of diseases that arise from attacks by the immune system on the body's own organs, as occurs in diseases such as lupus erythematosus. Metabolic disorders such as diabetes have become increasingly understood as knowledge increases of the physiology of organs such as the pancreas, but causality in such cases is complex, involving an interaction of hereditary and environmental factors. Similarly, although knowledge is developing rapidly concerning the nature of the cells and genes involved in the growth of cancers, the causal interactions are enormously complex and hard to identify.

The authoritative *Cecil Textbook of Medicine* is divided into parts that implicitly classify diseases in two complementary respects: organ systems and pathogenesis. Table 10.5 lists the relevant parts of the textbook. Most of these are organized around physiological systems, such as the cardiovascular and respiratory systems. But there are also parts that group diseases in terms of pathogenetic mechanisms that can affect various organ systems: oncology, metabolic diseases, nutritional diseases, infectious diseases, and so on. Some diseases are naturally discussed in more than one part, as when myocarditis occurs both under cardiovascular diseases and infectious diseases. Modern medical classification thus blends two overlapping taxonomies of disease.

The shift from the humoral to the germ theory of disease required a conceptual revolution: the old conceptual and explanatory system was replaced by a radically different one. In contrast, the development in the twentieth century of concepts of genetic, nutritional, immunological, and metabolic diseases were relatively conservative extensions of the nineteenth century ideas: new causes were introduced without denying that the germ theory was right about the causes of diseases to which it had been applied. Let us now look at changes in the concept of disease more systematically.

Changes in disease concepts

The development of the concept of disease illustrates all nine kinds of conceptual change that were distinguished in Table 10.1. I will characterize changes as *conservative* if they involve extensions to existing concepts and beliefs, and *nonconservative* if they require rejection of previous concepts and beliefs. The first kinds of conceptual change, adding new instances such as new cases of tuberculosis and empirical generalizations such as about who tends to get tuberculosis, are usually conservative. Adding a new causal rule, however, can drastically alter the concept of a disease by changing the links in the causal network for the disease. When Koch showed that tuberculosis is caused by a bacillus, he developed a very different causal network from that of the Hippocratics: the disease is an infection, not an imbalance, and can be treated by killing the microbes that cause the infection, not by overcoming the imbalance. Adding a new causal rule can be conservative if the rule does not clash with a previously held causal rule, but the replacement of the humoral theory by the germ theory required numerous instances of nonconservative rule addition.

Adding a new part relation is usually a conservative conceptual change in the history of medicine, since finding new parts does not require rejection of previous views about parts. For example, when Schwann proposed in 1839 that animals are composed of cells, his new subdivision did not require rejection of previous views about organs. However, identifying new parts can sometimes lead to nonconservative rule addition if the new parts suggest new causal rules, as when the discovery of new organs made possible novel diagnoses.

Adding a new kind-relation can be conservative when it simply involves subdividing accepted kinds into finer distinctions, as when diabetes mellitus is divided into two kinds, type I or insulin-dependent diabetes and type II or non-insulin dependent diabetes. Sometimes, however, adding kind-relations involves changing causal rules, as when the germ theory introduced infectious diseases as a new class with causes very different from those associated with the humoral theory.

Adding a new concept can be conservative when the concept fits with the existing conceptual system. Adding the classes of genetic and nutritional diseases was conservative with respect to the germ theory, since the new concepts largely applied to diseases that had not previously been asserted to be infectious. In contrast, the concept of infectious disease was nonconservative with respect to the humoral theory, since it required rejecting not only previous beliefs but also previous concepts. Modern concepts of blood, phlegm, and bile do not play anything like the explanatory and clinical role that they did for the Hippocratics.

For the germ theory, fever is not itself a disease as it was for Hippocrates and Fracastoro, but only a symptom of infection. Hence there is no need to include in the taxonomy of diseases a classification of kinds of fever. Abandonment of the fever branch of the disease taxonomy exemplifies the seventh kind of conceptual change listed in Table 10.1, collapsing a kind-hierarchy to abandon a previous distinction. This change is clearly nonconservative, requiring the abandonment of previously accepted concepts and beliefs.

Branch jumping – reorganizing hierarchies by shifting a concept from one branch of a hierarchical tree to another branch – is similarly nonconservative. To take a recent example, the new bacterial theory of the origins of many peptic ulcers requires reclassification of ulcers as an infectious disease, rather than as a disorder due to excess acidity or as a psychosomatic disease due to stress (Thagard, forthcoming-a). Similarly, the classification of diseases such as tuberculosis, cholera, rabies, and malaria in terms of their microbial causes shifts these concepts to a new place in the tree of diseases, abandoning their classification in terms of kind of fever or superficial symptoms.

Tree switching, changing the basis on which classifications are made, is nonconservative, since it goes together with the development of new branches that supersede previous classifications. The transition to the germ theory was a case of tree switching, since it introduced classification of diseases in terms of their causes, particularly their microbial causes. Modern medicine no longer classifies diseases in terms of symptoms, but rather in terms of causes and organ systems affected. Symptoms are related to organ systems, since, for example, a lung disorder has symptoms involving the lungs, but the seat of the disorder and its causes are more fundamental to classification of diseases than are symptoms. In contrast, dictionaries of symptoms and other books written for laypeople are still organized in terms of symptoms rather than organ systems or causes of disease.

In sum, the transition in the nineteenth century from the humoral theory to the germ theory of disease was highly nonconservative, involving new concepts, new causal rules, and new classifications, as well as the abandonment of old ones. The transition from the humoral to the germ theory was largely accomplished by the ability of the latter to provide a superior new account of the causes and treatments of diseases. In contrast, the twentieth-century expansion of causes of diseases to include nutritional, immunological, and metabolic considerations was largely conservative with respect to the germ theory. New causes were introduced, without rejecting the established concepts and beliefs about infectious diseases. Harvard Medical School now advocates a "biopsychosocial" model of medicine (Tosteson, Adelstein, and Carver, 1994). The modern trend to multifactorial theories envisioning such diseases as cancers as the result of complex interactions of genetic, environmental, immunological and other factors is similarly conservative, except with respect to narrow views that attempt to specify a single cause for each particular disease.

Changes in germ concepts

Accompanying the changes in the concept of disease that were brought about by the germ theory were dramatic changes in concepts describing the infectious agents newly held to be responsible for disease. The development of concepts such as bacteria and viruses involved some of the same kinds of changes so far described for disease concepts.

Historical development

Microscopic living creatures were first observed in 1674 by Leeuwenhoek. Examining a sample of lake water with a simple microscope, he observed "very many little animalcules"; his descriptions apply to what are now called protozoa (Dobell, 1958, p. 110). In 1676, Leeuwenhoek observed many animalcules in water in which pepper had been standing for some weeks, including some "incredibly small" animalcules that were evidently bacteria.

Although we can say that Leeuwenhoek discovered protozoa and bacteria, these concepts did not originate with him, for he wrote only of animalcules differing in their size and parts. Leeuwenhoek never associated the animalcules he observed with the causation of disease. The concept of germ that arose in the nineteenth century was both biological and medical: a germ is a biological organism that can cause disease. Fracastoro's concept of *seminaria* was medical but not biological; Leeuwenhoek's concept of *animalcule* was biological but not medical. Fracastoro and Leeuwenhoek both introduced new concepts that retrospectively can be seen as ancestors of modern microbiology but were very different from current concepts.

In the twelfth (1767) edition of the *Systema Naturae* Linnaeus assigned all the animalcules then known to three genera, *Volvo, Furia,* and *Chaos.* The entities that Leeuwenhoek had observed were termed "infusoria" in the eighteenth century because they were observed in infusions (solutions) of decaying organic matter. Linnaeus lumped all the infusoria to a single species, *Chaos infusorium* (Bulloch, 1979, p. 37). The term "bacterium" was introduced by Gottfried in 1829.

Modern microbiology began with the French chemist Pasteur, who in 1857 discovered that lactic acid fermentation is caused by a microorganism, yeast. Previously, fermentation was believed to be the result of decomposition of a substance, not the effect of an organism such as yeast. In 1861, Pasteur announced that the ferment that produces butyric acid is an infusorium ("infu-soire", Brock, 1988, p. 265). The anaerobic bacteria observed by Pasteur were small cylindrical rods about .002 mm in diameter. This discovery, and subsequent work by Pasteur, Koch, and others on the involvement of microorganisms in disease, led to an explosion of work that resulted, by the end of the nineteenth century, in the identification of many different kinds of bacteria and protozoa, along with demonstrations that many important diseases such as tuberculosis and malaria are caused by microbes. (The term "microbe" was introduced in 1878 by Sédillot.)

Attempts were made to identify microbes responsible for diseases such as rabies and smallpox, but the agents in these cases were what we now call viruses, which are too small to be seen through an optical microscope. The term "virus" originally meant "poison", and any cause of disease, including Fracastoro's *seminaria*, could be referred to as a virus. In 1884 Chamberland used filtration through a porous vase of porcelain to purify water of microbes, but in 1892 Ivanowski was surprised to find that a filtered extract from diseased tobacco plants could cause disease in previously healthy plants. In 1898 Löffler and Frosch conjectured that hoof and mouth disease is caused by "a previously undiscovered agent of disease, so small as to pass through the pores of a filter retaining the smallest known bacteria" (Lechevalier and Solotorovsky, 1974, pp. 284–285). The conjectured poison became known as a "filterable virus". After 1915, when Twort showed that bacteria can be attacked by filterable viruses, the concept of a virus as an ultramicroscopic organism became established. In 1935, Stanley presented crystallographic evidence that tobacco mosaic virus is a protein. During the 1930s, the electron microscope was developed, and in 1939 Kausch, Pfankuch, and Ruska used it to describe the appearance of the tobacco mosaic virus. Thus use of the term "virus" evolved gradually from concerning any disease-causing poison to concern very small microorganisms detected by electron microscopes.

Representational change

When Leeuwenhoek introduced the term "animalcule", he introduced into his mental apparatus a new concept that differentiated the newly observed entities from larger animals. Concepts need not be formed directly by observation, however, but can be formed as part of the generation of explanatory hypotheses. Fracastoro's concept of *seminaria* did not refer to any entity he had observed, but rather to one he had postulated in order to explain contagion. Similarly, the concept of a filterable virus initially concerned a hypothetical entity, although viruses later were identified by electron microscopy.

After Pasteur, Lister and others showed the medical significance of bacteria in the 1860s, great progress was made in identifying new kinds of bacteria and demonstrating their roles in a host of diseases, including diphtheria, tuberculosis, and cholera. By the end of the 1870s, people no longer spoke of "the" bacteria, but of different bacteria (Bulloch, 1979, p. 203). In place of the general concepts of animalcule and infusorium, concepts referring to particular kinds of bacteria and protozoa were developed, and the concept of microbe was introduced to reunify the plethora of newly differentiated concepts. Taxonomy of bacteria was very important for the development of the germ theory of disease: if one bacterium could unpredictably turn into another kind, then it would be difficult to accept the fact that a specific disease was caused by specific bacteria (Brock, 1988, p. 73). Today, more than 2,000 species of bacteria have been identified, along with many species of protozoa.

Proliferation of microbiological concepts did not simply involve extension of existing classification, but often required revision of kind relations. Leeuwenhoek and the eighteenth-century taxonomists classified bacteria and other infusoria as animals, but in 1852 Perty contended that some of the infusoria are "animal-plants", and Cohn argued in 1854 that bacteria of the genus Vibriona are plants analogous to algae. In 1857, the German botanist Nageli proposed that bacteria should be regarded as a class of their own within the vegetable kingdom, for which he coined the term "Schizmocyetes", or "fission fungi" (Collard, 1976, p. 151). Today, in the widely used five kingdom classification, bacteria are no longer classed with fungi, but rather with blue-green algae in the kingdom Monera.

Reclassification of viruses has been even more complex. Originally, "virus" meant "slime" or "poison", but only at the end of the nineteenth century did it start to acquire the meaning of "infectious agent". By the 1940s, the electron microscope made it possible to discern the structure of many kinds of viruses, which are particles consisting only of DNA or RNA (but not both) and a protein shell. Unlike bacteria, which consist of living cells, viruses cannot reproduce on their own, but only when they are parasites in living cells. When Pasteur and other early researchers attempted to identify the cause of diseases such as rabies and smallpox, they thought they were looking for a kind of bacteria, but viruses turned out to be a much smaller and simpler kind of entity. Hundreds of kinds of viruses have been identified. By 1950, viruses were soundly differentiated from bacteria, and the field of virology split off from bacteriology. The mental representations of microbiologists reflect these differences, and hundreds of kinds of viruses are now distinguished based on their structure as revealed by electron microscopy. Viruses "cannot logically be placed in either a strictly biochemical or in a strictly biological category; they are too complex to be macromolecules in the ordinary sense and too divergent in their physiology and manner of replication to be conventional living organisms" (Hughes, 1977, p. 106). Virologists are wont to say: viruses are viruses.

Reclassification of bacteria first as Schizmocyetes and then Monera, and reclassification of viruses as a unique kind of entity, are examples of branch jumping, the movement of a concept from one branch of a taxonomic tree to another. The development of concepts of bacteria and viruses does not seem to have involved radical change in classificatory practices, although after 1908 pathogenicity was admitted as a taxonomic criterion for bacteria (Collard, 1976,

p. 153). The empirical classification is designed to aid the differentiation between medically and industrially important species and others.

In sum, conceptual change in microbiology has involved the formation of many new mental representations corresponding to terms such as "animalcule", "bacteria", and "virus". Concept formation often involved differentiation, as new kinds of entity were distinguished from ones previously known. In addition, the organization of microbiological concepts has changed dramatically over time, as new kinds of infectious agents have been identified and as existing kinds have been reclassified in terms of higher order kinds. The concept of infection has also changed, as the modern meaning of invasion by micro-organisms replaced the older, vaguer meaning of infection as staining or pollution. Today, infectious diseases can be differentiated as bacterial infections or viral infections, just as germs can be differentiated as bacteria or viruses. Thus germ concepts and the concept of infection changed in tandem with changes in the concept of disease.

Terminological and mental change has been coupled with changes in ways of fixing the reference of concepts of germs, as the last section of this chapter will show. First, I shall compare the preceding account of changes in disease and germ concepts with other recent discussions of conceptual change.

Other representational accounts of conceptual change

Kuhn

Accounts of conceptual change go back at least as far as the nineteenth-century writings of Hegel and Whewell, but have proliferated since Thomas Kuhn's (1970) work on scientific revolutions. Kuhn (1993, p. 336) now characterizes a scientific revolution in part as "the transition to a new lexical structure, to a revised set of kinds". Terms for kinds "supply the categories prerequisite to description of and generalization about the world. If two communities differ in their conceptual vocabularies, their members will describe the world differently and make different generalizations about it" (Kuhn, 1993, p. 319). The difference is particularly serious if the new set of kind-terms overlaps kind-terms already in place, since there then can be no straightforward translation between the terms in the two theories (see also Hacking, 1993). Buchwald (1992) shows that two competing optical theories in the early nineteenth century worked with taxonomies that cannot be mapped or grafted onto one another.

My discussion of concepts of disease similarly assumes that scientific categories can be thought of as forming a taxonomic tree, although in medicine the tree is tangled because of the intermingling of physiological and patho-genetic taxonomies. I have described several different kinds of changes to the taxonomy of diseases that occurred with the development of the germ theory of disease. It is indeed difficult to translate completely between the humoral and the germ conceptions of disease, because the Hippocratic taxonomy of diseases in terms of bodily locations divides the world up very differently

from the classification of diseases in terms of microbial causes. Partial translation is nevertheless possible: we can recognize ancient discussions of diseases
like phthisis (tuberculosis) because the symptoms associated with it today are
similar to ones identified long ago, even if the etiology and taxonomy of the
disease has changed dramatically. Like Kuhn (1993, p. 315), who refers to the
lexicon as a "mental module", I take conceptual change to be change in mental
representations.

Carey

Carey also takes concepts and beliefs to be mental structures, and lists three
types of conceptual change (Carey, 1992, p. 95). The first, differentiation,
occurs when a new distinction is drawn. The development of disease concepts
has seen many such differentiations, both in distinguishing between particular
diseases such as measles and smallpox, and in distinguishing between kinds
of diseases such as bacterial infections and viral infections. The second, coalescence, occurs when a distinction is abandoned, as we saw in the abandonment
of the Hippocratic distinction between kinds of fever and in the scrapping of the
distinction between scrofula and phthisis. In Carey's third kind of conceptual
change, simple properties are reanalyzed as relations, as when Newton reanalyzed the concept *weight* as a relation between an object and the earth. Whether
there have been medical examples of this kind of conceptual change is unclear.

Chi

Chi and her colleagues distinguish between conceptual change within an ontological category and *radical* conceptual change that necessitates a change across
ontological categories (Chi, 1992; Slotta, Chi, and Joram, 1996). She argues
that physics education requires radical conceptual change, since students must
recategorize familiar concepts such as heat, light, force, and current, which
their everyday conceptual systems take to be substances, as events defined by
relational constraints between several entities. Radical conceptual change
cannot occur merely by adapting or extending a previous conceptual scheme,
but requires constructing a new set of concepts and shifting to it as a whole.

Is change in the concept of disease radical in Chi's sense? Brock (1988,
p. 74) suggests that Fracastoro's contagion theory introduced the concept of
an infectious disease as a process rather than a thing. But the Hippocratics'
extensive discussions of the courses and prognoses of diseases suggest that they
also thought of diseases as falling under the ontological category of process.
Chi's fundamental ontological categories are matter (kinds and artifacts), events,
and abstractions. For the Hippocratics as well as the nineteenth-century germ
theorists, diseases were complex events, not kinds of things or abstractions. So
the transition to the germ theory of disease did not involve radical conceptual
change in Chi's sense. Nevertheless, it did require the sort of replacement
mechanism that she describes for radical conceptual change in which a whole

new conceptual scheme is constructed, not simply produced by piecemeal modification of the previous humoral scheme.[3]

Gentner

Gentner *et al.* (1997) identified four analogical processes of conceptual change that they conjecture were important in the development of Kepler's work on the solar system: highlighting, projection of candidate inferences, re-representation, and restructuring. As we saw above, the analogy between fermentation and disease was important for Pasteur and Lister who were the central contributors to the germ theory of disease. The analogy between fermentation and disease was already familiar, but Pasteur and Lister created a new mapping between the two processes. This new mapping highlighted the role of microorganisms in fermenting substances and in disease organisms. It also made possible candidate inferences that diseases are caused by germs, just like fermentation. It is not apparent that the new mapping required any re-representation of predicates, but it certainly did require restructuring of causal links in the target domain to include microorganisms as the causal agent of disease. So at least three of the four analogical processes that Gentner *et al.* discuss in the Kepler case seem to have operated in the development of the germ theory of disease.

Nersessian

Nersessian (1989) discusses several important kinds of conceptual change that occurred with the development of Newtonian physics. Some concepts were added (gravity), some were deleted (e.g. natural motion), and there were many changes in kind hierarchies similar to the ones we have seen in the development of disease concepts. Nersessian also points out important changes from properties to relations. For example, gravity was reconceived as a force, which is a relation rather than a property. As I mentioned in discussing Carey, this kind of conceptual change may not have occurred in the disease case. Nersessian (1992) describes how analogy, imaging, thought experiments, and limiting case analyses have contributed to conceptual change in the history of physics. Of the mechanisms she discusses, we saw that analogy was very important in the development of the germ theory of diseases by Pasteur and Lister.

Referential change

Kitcher (1993) describes conceptual change, not in terms of mental representations, but in terms of *modes of reference*, which are connections between a term and an object that make it the case that the term refers to the object. He describes three types of mode of reference: *descriptive*, when the speaker uses a description to pick out an object that a term is intended to refer to; *baptismal*, when a speaker ostensively applies a term to a particular present object; and *conformist*, when a speaker's usage is parasitic on the usage of others who have established the reference of a term either descriptively or baptismally. A term may have multiple modes of reference, which together comprise its *reference potential*. According to Kitcher (1993, p. 103), conceptual change is change in reference potential.

The germ theory undoubtedly brought with it new modes of reference for disease terms. Tuberculosis could now be described as the disease caused by the tubercle bacillus. Disease concepts did not change completely, however, since the descriptive modes of reference associated with familiar observable symptoms did not change. Terms for the various microbes that cause disease had baptismal modes of reference that occurred when researchers such as Koch first observed them under the microscope.

When Fracastoro described *seminaria* as the causes of contagion, he used a verbal description that was intended to refer to agents of disease. Microbiologists from Leeuwenhoek on, however, were able to fix reference baptismally by pointing to examples of the new kinds of microorganisms that were being discovered. Their ability to do this depended on the development of a series of technological advances that illustrate the crucial role of instruments in conceptual change in microbiology.

Why was Leeuwenhoek the first to discover the tiny "animalcules" that we now call bacteria? Others in his time were using microscopes to look at previously unobserved phenomena, but Leeuwenhoek developed his own techniques of microscope construction that were unrivaled for decades afterward. He was then able to see numerous sorts of previously unidentified organisms. Here is Leeuwenhoek's own description of the first observation of bacteria, which took place in 1676 as the accidental result of an attempt to discover why pepper is hot to the tongue:

> I did now place anew about 1/3 ounce of whole pepper in water, and set it in my closet, with no other design than to soften the pepper, that I could better study it. . . . The pepper having lain about three weeks in the water, . . . I saw therein, with great wonder, incredibly many very little animalcules, of divers sorts. . . . The fourth sort of little animals, which drifted among the three sorts aforesaid, were incredibly small; nay, so small, in my sight, that I judged that even if 100 of these very wee animals lay stretched out one against another, they could not reach to the length of a grain of coarse sand.
>
> (excerpts from Dobell, 1958, pp. 132–133)

Observation of bacteria through a microscope is not easy, both because of the difficulty of producing accurate lenses and because of the need to focus on specimens where bacteria exist. Microscopes that reduced aberration sufficiently to facilitate observation of bacteria were not available until the 1820s. Fixing the reference of concepts referring to different kinds of bacteria depended on these advances in microscopy.

Other experimental techniques were also required for the development of bacteriology (Collard, 1976). Through the 1870s, it was very difficult to obtain pure cultures that contained only one kind of bacterium, since liquid solutions tended to contain many kinds of bacteria. But in 1881 Robert Koch developed a technique of growing bacteria on cut potatoes, and the next year agar was introduced as a solid medium for culturing bacteria. The identification of many medically important bacteria in the next few years used these new techniques.

The transparency of bacteria makes them difficult to observe, but staining techniques have provided powerful ways of determining their presence and structure. Vegetable stains were first applied to bacteria by Hoffman in 1869, and improved techniques including Gram's technique of counter-staining were developed over the next decades. Like culturing in solid media, staining is an important aid to the fixing of reference of terms for new kinds of bacteria. Culturing and staining enabled Robert Koch to discover the bacterium responsible for tuberculosis:

> On the basis of my extensive observations, I consider it as proved that in all tuberculous conditions of man and animals there exists a characteristic bacterium which I have designated as the tubercle bacillus, which has specific properties which allow it to be distinguished from all other microorganisms.
>
> (Koch, quoted in Brock, 1988, p. 121)

The baptismal mode of reference to the tubercle bacillus thus depended on the development of new experimental techniques.

New techniques were also crucial for the referential development of concepts concerning viruses. Filtration techniques in the 1880s made possible the differentiation of viruses from bacteria, which were too large to pass through the filters. At this point, the only mode of reference for filterable viruses was descriptive: virus was whatever passed through the filters and caused disease. After 1920, centrifuges were increasingly used to isolate viruses and estimate their size based on centrifugation time and force of gravity. A few very large viruses can be identified with optical microscopes, but baptismal fixing of reference of most concepts of viruses requires use of the electron microscope, which also made possible determination of the structure of bacteria. Before 1939, when Kausche, Pfankuch, and Ruska first used the electron microscope for visualization of a virus, the mode of reference was descriptive, as in "the virus of measles". The third type of mode of reference defined by Kitcher (1993) is conformist, when a speaker's usage is parasitic on the usage of others who have established the reference of a term either descriptively or baptismally. For most people, the reference of concepts like *bacteria* and *virus* is fixed in this way, since they have neither seen such entities themselves nor been given an accurate description.

How are Kitcher's three modes of reference – descriptive, baptismal, and conformist – related to representational changes involving concept formation, differentiation, and reclassification? Descriptive modes of reference that involve words and verbal descriptions are easily cast in terms of mental representation by supposing that thinkers have (1) mental concepts corresponding to words and (2) proposition-like representations corresponding to descriptions. With respect to description, the mental representation view of conceptual change currently is richer than the referential view, since it pays attention to the kind-relations of concepts. But ideas like differentiation and reclassification could be reframed in terms of a verbal lexicon rather than a mental lexicon by taking *kind* as a relation among verbal terms rather than mental structures. Given the theoretical richness of taking concepts as mental representations, there is no reason to prefer discussion of terms as words rather than as concepts.

But the reference-potential view of conceptual change does have an advantage over the mental-representation when it comes to understanding the relation between representations and the world. The baptismal mode of reference operated repeatedly in the history of microbiology, from Leeuwenhoek fixing the reference of "animalcule" to Koch fixing the reference of "tubercle bacillus", to electron microscopists fixing the reference of "tobacco mosaic virus". This mode of reference is best viewed not as a single act, but as a matter of ongoing interaction with the world using instruments and experimental techniques. Koch not only baptised the tubercle bacillus, he photographed and showed how to culture it and transmit it to laboratory animals. This was more than description, and more than baptism: it was development of replicable physical procedures for interacting with the entity referred to by the term (or concept) "tubercle bacillus". Changes in such procedures and attendant new baptismal episodes are aspects of conceptual change not captured by concentration solely on mental representation.

When concepts are formed purely descriptively, for example when *seminaria* are characterized as the seeds of disease, conceptual change can be viewed in terms of mental structures. But when concepts are formed ostensively as the result of interactions with the world, we have to understand conceptual change in terms of reference as well as representation. Differentiation is not only conceptual: entities can be differentiated into different classes if observation makes them sufficiently distinguishable that they can be dubbed independently.

Although changes in baptismal reference fixation are important to understanding the development of germ concepts, they are not so directly relevant to understanding the development of disease concepts. Diseases involve complexes of symptoms, so there is no entity that one can identify ostensively. Reference to diseases is fixed descriptively in terms of their symptoms or causes, although reference to symptoms and microbial causes can be fixed baptismally.

The mental-representation approach has also tended to neglect the social nature of conceptual change implicit in Kitcher's conformist mode of reference. Even from the perspective of mental representation, conceptual change is a social as well as a psychological phenomenon, but this is not the place to address social aspects of conceptual change in medicine. Thagard (1992) discusses the complementarity of social and psychological explanations of scientific change.

Although representational accounts of conceptual change do not tell the whole story, there remains ample reason to describe conceptual change in part as change in mental representations, especially kind-relations. Conceptual change is clearly both representational and referential, since the meaning of concepts is a function both of how they relate to each other and how they relate to the world. A full theory of conceptual change must integrate its representational, referential, and social aspects.

Conclusions

I have described the structure of the concept of disease and the way in which disease and germ concepts have changed. Historical evidence supports three main conclusions:

1   Disease concepts are causal networks that represent the relations among causes, disorders, symptoms, and treatments of diseases.
2   The most important changes in disease concepts occurred because of alterations in beliefs about the causes of disease.
3   The development of germ concepts should be thought of in terms of referential change as well as representational change.

Emphasis on the causal structure of disease concepts does not exclude other cognitive aspects such as sets of prototypical symptoms which are also associated with diseases. But it sees disease as an inherently causal concept, not just a featural one.

Many issues have not been addressed in this chapter. What were the cognitive mechanisms by which the concepts and hypotheses of the germ theory of disease were introduced? Analogy, which is clearly at work in the writings of Pasteur and Lister, is one relevant mechanism, but other kinds of concept formation and hypothesis construction may also have been important. Why was the germ theory accepted as superior to the humoral theory? Conceptual changes such as the addition of new concepts, kind-relations, and classifications, in company with abandonment of old humoral ones, show that development of the germ theory was not made by piecemeal revision of the old. Instead, a new conceptual structure had to be put together that supplanted the old one. All the major scientific revolutions in the natural sciences involved replacement of one theory by another on the basis of explanatory coherence (Thagard, 1992), but whether a similar account applies to the adoption of the germ theory of disease remains to be shown.

Recent interest in conceptual change has come as much from developmental and educational psychologists as from historians and philosophers of science. It would be interesting to determine what kinds of conceptual changes must be undergone by medical students training to be physicians or by laypeople attempting to understand and comply with treatment of their illnesses (see Skelton and Croyle, 1991). The structure and change of disease concepts is thus a topic of practical as well as theoretical interest.

Notes

* This research is supported by a grant from the Social Sciences and Humanities Research Council of Canada. Thanks to Chris Eliasmith for comments on an earlier draft.
1 My account of the structure of disease concepts is consistent with findings by health psychologists that lay theories of illness include the elements of symptoms, consequences, temporal course, cause, and cure; see Skelton and Croyle (1991). Michela and Wood (1986) provide a comprehensive review of causal attributions in health and illness.
2 The historical and philosophical literature on disease concepts is vast. Useful historical works include Have *et al.* (1990), Heidel (1941), Hudson (1983), King (1982), Kiple (1993), Magner (1992), Nuland (1988), and Temkin (1973). Philosophical discussions of the nature of disease include Caplan *et al.* (1981) and Reznek (1987). Also relevant to the germ theory of disease are works on the history of microbiology, such as Brock (1988), Collard (1976), Grafe (1991), and Lechevalier and Solotorovsky (1974).
3 If laypeople think of diseases as things rather than processes, medical education may require conceptual change across Chi's ontological categories.

References

Brock, T. (1988). *Robert Koch: A life in medicine and bacteriology.* Madison: Science Tech Publishers.

Buchwald, J.Z. (1992). Kinds and the wave theory of light. *Studies in History and Philosophy of Science, 23,* 39–74.

Bulloch, W. (1979). *The history of bacteriology.* New York: Dover.

Caplan, A.L., Engelhardt, H.T. and McCartney, J.M. (Eds.) (1981). *Concepts of health and disease: Interdisciplinary perspectives.* Reading, MA: Addison-Wesley.

Carey, S. (1985). *Conceptual change in childhood.* Cambridge, MA: MIT Press/Bradford Books.

Carey, S. (1992). The origin and evolution of everyday concepts. In R.N. Giere (Ed.), *Cognitive models of science* (pp. 89–128). Minneapolis: University of Minnesota Press.

Chi, M. (1992). Conceptual change within and across categories: Implications for learning and discovery in science. In R. Giere (Ed.), *Cognitive models of science,* Minnesota Studies in the Philosophy of Science xv (pp. 129–186). Minneapolis: University of Minnesota Press.

Collard, P. (1976). *The development of microbiology.* Cambridge: Cambridge University Press.

Devor, E.J. (1993). Genetic disease. In K. F. Kiple (Ed.), *The Cambridge world history of disease* (pp. 113–126). Cambridge: Cambridge University Press.

Dobell, C. (1958). *Antony von Leeuwenhoek and his 'little animals'.* New York: Russell and Russell.

Fracastorius, H. (1930). *Contagion, contagious diseases, and their treatment* (Wright, W.C., Trans.). New York: G.P. Putnam's Sons.

Geison, G. (1995). *The private science of Louis Pasteur.* Princeton: Princeton University Press.

Gentner, D., Brem, S., Ferguson, R., Wolff, P., Markman, A. and Forbus, K. (1997). Analogy and creativity in the works of Johannes Kepler. In T. Ward, S. Smith and J. Vaid (Eds.), *Creative thought: An investigation of conceptual structures and processes* (pp. 403–459). Washington, DC: American Psychological Association.

Grafe, A. (1991). *A history of experimental virology* (Reckendorf, E., Trans.). Berlin: Springer-Verlag.

Hacking, I. (1993). Working in a new world: The taxonomic solution. In P. Horwich (Ed.), *World changes: Thomas Kuhn and the nature of science* (pp. 275–310). Cambridge, MA: MIT Press.

Have, A.M. J.t., Kimsma, G.K. and Spicker, S.F. (Eds.) (1990). *The growth of medical knowledge*. Dordrecht: Kluwer.

Heidel, W.A. (1941). *Hippocratic medicine: In spirit and method*. New York: Columbia University Press.

Hippocrates (1988). *Hippocrates, vol. V* (Potter, P., Trans.). Cambridge, MA: Harvard University Press.

Holyoak, K.J. and Thagard, P. (1995). *Mental leaps: Analogy in creative thought*. Cambridge, MA: MIT Press/Bradford Books.

Hudson, R.P. (1983). *Disease and its control: The shaping of modern thought*. Westport, CT: Greenwood.

Hughes, S.S. (1977). *The virus: A history of the concept*. London: Heinemann.

Keil, F. (1989). *Concepts, kinds, and cognitive development*. Cambridge, MA: MIT Press/Bradford Books.

King, L.S. (1982). *Medical thinking: A historical preface*. Princeton: Princeton University Press.

Kiple, K.F. (Ed.) (1993). *The Cambridge world history of disease*. Cambridge: Cambridge University Press.

Kitcher, P. (1993). *The advancement of science*. Oxford: Oxford University Press.

Kuhn, T. (1970). *Structure of scientific revolutions* (2nd ed.). Chicago: University of Chicago Press.

Kuhn, T.S. (1993). Afterwords. In P. Horwich (Ed.), *World changes: Thomas Kuhn and the nature of science* (pp. 311–341). Cambridge, MA: MIT Press.

Lechevalier, H.A. and Solotorovsky, M. (1974). *Three centuries of microbiology*. New York: Dover.

Lloyd, G.E.R. (Ed.) (1978). *Hippocratic writings*. Harmondsworth: Penguin.

Magner, L.M. (1992). *A history of medicine*. New York: Marcel Dekker.

Medin, D. (1989). Concepts and conceptual structure. *American Psychologist, 44*, 1469–1481.

Michela, J.L. and Wood, J.V. (1986). Causal attributions in health and illness. In P.C. Kendall (Ed.), *Advances in cognitive-behavioral research and therapy, vol. 5* (pp. 179–235). New York: Academic Press.

Murphy, G. and Medin, D. (1985). The role of theories in conceptual coherence. *Psychological Review, 92*, 289–316.

Nersessian, N. (1989). Conceptual change in science and in science education. *Synthese, 80*, 163–183.

Nersessian, N. (1992). How do scientists think? Capturing the dynamics of conceptual change in science. In R. Giere (Ed.), *Cognitive models of science*, Minnesota Studies in the Philosophy of Science XV (pp. 3–44). Minneapolis: University of Minnesota Press.

Nuland, S.B. (1988). *Doctors: The biography of medicine*. New York: Knopf.

Nutton, V. (1990). The reception of Fracastoro's theory of contagion: The seed that fell among thorns? *Osiris, Second series, 6*, 196–234.

Pasteur, L. (1922). *Oeuvres*. Paris: Masson.

Reznek, L. (1987). *The nature of disease*. London: Routledge and Kegan Paul.

Skelton, J.A. and Croyle, R.T. (Eds.) (1991). *Mental representation in health and illness*. New York: Springer-Verlag.

Slotta, J.D., Chi, M.T.H. and Joram, E. (1996). Assessing students' misclassifications of physics concepts: An ontological basis for conceptual change. *Cognition and Instruction, 13*, 373–400.

Smith, E. (1989). Concepts and induction. In M. Posner (Ed.), *Foundations of cognitive science* (pp. 501–526). Cambridge, MA: MIT Press.

Smith, E. and Medin, D. (1981). *Categories and concepts*. Cambridge, MA: Harvard University Press.

Temkin, O. (1973). Health and disease. In P.P. Wiener (Ed.), *Dictionary of the history of ideas* (pp. 395–407). New York: Scribner's.

Thagard, P. (1992). *Conceptual revolutions*. Princeton: Princeton University Press.

Thagard, P. (1996). *Mind: Introduction to cognitive science*. Cambridge, MA: MIT Press.

Thagard, P. (forthcoming-a). Ulcers and bacteria I: Discovery and conceptual change. *Studies in History and Philosophy of Science*.

Thagard, P. (forthcoming-b). Ulcers and bacteria II: Physical and social interactions. *Studies in History and Philosophy of Science*.

Tosteson, D.C., Adelstein, S.J. and Carver, S.T. (Eds.) (1994). *New pathways to medical education: Learning to learn at Harvard Medical School*. Cambridge, MA: Harvard University Press.

Vallery-Radot, R. (1926). *The life of Pasteur* (Devonshire, R.L., Trans.). Garden City, NY: Doubleday.

Van Helvoort, T. (1994). History of virus research in the twentieth century: The problem of conceptual continuity. *History of Science, 23*, 185–235.

Wyngaarden, J.B., Smith, L.H. and Bennett, J.C. (Eds.) (1992). *Cecil Textbook of Medicine* (19th ed.). Philadelphia: W.B. Saunders.

Author index

Subject index